D1562424

THE FRANKENSTEIN ARCHIVE

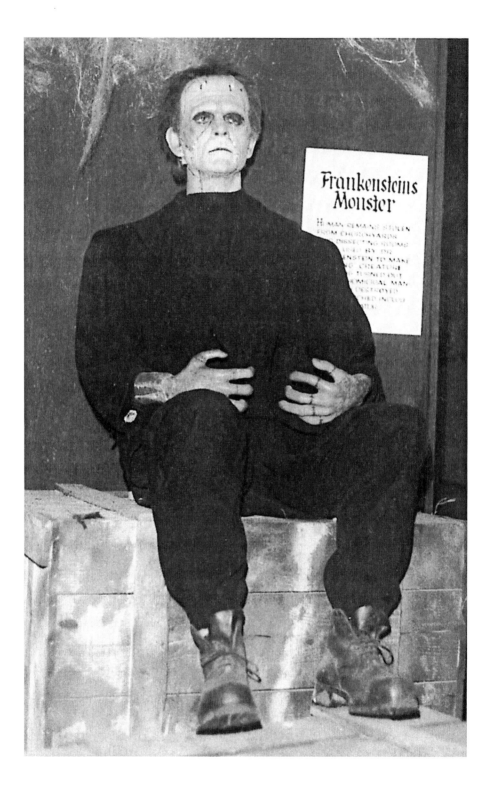

# THE FRANKENSTEIN ARCHIVE

*Essays on the Monster, the Myth, the Movies, and More*

DONALD F. GLUT

McFarland & Company, Inc., Publishers
*Jefferson, North Carolina, and London*

To Bob Burns and Jim Harmon.
Thanks for all the friendship and support
since that day I met you both back in June 1962.

*Frontispiece:* Frankenstein's Monster has achieved the status of icon and modern myth, especially when his image is patterned after the character from Universal Pictures' series of motion pictures. This Universal-inspired dummy was displayed (in the company mostly of waxen celebrities and historical figures) at the "Madame Tussaud Wax Museum" in Old Town, Chicago, during the late 1960s. Similar Frankenstein Monster figures appeared around the same time in myriad other such museums. (Photograph by the author.)

Library of Congress Cataloguing-in-Publication Data

Glut, Donald F.
    The Frankenstein archive : essays on the monster, the myth, the movies, and more / Donald F. Glut.
        p.      cm.
    Includes index.

    ISBN 0-7864-1353-0 (softcover : 50# alkaline paper) ∞

    1. Frankenstein films—History and criticism.   2. Frankenstein (Fictitious character) in literature.   3. Shelley, Mary Wollstonecraft, 1797–1851. Frankenstein   I.   Title.
    PN1995.9.F8 G59   2002
    791.43'651—dc21                                        2002009001

British Library cataloguing data are available

*Cover illustration ©2002 Art Parts*

Manufactured in the United States of America

*McFarland & Company, Inc., Publishers*
  *Box 611, Jefferson, North Carolina 28640*
    *www.mcfarlandpub.com*

# TABLE OF CONTENTS

# PREFACE

This book *is*, in a sense, a Frankenstein Monster.

Not assembled and stitched together from the cold organs and tissues of many once-living beings—as was the creature patched together and then given new life by an overly zealous young scientist in Mary Wollstonecraft Shelley's classic novel, *Frankenstein; or, The Modern Prometheus*, first published in 1818—this volume was, nonetheless, put together from many individual "pieces" (in the literary sense of that word), most of them dating back not only to an earlier century, but to a previous millennium. Granted, as these words are being typed into my computer, the new millennium is just beginning. Yet there are some similarities between this collection of individual articles and Frankenstein's Monster.

For many years, decades even, my name has been associated with the "Frankenstein" theme. I have written nonfiction books on this topic—most notably *The Frankenstein Legend: A Tribute to Mary Shelley and Boris Karloff* (Scarecrow, 1973) and *The Frankenstein Catalog* (McFarland, 1984)— for both adult and juvenile readers, a series of novels and short stories featuring the Frankenstein Monster, numerous scripts for various comic-book titles and television animation shows, and liner notes for a record album. I have also directed stage presentations, and in my much younger years, even made a series of amateur Frankenstein movies. I have been interviewed on radio and television news and talk shows about this subject, and also in various home video and DVD documentaries. Over the years I have known, spoken to, interviewed and worked with numerous people associated with the world of "Frankenstein"—authors, actors, special-effects people, make-up artists and others. Also, over the past few decades I have written a good number of articles about various aspects of

The author (center)—as a teenager in the summer of 1958 in Chicago—sporting his first attempted Frankenstein Monster make-up, flanked by visiting cousins George and Louis Csurics. The make-up was directly inspired by one recently seen on *The Spike Jones Show* for that TV program's "Halloween Spooktacular." (Photograph by Julia B. Glut.)

the Frankenstein mythos that have been published in magazines with titles like *Castle of Frankenstein*, *Famous Monsters of Filmland* and *Monsters of the Movies*. Some, although not all, of those articles form the "skeletal structure" of this book.

Like the Monster created by Victor (or, as Universal Pictures called him, "Henry") Frankenstein, this volume comprises many individual parts, some of them quite disparate in their specific themes, although they all relate in some major way to the subject of Frankenstein. Sometimes several individual articles have been taken apart, rearranged and then joined together to make a single newly reconstructed article. In every case I, the author of each of these pieces, have revised and sometimes extensively rewritten the original text (improved upon it, if you will, as Frankenstein did upon his own raw materials), brought this material together into a hopefully cohesive whole, and then given it new life. In some instances, new bits of information have been incorporated, facts that were unknown when the original article was written. An example is the revelation of the name of the actor who did the Monster's wax museum cameo in the 1953 movie *Abbott and Costello Meet Dr. Jekyll and Mr. Hyde* (no, I won't reveal that tidbit here; you'll have to hunt it down).

I hope that at least most of the errors (I will *not* point them out!) that had crept into the original manuscripts those many years ago have been corrected.

Each article has been prefaced with introductory notes. These notes are intended to place each article into its historical perspective, comment upon its origin and content, and, where appropriate, supplement its text with new information.

Some of the articles, such as those on amateur Frankenstein movies and the attempted revival of the Dick Briefer *Frankenstein* comic-book series, relate directly to some of my own involvements with the Frankenstein theme and Monster.

The reader is forewarned that this volume does *not* purport to be a biographical account of Mary Shelley's life or a critical analysis of her novel *Frankenstein*; nor is it a detailed history of the Frankenstein subject in motion pictures or in any other medium. Not included in this book are "checklists" of titles or credits of comic-book or any other kinds of stories in which the Monster has appeared. This volume is simply my musings on variations of the Frankenstein theme, some of them not often discussed elsewhere.

I hope you will enjoy reading this collection as much as I did assembling it. Comments and criticisms are welcome, sent to me through the publisher. But please, no blazing torches or angry mobs.

D.F.G.
Burbank CA
*Summer 2002*

# I

# FRANKENSTEIN: THE (UNTOLD) TRUE STORY

In the late 1990s, Dennis Druktenis, an Illinois-based editor/publisher nostalgic for the "good old days" of monster movies and the first wave (1950s to 1960s) of magazines devoted to them, and with already one continuing monster-magazine title to his credit (*Scary Monsters*), decided (*à la* Dr. Frankenstein) to revive Calvin Thomas Beck's two brainchildren, *The Journal of Frankenstein* and *Castle of Frankenstein*, his issues continuing the numbering where Beck's had left off. As much of the material in both of these revived magazines centered around the Frankenstein Monster, story and theme, I wondered if Dennis might be interested in a few articles I had long considered writing but had no specific place in mind to publish them. Phoning Dennis, I promptly learned that he was more than willing to run these articles in his Frankenstein-related magazines.

The following article, previously titled "Frankenstein: The Cryptic Continuity," first appeared in Dennis' *Castle of Frankenstein Yearbook 2000*, supplemented with numerous still photographs and movie-frame blowups from various Frankenstein movies. The idea for the article had been growing in the back of my mind for a couple of years, jump-started by the "universal" frustration among Frankenstein-movie fans over the "mistakes" the films' writers seemed to make from one series entry to the next. Such mistakes were often the topics of conversation when some of us Frankenstein buffs talked to each other at parties, conventions or over the phone. Why, for example, was a particular town called one thing in one movie and something else in the next?

The topic soon became for me an intellectual game whereby I attempted to rationalize those errors and, looking to the movies themselves for clues, possibly explain them away. Indeed, the article involved more work than I had anticipated and became somewhat longer than either I or Dennis Druktenis had planned. One thing I knew for certain, however, as I started putting the pieces of this puzzle together, was that I *had* to write this article, if for no other reason than just to get the whole notion "out of my system."

❋    ❋    ❋

For those of us who love the old Frankenstein movies—primarily the original black and white gems comprising the series made by Universal Pictures during the 1930s and 1940s, but also the color films of the 1950s through 1970s produced by Hammer Films—a major source of irritation has been the apparent lack of continuity from one motion picture to the next.

In the Universal entries, how did a town's name inexplicably change from "Vasaria" to "Frankenstein"?

How did the watchtower, where the Frankenstein Monster was created, move from the outskirts of the town of Goldstadt to the Frankenstein property itself?

How did the Wolf Man, Lawrence Talbot, survive being fatally shot with a silver bullet, and what happened to Dr. Edelmann's cure of his lycanthropic affliction?

And in the Hammer series of Frankenstein movies, why are there three vastly different looks for the original Creature?

These, and many more searing questions, have long demanded answering. We more cynical Frankenstein-movie fans might be tempted to explain such annoying conundrums by accusing the studio Powers That Be, at both Universal and Hammer, of simply not caring. These are, after all, just movies, the individual series entries often separated from one another by years. Who could ever remember names and events from one movie to the next? Seemingly neither the studio executives nor the films' writers remembered, either. I would wager a "Frankensteinian crown" or "Vasarian mark" that most (if not all) of us Frankenstein aficionados still cringe whenever these apparent continuity errors pop out at us, marring yet another viewing of those beloved movies.

Note that I've purposely described these errors as "apparent," for, in truth, that is exactly what they are—at least when considered from the correct perspective. Actually, there are *no* continuity mistakes in these movies! Now, before the readers grab their torches and pitchforks and haul me off to Dr. Ludwig Frankenstein's hospital for those suffering from "Diseases of the Mind," consider the following arguments. Hopefully they will put your brains (even the transplanted ones) at ease for all eternity.

For there is, you see, a kind of "cryptic continuity" in the "universes" of the Universal and Hammer Frankenstein films that the cameras have *not recorded*—but one that is plausible and possible, nonetheless, and there for us to discover.

But first, some ground rules:

Movies made in previous decades tended to reveal more in terms of story narrative, while modern films require and expect audiences' imaginations to fill in various "blanks" regarding plot. In an older film like Universal's *House of Dracula*, the character of Dr. Edelmann gets a telephone call from Inspector Holtz. Edelmann is then shown leaving his premises (he could also have been shown actually traveling toward his destination), finally arriving at the Visaria police station where, at last, he meets the jailed Wolf Man in his human state of Lawrence Talbot. If *House of Dracula* were made today, the action would probably cut directly from Dr. Edelmann on the phone (not even waiting for him to hang up) to his arrival outside Talbot's cell. Today's audiences are used to supplying for themselves such narrative gaps. (Modern police-type television shows, such as *Profiler*, often cut directly from a law officer responding to even a minor clue to a killer's whereabouts to arriving there in the "nick of time.") To make my explanations "work," we must apply our creative mental talents as modern viewers, imagining what the old Frankenstein movies *did not* show us.

Much, in fact, happens to the characters in the Frankenstein movies that is not revealed to us directly on screen or through dialogue. In a movie we only see what the camera shows us or what the microphone allows us to hear, and that camera and mike can only be in one place at any given time. Therefore, while Dr. Henry Frankenstein is busy bringing his Monster to life in the watchtower in Universal's original *Frankenstein*, other characters (*e.g.*, little Maria, the Burgomaster and Henry's father, the old Baron Frankenstein) are elsewhere engaged in their own unseen (by us, anyway) business.

Also, events occur *between* each movie, sometimes over a span of more than a year. During this "down time," our imaginations must really work to "reconstruct"—based upon evidence found in the movies themselves or extrapolated from information given in those pictures—those events we never actually saw, but which can explain all of those apparent continuity snafus.

We must not, however, regard certain "cosmetic anomalies" (mostly in the Universal films) as mistakes. Not always is a character appearing in more than one film played by the same actor. At Universal, Mae Clarke played Elizabeth in *Frankenstein*, while Valerie Hobson enacted that same role in the sequel *Bride of Frankenstein*; and other actors have portrayed the Frankenstein Monster after the original actor Boris Karloff left that role. Indeed, the Monster's very appearance changes, sometimes drastically, due to the physical features of the actor portraying the character, or based on new refinements and details introduced by the make-up artists. (One could, of course, make a case that the Monster's physical appearance was affected, even altered, by the chemical injections and electrical barrages inflicted on him over the years by various scientists making off-screen "repairs.") Places, such as Castle Frankenstein, are influenced not only by the creativity of set designers, but also by styles and tastes in vogue when a particular movie was made, not to mention the individual film's budget. Also, both Universal and Hammer drew their talent from a "stock company" of contract players. Thus, the return of an actor to the same kind of role does not necessarily indicate a reprise of the same character (*e.g.*, Lionel Atwill as three different—though virtually interchangeable—police inspectors in *Son of Frankenstein*, *House of Frankenstein* and *House of Dracula*; Michael Mark and Lionel Bellmore playing different—yet virtually identical—town officials in *Son of Frankenstein* and *The Ghost of Frankenstein*; and John Carradine playing a human traveler in *Bride of Frankenstein* and a human vampire in *House of Frankenstein* and *House of Dracula*).

Also, we must ignore various so-called "bloopers" or mistakes that creep into movies beyond anyone's control and which, therefore, have no valid bearing on the plots. These include such unintentional blunders as Dracula briefly reflecting in a cabinet glass in *House of Dracula*, the Monster wearing actor Glenn Strange's wedding ring in a few shots in *House of Frankenstein*, and the Monster's right electrode popping off his neck during a laboratory scene in *Abbott and Costello Meet Frankenstein*.

Lastly, we need not discuss most of the footage excised from film entries, including *Bride of Frankenstein* (*e.g.*, additional murders, only some actually committed by the Monster), *Son of Frankenstein* (*e.g.*, scenes involving actor Dwight Frye), *The Wolf Man* (*e.g.*, Talbot wrestling a bear) and *Frankenstein Meets the Wolf Man* (*e.g.*, references to the Monster's blindness and also his dialogue), this material having already been well covered elsewhere.

The above rules stated, let us begin with the Universal Frankenstein series.

First, it is important to establish the time period and location in which this series takes place. *Frankenstein* appears to be set about the same time of the film's release, or 1931, as evidenced by the clothing, Elizabeth's make-up, Henry's wristwatch, etc., in some unspecified part of Germany. The time period, however, remains undefined, as this setting has somehow remained "untouched by time." In other words, the *Frankenstein* "universe," as established in the original film, is a variation on the familiar "Ruritanian" environment commonly depicted in countless romantic adventures and operettas, a vaguely set realm where people—though possibly existing in the modern world—still wear the styles of an earlier century, and horses, wagons and carriages are the common modes of transportation. This setting is also reminiscent of the timeless Grimms fairy tales, which were never specific as to where and when they were set. In fact, the action in *Frankenstein* can be interpreted as occurring in 1931— or somewhat earlier.

However, if we really wish to lock down *firmly* the time period for *Frankenstein*, we must search for clues in the first three sequels—*Bride of Frankenstein*, *Son of Frankenstein* and *The Ghost of Frankenstein*.

In *Bride of Frankenstein*, filmed but deleted scenes from the opening "Lake Geneva" sequence (according to real history and the script, this is set in 1816, before the novel *Frankenstein; or, The Modern Prometheus* was published) have author Mary Shelley state that she has "taken the story far into the future—and made use of developments [*e.g.*, the telephone-like "electrical machine" and "cosmic diffuser"] which science will some day know—a hundred years to come." Taking Mary's statement literally, that sets the main action of *Bride of Frankenstein* in 1916, although her "hundred years" may be an estimate meaning "approximately a century" later. The clothing in Mary's "future," like that worn by Dr. Pretorious and the villagers, seems to date earlier than 1935, when *Bride of Frankenstein* was made, possibly as far back as the late 1800s, while that worn by the more fashionable Elizabeth suggests the 1920s. The skeleton of Madeleine

Ernestine, disinterred by Pretorious' grave robbers as a foundation for the Bride, is identified by ghoul Karl Glutz as having "died 1899." This implies that the main events of *Bride of Frankenstein* take place approximately a century after those at Lake Geneva, long enough after 1899 for Ms. Ernestine's body to decompose to a skeletal state. *Bride of Frankenstein*, therefore, could be set in 1916, or earlier, or as late as the 1920s. By inference, whatever date we eventually assign to *Bride of Frankenstein* basically also applies to *Frankenstein*, as that first sequel picks up directly from where the original movie ends.

Interestingly, the screenplay for *Bride of Frankenstein* does not include Karl's "died 1899" line. It does, however, have Elizabeth refer to an automobile, "I heard the car drive up," a line that was altered to "I heard the carriage drive up" in the actual film. Cars did exist, of course, in the early 1900s. However, deleting references to them helped to maintain the film's "Ruritanian" brand of timelessness; also, there may have been a conscious, albeit "last minute" effort to push this story, originally intended to be set in the 1920s or '30s, back to an earlier time period.

A car is prominently featured, however, in the next sequel, *Son of Frankenstein*, and, like the movie itself, it dates to 1939. The clothing in *Son of Frankenstein*, at least that worn by the more "trendy" Frankenstein family members, is also of late 1930s vintage (though other characters have followed the more "primitive" fashion sensibilities of their predecessors in *Frankenstein* and *Bride of Frankenstein*). These details unequivocally establish the modern (*i.e.* 1939) setting for *Son of Frankenstein*.

In the later sequels, characters entering the Frankenstein world from more modern environments—*e.g.*, Lawrence Talbot from Wales and Dr. Frank Mannering (*Frankenstein Meets the Wolf Man*) from England—wear clothing of the 1940s, while the local villagers and peasants continue adhering to the old styles. And the hardware has been updated, also. The "mad lab" devices are more modern appearing than the "cosmic diffusers" and other electrical gadgets of the first two films, and telephones are no longer primitive "electrical machines." This all indicates that each sequel, beginning with *Son of Frankenstein*, actually takes place about *the time it was filmed*, despite the "Ruritanian"-type trappings. Additionally, Universal's Dracula and Invisible Man movie series of the 1930s and '40s, also *The Wolf Man* in 1941—all of which crossed-over into the Frankenstein films and also each other's titles (*e.g.*, *The Invisible Man's Revenge* refers to "Dracula" as if he is a real person as opposed to a movie character)— undoubtedly take place when these films were released. They feature modern automobiles, telephones, even references to the ongoing World War

Two, as in *Invisible Agent* and *The Mummy's Tomb*. (Although Kharis the Mummy never actually appears in any of its Frankenstein movies, Universal clearly intended the adventures of these two characters to occur in the same "universe"; this is evidenced by early reports that, at least in the development stages, the studio had intended to include Kharis, as well as other monsters, in *Chamber of Horror*, the film that would become *House of Frankenstein*, and also, along with Dracula's son, in *The Brain of Frankenstein*, which would become the comedy/horror classic *Abbott and Costello Meet Frankenstein*.)

Simply put, *The Ghost of Frankenstein* is set in 1942, *Frankenstein Meets the Wolf Man* in 1943, *House of Frankenstein* in 1944, *House of Dracula* in 1945, and (yes, it's part of the series) *Abbott and Costello Meet Frankenstein* in 1948.

Maintaining a sense of "timelessness" was most tricky during the sequels of the early through middle 1940s. The earlier Frankenstein movies, with their ethnic names and "herr" burgomasters, established the obvious Germanic setting. This not only sustained the traditional Gothic setting, dating back to silent films, as our world quickly moved into the future, but avoided dealing with such real-life horrors as the Nazis and World War Two.

Therefore, the Universal Frankenstein movies must be set in some remote, Ruritanian part of Germany unknown to or ignored by the Nazis. Furthermore, the superstitious and occult-obsessed Adolf Hitler might have thought it best to avoid altogether areas associated with bizarre horrors such as Frankenstein's Monster, Dracula and the Wolf Man.

*Son of Frankenstein* and *The Ghost of Frankenstein* introduce Henry Frankenstein's two adult siblings, Wolf and Ludwig, respectively. In 1939, during the events of *Son of Frankenstein*, Wolf seems to be no more than about 35 years old (actor Basil Rathbone being actually 47 at the time he played Wolf), having a youthful wife and very young son. Brother Ludwig, in 1942 when *The Ghost of Frankenstein* was filmed, seems considerably older than Wolf (though, in reality, Sir Cedric Hardwick, who played Ludwig, was a year younger than Rathbone). Ludwig has a daughter in her twenties (actress Evelyn Ankers was then 24). Therefore, Ludwig must be somewhere in his late forties.

Henry Frankenstein and Elizabeth are not officially married until the storyline of *Bride of Frankenstein* is well underway—perhaps after the passage of a year or more, during which time the old Baron Frankenstein dies and Henry assumes that title. The Frankensteins have no children until after the final events of *Bride of Frankenstein*. For the couple to have two sons that attain middle age by the late 1930s to early '40s, their children could only have been born shortly after the climax of the first sequel. Doing the "monster math," this dates *Frankenstein* and *Bride of Franken-stein* about 40 or so years before *Son of Frankenstein* and *The Ghost of Frankenstein*—that is, about the "Turn of the Century," with any blatant 1920s and 1930s references in these films (*e.g.*, Elizabeth's 1920s-style clothes) consequently written off as the aforementioned (and non-applic-able) "cosmetic anomalies."

Incidentally, a Turn of the (18th–19th) Century time frame for *Frank-enstein* also explains the Monster's otherwise anachronistic appearance as a wax figure in *Abbott and Costello Meet Dr. Jekyll and Mr. Hyde*, which, based on various trappings (*e.g.*, telephones, electrical fixtures, etc.), also seems set about that time. Obviously, either the Monster's infamy spread rapidly and as far as England, or someone from the museum vacationed near Castle Frankenstein and saw the Monster up close enough to have a wax figure made.

We now pause to address some undisclosed events in *Frankenstein*— specifically, the activities of the Monster following his murder of Profes-sor Waldman and escape from the watchtower, but prior to his eventual appearance in Elizabeth's bedroom at Castle Frankenstein. During this transitional period, we are witnesses as the Monster inadvertently kills the child Maria. And Henry learns from his friend Victor Moritz that, "He's been seen in the hills, terrorizing the mountainside." What we do not see is that this "terrorizing" also includes the Monster tearing the arm off a boy named Krogh who will later (as seen in *Son of Frankenstein*) grow up to be the village of Frankenstein's police inspector. (Allowing that Krogh is prematurely aged in *Son of Frankenstein* when he relates this story, prob-ably because of this terrible and traumatic experience and also due to the stress of his job, he can only have been "but a child at the time, about the age of your own son, Herr Baron" at the very start of the Monster's vio-lent career.)

We move now to other "problems." In *Frankenstein*, contrary to the opinions of some published writers, there are *two* towns or villages, not one. Goldstadt is the town wherein the "Goldstadt Medical College," which Henry once attended, is located. (The name "Goldstadt" was plainly based on "Ingolstadt," a very real college town in Germany, also the place where, in Mary Shelley's novel, Victor Frankenstein creates his Monster.) From the appearance and attitude of the students, Goldstadt is a relatively sophisticated place. Henry himself establishes that this is not the village near the Frankenstein castle in the wording of his letter to Elizabeth: "I am living in an abandoned old watchtower close to the town of Goldstadt." If the towns were one and the same, Henry would have written something like, "I am living in the old watchtower outside of town."

Some distance from Goldstadt, overlooked by Castle Frankenstein, is the second town—in fact, a more primitive village populated by rural "Tyrolean" and peasant-type people. It is this village (its name revealed retroactively in the second sequel) where Hans the woodcutter brings his drowned daughter Maria in *Frankenstein*, and where the Monster is chained by the Burgomaster's gendarmes in *Bride of Frankenstein*. This village is first referred to by name in *Son of Frankenstein*. Here we finally learn that the village is called "Frankenstein,"

Boris Karloff as the Monster in the 1931 Universal Pictures classic motion picture *Frankenstein*, here seen in the woods just outside the village bearing his creator's name.

named, of course, after the long-established Frankenstein family (an important fact to remember in this discussion). Given the resentment the villagers have in *Son* for Wolf von Frankenstein, for Henry and his kin, it is doubtful that this naming was done after the events of *Frankenstein* and *Bride of Frankenstein*.

Other unrecorded events occur around the Frankenstein village and estate during the almost 40 years separating the first movies from *Son of Frankenstein*. Following the watchtower explosion ending *Bride of Frankenstein*, the Monster frees himself of the rubble and clandestinely makes his way back to the neighborhood of Castle Frankenstein. As years pass, the Monster loses his ability to speak, either due to brain or throat damage suffered during the watchtower explosion, because he prefers being mute, or, for lack of practice, he simply has forgotten how to talk.

Henry Frankenstein, around the time of Ludwig's birth, uses a fraction of the vast family wealth to remove the rubble of the old watchtower laboratory, and then relocate it to the Frankenstein property. This is not just some magnanimous attempt to atone to the people of Goldstadt for the horrors he unleashed upon them; it will also allow Henry, in secret and on his own "turf," to resume his unorthodox research. Sending Elizabeth and the boys away to England, where Wolf and Ludwig will eventually begin their own medical studies (Wolf alludes to this in *Son of Frankenstein*), Henry goes to work. He reconstructs the watchtower—at least part of it, given the destructive effects of the explosion—above the Frankenstein family burial crypts and those ancient Roman sulfur pits. Now Henry's work is rather low key, although it still involves experiments utilizing brain transplants on corpses. Eventually, he takes on two helpers—a scientist named Niemann (who, before he dies, will pass on what he learns from Frankenstein about transplanting brains, even serving as an inspiration to his mad brother Gustav, as related in *House of Frankenstein*), and a local blacksmith looking for a second job.

The blacksmith, named Ygor, moonlights snatching bodies for Henry (who *else* in the region would he have been performing this grisly work for?), eventually getting caught and arrested for his ghoulish activities by Inspector Krogh. Convicted of grave robbing shortly after Henry's death (a "horrible death," as later revealed by granddaughter Elsa in *Frankenstein Meets the Wolf Man*), Ygor is hanged. Miraculously surviving the rope, he is tossed into that old place of the dead, Frankenstein's watchtower. Now an unemployed, legally dead outcast, Ygor meets the hiding Frankenstein Monster, befriending the giant, giving him a new fur vest as a token of their friendship, and finally using the creature to murder the jury members who sentenced him to the gallows.

While Wolf von Frankenstein mostly lives in England during this period, brother Ludwig returns to the general area within approximately 20 years, settling in the village of Vasaria (note spelling) where he starts his medical practice. Ludwig is either married at the time or marries shortly thereafter, for daughter (now Baroness) Elsa Frankenstein in *Frankenstein Meets the Wolf Man* comments that she remembers Vasaria's Festival of the New Wine from when she was a child. (As we never see Ludwig's wife, it is assumed that she dies somewhere within the past couple of decades.)

When Wolf makes his 1939 return to the family estate in *Son of*

Artwork depicting the Frankenstein Castle at the edge of the Frankenstein village, as designed by art director Jack Otterson for the third movie in the series made by Universal Pictures, *Son of Frankenstein* in 1939. In the first *Frankenstein*, made eight years earlier, the watchtower in which Henry's laboratory is set up is located some distance away from the family-owned property. In this film, however, the watchtower can be seen just by peering out through a castle window.

*Frankenstein*, he does not, at first, comprehend the magnitude of Henry's achievement. He admits to Inspector Krogh that his father gave life to a dead man, although Henry's real achievement—the creation of an artificial being from parts of different corpses—was far more. In later years, obviously haunted by guilt over reviving the Monster, he retreats (according to brother Ludwig in *The Ghost of Frankenstein*) into exile.

A note regarding the Monster's 1941 "cameo appearance" in the Olsen and Johnson comedy film *Hellzapoppin'*, which was filmed between *Son of Frankenstein* and *The Ghost of Frankenstein*: As it was illogical, impractical and, more importantly, impossible for the Monster to escape from that sulfur pit, clean himself off, travel uninterrupted to the United States just for this brief appearance (and not create some kind of a major disturbance that would undoubtedly result in his capture and probable destruction), then return to Europe and the pit, this appearance can only be interpreted as an actor portraying the Monster as part of Olsen and Johnson's comedy show.

The village named Frankenstein sees much action through *Franken-stein*, *Bride of Frankenstein* and *Son of Frankenstein*; it is also the setting for the opening scenes of *The Ghost of Frankenstein*. In *The Ghost of Frankenstein*, the Burgomaster grants the villagers permission to destroy the Frankenstein castle, which they promptly do with dynamite. Both the Frankenstein Monster and Ygor demonstrate their incredible physical constitutions and their bodies' natural recuperative abilities in *The Ghost of Frankenstein*. The Monster has survived yet another "death," the boiling sulfur that claimed him in *Son of Frankenstein*, the sulfur cooling and solidifying, doing no more damage than destroying his fur vest. (Ygor would later steal for him another black jacket, apparently the Monster's apparel of choice.) Though a lightning bolt was said to have knocked him cold in *Son of Frankenstein*, another—this time hitting his neck electrodes (thereby contradicting that adage about "lightning striking twice")—somewhat renews his strength. Ygor, shot by Wolf von Frankenstein in *Son of Frankenstein*, also proves that his tough old body can survive bullets as well as a hangman's noose. He has also discovered grooming; for somewhere in those three years between *Son of Frankenstein* and *The Ghost of Frankenstein* he has managed to get some dentist to straighten his uneven teeth and a barber to trim his hair and beard.

When Ygor leaves the Frankenstein village with the Monster at the beginning of *The Ghost of Frankenstein*, all living members of the Frankenstein family have already vacated the area or died, and so there is no reason for the village to retain its accursed name. As Ygor leads his giant friend off to Vasaria (again, note the spelling) to seek "the second son of Frankenstein," Frankenstein village officials, albeit off-camera, start legal procedures to change forever the name of their own town to something less portentous. Thus, the name of "Frankenstein" becomes available to anyone who wants it, for whatever reason, for their own town.

Much of the action in *The Ghost of Frankenstein* and its inevitable sequel *Frankenstein Meets the Wolf Man* takes place in Vasaria. It is to this village that lovely Elsa Frankenstein, having left her hometown after the events of *The Ghost of Frankenstein*, returns in the follow-up two-monster picture. The year between these movies constitutes a rather difficult one for the young woman. She has been trying to forget her experiences with the Monster. Erik Ernst, the village prosecutor from *The Ghost of Frankenstein* and her former fiancé, is nowhere to be seen (possibly fearing that any children he and Elsa might have would be tainted with the seemingly inherited desire to create life by unnatural means). And somehow she has picked up a regional accent.

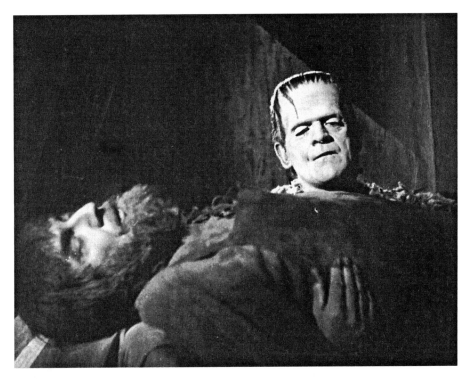

Although shot "to death" in *Son of Frankenstein* (1939), Ygor (Bela Lugosi) — as well as the Monster (Boris Karloff) — would survive (not surprisingly) this movie's final fade-out. This previously unpublished photograph is from the private collection of the film's art director, Jack Otterson.

Strangely, the ruins of Ludwig Frankenstein's house seem to have transformed into those of a castle on a hill, although the burning building that collapsed on the Monster at the end of *The Ghost of Frankenstein* was established in that film as a chateau/hospital on flat ground. These severe changes seem to have a more practical basis than those aforementioned concessions to designer's tastes and current vogues. The fact is that the Frankenstein, Dracula and Wolf Man pictures are basically Gothic-style movies, and castles on hilltops are an integral part of the Gothic tradition. Every entry in the Universal Frankenstein series has a castle (or at least a building suggesting one) in which major scenes are played out, therefore one was also incorporated into the plot of *Frankenstein Meets the Wolf Man*. Ludwig's house was not a castle in *The Ghost of Franken-stein* for a simple reason: The opening sequences of that movie takes place at Castle Frankenstein in the Frankenstein village; a second castle in

Vasaria would have been visually redundant. Regardless of the look and setting for this building, the story continuity remains basically intact, the ruins representing the Frankenstein home where the Monster was apparently last "destroyed."

Before continuing, some points are in order regarding the character of Lawrence Talbot, aka the Wolf Man, who, following his first appearance in *The Wolf Man*, becomes a major player in Universal's Frankenstein movies: That original film establishes that Talbot's transformation into a werewolf basically starts from his bare feet up. The first time we observe Talbot metamorphosing he is wearing a white T-shirt. The fully transformed Wolf Man is next seen clad in the character's trademark dark shirt, which would require human hands to put on and button. As we shall see, Talbot's hands are almost always the last (see below, concerning the Wolf Man's condition in *Abbott and Costello Meet Frankenstein*) to transform. This also implies that, until his hands are *fully* transformed, Talbot also retains enough human intelligence to remember how to dress. (The Wolf Man's predecessor in *WereWolf of London*, in the same "universe" by nature of the same basic werewolf mythology, and suffering essentially the same full moon–based curse, keeps enough intelligence after the transformation to don clothes and actually *talk*.)

In *Frankenstein Meets the Wolf Man*, Lawrence Talbot repeats his clothes-changing feat in the Cardiff hospital. He changes (we do not see his hands during the transformation, as they are kept "out of frame") to werewolf form in hospital garb and is next seen prowling the moonlit streets clad in his standard dark outfit. The final proof for this "hand last" hypothesis can be seen in the next series entry, *House of Frankenstein*. When Talbot metamorphoses in front of a dresser mirror in that film, he leaves the room transformed—*except* for his still human hands, which become Wolf Man hands by the time he gets outside. In a laboratory scene in *Abbott and Costello Meet Frankenstein*, Talbot gazes out the window; from there the scene cuts to the full moon, then to a close shot of his already-hairy hands, finally panning up to his werewolf face. This seems to imply that Talbot's feet change while he is *looking* at the moon, that his face changes while *we see* the moon, and that, once again, his hands—although we see them before we see his face—transform *last*. When the lycanthropic spell is over, however, Talbot's body transforms in its *entirety* all at once, as shown when his ice-thawed body returns to human form in *House of Frankenstein*.

Talbot's "magical shoes" are less easy to explain. The Wolf Man is almost always shown barefoot, his lupine feet part of the character's overall image. In *The Wolf Man*, Talbot is shown removing his shoes before undergoing his change; in *Frankenstein Meets the Wolf Man* it is a barefoot Wolf Man that plunges into the ice cavern beneath the Frankenstein castle ruins, but a shoe-wearing Talbot who is subsequently led by the Frankenstein Monster through those ruins; and in *Abbott and Costello Meet Frankenstein*, Talbot—in the woods, still wearing shoes—turns into a barefooted Wolf Man. How do Talbot's shoes mysteriously disappear and reappear? The explanation must be an arcane one somehow founded upon the very supernatural nature of Talbot's werewolf curse—some unknown power that can materialize, dematerialize and apparently even teleport human-manufactured wearing apparel (this explanation also being applicable to Dracula's vanishing or metamorphosing clothing when he turns into a bat or wolf, or dissolves to a skeletal state).

Why does Lawrence Talbot transform into a "human wolf" rather than a "full wolf," as had Bela the Gypsy (who, in biting Talbot before he died, passed on his werewolf curse in *The Wolf Man*)? By examining Universal's various "man into wolf" movies, and also by referring to actual legends (in which werewolves can appear as anything from crazed, non-physically transformed humans to entire wolves), we find that the werewolf phenomenon can manifest itself in various *degrees* of transformation. Indeed, even the Wolf Man's facial look differs slightly from one screen appearance to the next. This suggests that, just as Larry Talbot's human face reflected his ageing from movie to movie, so did his lycanthropic countenance evolve; thus the character in *The Wolf Man* looks quite different from that which appeared seven years later in *Abbott and Costello Meet Frankenstein*.

It is interesting to note that most "real" werewolf traditions do not mention a full moon as a catalyst for the transformation. Surprisingly, there is *no* full moon at all shown in *The Wolf Man*, nor is there even a mention of one (the "werewolf poem" in this film only refers to "the autumn moon"); not until *Frankenstein Meets the Wolf Man* does the full moon become an official part of the Wolf Man's mythology.

The lycanthropes in *WereWolf of London* are of the "human wolf" variety, people with hairy faces and animal-like fangs. Their faces, however, especially Dr. Glendon's in the London-set movie, retain much of their human appearance after transforming. The fake werewolf of the later *She-Wolf of London* does not even attempt to disguise herself with hair or fangs, stalking her victims in a monk-like cowl, the implied "change" apparently more mental or spiritual than physical. Furthermore, the werewolf curse is associated with vampiric powers (*e.g.*, the Count becoming

**Dr. Frank Mannering (Patrick Knowles) tends to the Monster (Bela Lugosi) as Baroness Elsa Frankenstein (Ilona Massey) speaks with Lawrence Talbot (Lon Chaney, Jr.) in *Frankenstein Meets the Wolf Man* (1943).**

a complete wolf in *Dracula*). According to Serbian tradition, a werewolf in life may become a vampire after death. Perhaps, then, if ever finding the death he sought for so long, Talbot might have subsequently emerged from the grave as one of the undead.

Criticism of *Frankenstein Meets the Wolf Man* has been raised questioning how Larry Talbot and the Gypsy Maleva travel from the village of Cardiff, England, to Vasaria, Germany, by wagon. Really, there is no problem here at all. When Talbot enters Maleva's camp he clearly states that he has searched for her "all over Europe." By "Europe," Talbot obviously means the continent, indicating that he has already crossed the English Channel. *Frankenstein Meets the Wolf Man* ends with Vasek, the busybody village innkeeper, blowing up the dam that drives the turbines that power-up the laboratory equipment inside Frankenstein's castle. This irresponsible act not only presumably destroys both Frankenstein's Monster and the Wolf Man during their climactic battle, but also endangers the lives of the British scientist Dr. Mannering, Elsa Frankenstein and Maleva. For this reason, following the movie's fade out, Vasek is almost immediately arrested for possible murder (of Lawrence Talbot), attempted murder (of Mannering, Elsa and Maleva), damage of private property, endangerment to the community, unlawful use of explosives, and various other charges. Naturally, he is convicted for at least some of these crimes and sentenced to serve time in Neustadt Prison where he encounters Dr. Gustav Niemann, jailed for giving a dog a human brain. The mad scientist learns from the boastful Vasek the events that had recently transpired in Vasaria (including the resting place of the Monster and the human name of the Wolf Man) that he later, in *House of Frankenstein*, relates to Talbot.

Believing her grandfather's monstrous creation finally destroyed, Elsa (in scenes we don't see) decides to remain in Vasaria, this time settling down with her new love, Frank Mannering. Guaranteed that no more monsters will be brought to life in their town, the people of Vasaria respond positively to the pretty and charismatic Elsa, actually get to like her, and finally, as suggested by the Mayor, agree to rename their town "Frankenstein" in her honor (a better name might have been "*Neu Frankenstein*," or "New Frankenstein"). Two years later, mad Dr. Niemann, accompanied by the sensitive and obedient hunchback Daniel, escapes from Neustadt Prison and gets illegal possession of Professor Bruno Lampini's traveling "Chamber of Horrors." Among the horror exhibits is the actual staked skeleton of the vampire Count Dracula, which Lampini, sometime prior to 1944 (when the events of *House of Frankenstein* take place), "borrowed" from Castle Dracula in the Carpathian Mountains.

Now for some necessary notes concerning Dracula, who, like the Wolf Man, also figures significantly in Universal's Frankenstein mythos: The original *Dracula* film ends in 1931 with the centuries-old Count destroyed by a wooden stake pounded through his heart by vampire hunter Professor Van Helsing. Dracula's corpse is not shown to revert to bones following this act, remaining uncorrupted even five years later, as verified in *Dracula's Daughter*, the first sequel to *Dracula*. Notably, the titled character in that film, Countess Zaleska, when she is fatally impaled by the wooden shaft of an arrow, also does not decompose, although she has been a vampire for at least a century. This implies, as later films (*i.e., Son of Dracula, House of Frankenstein* and *House of Dracula*) will reveal, that Universal's vampires are reduced to a skeletal state only by fire or the sun's rays. In *Dracula's Daughter*, the Countess burns her father's impaled and uncorrupted remains, then, unable to shirk her vampiric nature, returns to the family castle in Transylvania. What we are *not* shown, however, is that the flames did not *entirely* consume the Count's body, but left his articulated bones (and Van Helsing's stake) intact; nor are we shown Zaleska respectfully taking, via airplane, his skeleton back with her to Transylvania to its final resting place, only to be found years later, still impaled by that same wooden stake, by Professor Lampini.

In 1943, in the movie *Son of Dracula*, Dracula's male offspring, going by the name of "Alucard," has his brief (and final) adventure in the United States. Although it has become almost the norm during the past few decades to regard "Alucard" as the old Count himself rather than his son, this interpretation is not correct. The movie's title constitutes evidence as to "Alucard's" position in the Dracula family. "Alucard" is identified in the film by a character (a Van Helsing equivalent), uncertain as to the vampire's true identity, as either the original Count *or* his descendant. Most importantly, this movie (which begins with the vampire simply showing up in North America and ending with his destruction by sunlight on the same soil) stands alone, not otherwise fitting into the continuity of *Dracula*, *Dracula's Daughter*, or the later *House of Frankenstein* and *House of Dracula*. Finally, this vampire (perhaps because of his relative youth) does not display all the weaknesses of his father and sister (*e.g.*, he casts a reflection in a mirror), and has at least one unique power, transforming into a mist, which the other family members are never shown to possess. Although one character says, "He's not Count Alucard, he's Count Dracula," remember that Dracula is a last or family name. Just as Henry Frankenstein, Elizabeth Frankenstein, Ludwig Frankenstein and Elsa Frankenstein can all correctly be called "Frankenstein," so are Count Dracula, Countess Zaleska and Count "Alucard" all named "Dracula."

The original Count Dracula—that is, the one from the first *Dracula* movie—returns in *House of Frankenstein* with a new face and at least one new human vice: Now he drinks wine. In *Dracula*, the Count tells castle guest Renfield, whom he is plainly toying with at that moment like a spider with a fly, that he "never" drinks wine. This also implies either something about Dracula's personal taste in beverages, or that, as far as alcohol is concerned, the vampire is "on the wagon" in 1931. When he imbibes wine in *House of Frankenstein*, his motives are rather different, however. Not only is he trying to pass himself off as the human "Baron Latos," but he doesn't want to appear rude (by refusing the wine of the Hussman household) to the desirable young newlywed Rita. As to the vampire's new look? Since (a change in actors not withstanding) he has the super-

"Mad Scientist" Dr. Niemann (Boris Karloff) holds Count Dracula (John Carradine) at stake-point in Universal Picture's first "monster rally," *House of Frankenstein* in 1944. Contrary to the opinion of some Dracula-movie buffs, this is the *first* time the *original* Count appears on the screen since his remains were shown cremated by his distaff offspring in the 1936 sequel *Dracula's Daughter.*

natural power to change his physical form, metamorphosing from a "Bela Lugosi" look to a "John Carradine" countenance should certainly be less difficult to accomplish than becoming a bat or wolf.

Following the vampire Count's destruction by the rising sun in *House of Frankenstein*, Dr. Niemann and Daniel drive the purloined "Chamber of Horrors" wagons into the area where the Monster and Wolf Man were swept away by the rushing waters in *Frankenstein Meets the Wolf Man*. This is the recently re-christened village of Frankenstein, formerly Vasaria (again, remember the spelling), where Elsa Frankenstein and Dr. Frank Mannering presumably now happily live (although the camera does not show this). By now the residents of the new Frankenstein village are much embarrassed by the stigma of Vasek, one of their own people after all, perpetrating so heinous an act against his own community. Thus, a gendarme explains away the ruins of the Frankenstein property by simply stating, "the dam burst and swept the Wolf Man and Frankenstein Monster to their destruction." Niemann and Daniel encounter a band of Gypsies camped near the Frankenstein ruins. Remember that Maleva mysteriously disappears near the end of *Frankenstein Meets the Wolf Man* a year earlier, and is last seen in these ruins. The Gypsy band in *House of Frankenstein* could, then, be her own, having tracked their beloved senior member to this area; or this could be a different band altogether, which takes her in. Either way, we now have a plausible explanation as to how the Gypsy girl Ilonka knows that ubiquitous "werewolf poem," which is part of the United Kingdom's (and, presumably, not "the Continent's") folklore.

Dr. Niemann's hometown—to which he finally returns, taking along Daniel, Talbot, the comatose Frankenstein Monster and Ilonka in *House of Frankenstein*—is in "Visaria" (note the subtly different spelling). It is not uncommon in some European countries to have towns and villages with similarly spelled names (*e.g.*, in Germany the towns of Frankenstein, Falkenstein, Frankenthal and Frankfurt all coexist). "Visaria," therefore, is not "Vasaria," but another place altogether; and unlike that other town, it must be located in the northern part of the country, as, in the forthcoming *House of Dracula*, it will be shown to be a seacoast town.

Certainly, Dr. Niemann is well described as a "mad scientist." Among his crazy plans for revenge is to give Strauss, one of the men whose testimony sent the doctor to prison, the brain of the Wolf Man, Niemann explaining that the transplantation will, therefore, turn his old foe into a werewolf on moonlit nights. In reality, this operation, even if successful, would leave Strauss stone-cold dead, while Talbot's consciousness would simply occupy a new but older body. A saner scientist would have known better.

Both Count Dracula and Lawrence Talbot inexplicably show up again in *House of Dracula* with nary a scratch after apparently suffering "permanent" demises in *House of Frankenstein*—the vampire reduced to bones by the rays of the rising sun, the Wolf Man shot with a "silver bullet ... fired by someone who loves him enough to understand" (Ilonka's).

In the Wolf Man's case, an explanation for his survival is relatively easy: Ilonka, in the excitement of the werewolf's attack on her, simply misses firing the bullet into a vital spot ... that, or the bullet passes clean through the creature's body. Whichever is correct, that silver projectile

The comatose Monster (Glenn Strange), "Mad Scientist" Dr. Gustav Niemann (Boris Karloff) and "Wolf Man" Lawrence Talbot (Lon Chaney, Jr.) on their journey from the town of Frankenstein to that of Vasaria (note spelling) in *House of Frankenstein* (1944).

obviously does some significant damage, knocking the Wolf Man unconscious or into a temporary coma, and spurring his change back to human form, but does not kill him.

The Count's survival is more complicated to explain. Remember that when watching a movie we are only privy to what narrative information the cameras and microphones record, and then only what the film's editor includes for us to see and hear. In *House of Frankenstein*, when Dracula meets his doom by the sun's rays, we only see his *hand* dissolving away to bones, the rest of his body being hidden and not included in the frame.

Then the camera cuts away to Tony, the young hero, and the gendarmes rescuing Tony's new wife Rita, whom the vampire had placed under his spell. Had the camera remained on Dracula and shown him to us in his entirety, we might know how he escaped final destruction. Only Dracula's arm and hand are exposed to the direct rays of the sun, the rest of his body taking shelter behind his black coffin. Off-camera, using his cape as a protective shield, the Count, despite the agony of the sunlight and the bony condition of his arm and hand, manages to get back inside his coffin and shut the lid. Fortunately this is a remote area, Tony and the others having already left the actual scene tending to Rita. Here the vampire remains unmolested further until sunset, after which he emerges from his casket bed and secrets it away. It takes Dracula about a year to regenerate his tissues fully—just in time to enter the plotline of the next sequel, *House of Dracula*.

The title *House of Dracula* actually refers to the castle of Dr. Franz Edelmann, which, like Niemann's old home with laboratory, is "coincidentally" also situated in Visaria. The Frankenstein Monster is among the denizens destined to inhabit Edelmann's castle, and how he ends up there is well documented in the movie's dialogue (the quicksand enveloping the Monster's perfectly preserved body and Dr. Niemann's skeleton conveniently washed into a cave beneath Edelmann's house). Why a kindly doctor like Edelmann possesses the laboratory apparatus required to revive the Frankenstein Monster is never explained, however; which means we must again consider events that occur during the year separating *House of Frankenstein* from *House of Dracula*.

At the climax of *House of Frankenstein*, Dr. Niemann dies, carried into the quicksand bog by the Monster. Leaving behind no heirs (recall that his brother presumably died before passing on Henry Frankenstein's brain-transplantation secrets), his possessions, including a big house and everything inside it, soon go up for public auction. Fascinated by Niemann's collection of fantastic gadgets and gizmos (and in need of more space for his own practice), the mad scientist's naturally inquisitive neighbor Dr. Edelmann, the only bidder, purchases the house and its lab materials, possibly to use in some future experiment.

*House of Dracula* reflects the world's increasing cynicism and lack of belief in things supernatural resulting from the "growing up" much of its population did during the Second World War (an attitude also responsible, at least in part, for the genre of "film noir"). In this last of the "serious" sequels, the supernatural origins of the Count and the Wolf Man, Universal gospel since those characters were introduced in 1931 and 1941,

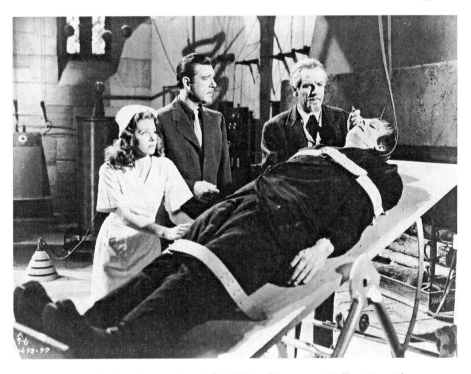

Hunchbacked Miliza (Jane Adams), "Wolf Man" Lawrence Talbot (Lon Chaney, Jr.) and not yet "Mad Doctor" Franz Edelmann (Onslow Stevens) discuss the alive but mostly dormant Frankenstein's Monster (Glenn Strange) in *House of Dracula* (1945). Did Edelmann purchase this property and laboratory equipment at auction from the estate of "Mad Scientist" Dr. Niemann? (Courtesy Dennis Druktenis, *The Journal of Frankenstein* and *Castle of Frankenstein* magazines.)

respectively, are explained away *scientifically*. (Other monsters introduced by Universal Pictures around this time also had science- or reality-based origins, *e.g.*, the Ape Woman, the Creeper and the aforementioned She-Wolf of London.) Does this mean that it now requires something different from the old book of monster-destroying rules—something based in science rather than mythology or religion—to lay these creatures to rest forever?

Actually, Dr. Edelmann, a brilliant man of science, is wrong in his theories regarding the origins of Dracula and the Wolf Man (there was no "second opinion" offered). Surely the origins of these characters are clearly based in the supernatural and not in science, as emphasized in all of these films excluding *House of Dracula*, and demonstrated by such unscientific phenomena as their vanishing and transforming clothes. More plausibly than contributing to the ends of these characters' careers, the scientific experiments of Dr. Edelmann on Dracula and Lawrence Talbot contribute in mysterious ways to their inevitable survival and subsequent swansong reappearance in the horror comedy *Abbott and Costello Meet Frankenstein*.

Recall that in *House of Dracula* the vampire Count is again completely reduced to bones by the deadly (to him) rays of the sun. This time, however, Dracula is already snuggled inside his coffin bed when the searing solar rays strike. If that does not offer him at least some protection, the chemicals injected into him by Dr. Edelmann—intended to make him *human* again—do affect his remains. However, we are not shown how, after Edelmann leaves the cellar, Nina the hunchbacked nurse dutifully goes downstairs to close Dracula's coffin. Now protected entirely from the sun's rays, with the doctor's drugs having a retroactive effect, the Count—abandoned and forgotten as the climactic events of *House of Dracula* unfold—begins his gradual process of regeneration. The process at last complete, the mostly "back to normal" Dracula salvages the alive but severely weakened Frankenstein Monster from the rubble of Dr. Edelmann's castle and prepares for their later trip to the United States in the Bud Abbott and Lou Costello film.

Although the curse of lycanthropy has, in theory, been lifted from Lawrence Talbot by more of Dr. Edelmann's amazing science, this miracle cure proves to be, at best, only temporary. Besides, this would not be the first time some doctor's attempt to cure Talbot failed to "take." During the operation in which Edelmann relieves the pressure on Talbot's skull that supposedly contributes to his transformations, the doctor warns, "He must be kept quiet. Any exertion could undo everything I hope we've accomplished." As it is unlikely that a man of action like Talbot could go through the rest of his life without "any exertion," it is consequently not surprising when he returns, werewolf curse and all, in *Abbott and Costello Meet Frankenstein*.

Dr. Edelmann's revolutionary experiments actually *do* work, at least to some minor extents, on our three classic fiends. Some of their effects, in fact, seemingly last for at least three years, carrying over into the storyline of *Abbott and Costello Meet Frankenstein*. In this last entry in the series (excluding *The Munsters* television shows and its movie spin-offs of decades later), Dracula—perhaps slightly more "human" than before—in two *deliberately* staged scenes, now casts (as do mortal humans and also his son Alucard) a mirror reflection. The Wolf Man, when biting "Cham-

The Wolf Man, or Lawrence Talbot (Lon Chaney, Jr.), attacks Dr. Edelmann (Onslow Stevens) in Universal Pictures' last serious Frankenstein movie, *House of Dracula* (1945). Edelmann will inevitably "cure" Talbot of his lycanthropic affliction, using a mold grown in this subterranean chamber. The cure, however, will not be permanent, as the Wolf Man will return four years later (to menace funnymen Bud Abbott and Lou Costello).

ber of Horrors" owner McDougal, apparently does not pass on his werewolf curse (unless there remains some unfilmed "sequel" out there that some other writer might care to tackle), perhaps an aftereffect of Edelmann's operation; and when Talbot undergoes his famous change in the woods, his face and hands transform simultaneously. Finally, Frankenstein's Monster, made stronger when Edelmann gives him "the strength of a hundred men," has not only had his physical strength boosted by the doctor (made into a Mr. Hyde–like madman by a transfusion of Dracula's blood), but also his courage and intelligence. For in *Abbott and Costello Meet*

*Frankenstein*, the Monster not only steps bravely into the flames of a blazing pier, he has also remembered how to speak.

A final comment regarding *Abbott and Costello Meet Frankenstein*: Just *which* Invisible Man is it that makes his cameo non-appearance at the end of this film? Naturally, this can only be a somewhat older Geoffrey Radcliffe from the first "Invisible" sequel, *The Invisible Man Returns*, who has apparently risked the insanity-inducing properties of the invisibility drug "duocaine" "to get in on the excitement." Unlike Radcliffe, the original character, the eventually mad scientist Jack Griffin in *The Invisible Man*, and his apparent nefarious, non-scientist descendant Robert Griffin in *The Invisible Man's Revenge*, both perish at the ends of their respective movies; good-guy relative (identical twin brother?) Frank Griffin in *Invisible Agent* apparently gives up his invisible career following his wartime adventure fighting the Axis; and this is certainly not the titled character (with no apparent relationship to the Griffin clan) of *The Invisible Woman* with a deeper voice. Also, the character in both this Abbott and Costello film and *The Invisible Man Returns* sounds the same (both voiced by actor Vincent Price). It would be, of course, an entirely new character that does "get in on the excitement" three years after *Abbott and Costello Meet Frankenstein* in *Abbott and Costello Meet the Invisible Ma*n, a film sharing continuity with the original *Invisible Man* and its sequels.

Unlike the American-made Frankenstein movies of Universal, those made by Hammer Films in England have paid only a modicum of attention to real plot to plot continuity. Most of the Hammer Frankenstein entries can more or less stand on their own and be enjoyed even when watched out of the sequence in which they were made and released. The biggest problems with the Hammer movies are how *The Evil of Frankenstein* and *The Horror of Frankenstein*, which diverge so drastically from the other entries, fit into this British series.

To understand the problems with *The Evil of Frankenstein*, we must first consider the very character of the film's (and series') principal figure, Baron Victor Frankenstein. In the first entry into the Hammer movies series, *The Curse of Frankenstein*, Victor is shown telling the story of the "Creature" he had made to a priest in his prison cell while awaiting execution for murder. In the flashback that makes up most of the film's narrative, we see the Baron and an assistant bring to life a white-faced, black-haired Creature having its own distinctive look. In *The Evil of Frankenstein*, in another flashback sequence also related by the Baron (to his assistant Hans), a much different-appearing, Universal-inspired Creature comes to life, with Frankenstein shown accomplishing this scientific

"THE CURSE OF FRANKENSTEIN"
In Eastman Colour                                    Cert 'X'
starring PETER CUSHING with
HAZEL COURT  ·  ROBERT URQUHART
and CHRISTOPHER LEE as the CREATURE

Baron Victor Frankenstein (Peter Cushing) is assisted by Paul Krempe (Robert Urquhart) in the making of and giving life to the Creature (Christopher Lee) in the 1957 Hammer Films production *The Curse of Frankenstein.*

feat with no one's help. After this flashback the Baron discovers *this* version of his Creature entombed in ice.

Here we clearly have *two similar though different* accounts of Baron Victor Frankenstein bringing to life his Creature ... one with the Baron aided by an assistant, the other with Victor working solo, and with two very different appearing Creatures. Which account is true? Actually, in a way, both of them; but both versions are dependent on the Baron's personality, which includes his having a tremendous ego and a tendency to deviate from the truth when it suits him (*e.g.*, his frequent change of name from film to film, his deceiving the wife of his latest human guinea pig in *Frankenstein Must Be Destroyed*, his lying in court in *Frankenstein and the Monster from Hell*, and so forth, on and on). Also, recall that in only one version of this creation account, *The Evil of Frankenstein*, is the Creature ever actually seen outside of the flashback; in *The Curse of Frankenstein* the Creature's appearance is entirely based on the imagery conjured up as a result of Victor's telling of his story.

The Baron's primary motive in *The Curse of Frankenstein* for telling his story is the misguided hope that the clergyman will believe him innocent of the murders committed by the Creature and, consequently, save him from the guillotine's blade. At the same time, however, Frankenstein oddly admits, in his narrative, to murdering Professor Bernstein for his brain and also to engineering the killing of servant Justine by the Creature (Victor perhaps being unable to resist an urge to boast of these clever machinations). For reasons known only to him, Frankenstein again lies— this time about the Creature's final fate, inventing from whole cloth the story of its destruction in the acid vat. The priest, then, leaves the jail cell remembering Victor's story of an experiment performed by two scientists, while conjuring up his own mental image of the Creature's (the one we see in the flashback) appearance.

What we therefore see in this extended flashback in *The Curse of Frankenstein* is basically "true"—although, as we will later see, the *actual* Creature (the version seen in *The Evil of Frankenstein*) looks nothing like the image created in the priest's imagination (and on screen for the audience's benefit) and is not dissolved in acid. In *The Evil of Frankenstein*, the Baron relates his story, albeit in a somewhat distorted and truncated flashback version, to a colleague he is trying to *impress*. Frankenstein does this by lying yet again, describing how he alone gave life to the Creature, thereby sharing with nobody the glory of his great scientific accomplishment. In *The Evil of Frankenstein* account, however, the Baron does not claim that the Creature was destroyed by acid. Because this version of the Creature is later seen in person by Hans looking exactly as he does in Victor's flashback, this version must be the character's *true* appearance.

In other words, the events of Victor's flashback story in *The Curse of Frankenstein* are essentially true, the most notable exception being the acid bath ending for the Creature, although the character's physical look is incorrect; while in *The Evil of Frankenstein*, although the events have been much revised to the Baron's liking, the Creature's appearance is accurate.

This only leaves *The Horror of Frankenstein*, which is basically a somewhat comedic remake of *The Curse of Frankenstein*, retaining the acid bath destruction but once again depicting a markedly different version of the "original" Creature. Fitting this movie into the rest of the Hammer Frankenstein series is simultaneously quite easy and yet also seemingly impossible. Again, explaining the perceived lapses in continuity requires some "filling in the blanks" by considering what happens outside the Baron's cell as he relates his story to the priest in *The Curse of Frankenstein*, and what happens after that picture ends.

Actually, the Baron's confessor is not the only person to hear the scientist's fantastic tale. It is also heard by a guard, who is stationed patiently just outside the cell door. The guard, of course, imagines his *own* version of the Creature. Telling what he overheard to a friend, the story gets distorted ... then, again, as the retold tale is passed on to another and another. One of these later recountings of the tale constitutes what we see in *The Horror of Frankenstein*, off-color jokes and all.

And so, there really are no conundrums, no continuity mistakes, to spoil the enjoyment of those revered Universal and Hammer Frankenstein movies. At least not anymore. (I'll leave it to some other writer to work out the sometimes-annoying continuity problems in Universal's "Mummy" series.)

So, let's thread up those movie projectors and slip in those videotapes and DVDs, grab a bowl of buttered popcorn, sit back and enjoy. And if any apparent continuity errors come our way, well, they can be eliminated. All it takes is some research—and a bit of imagination.

# II

# THE "STRANGE" FRANKENSTEIN MONSTER

The following piece is a composite based upon articles that, over the period of a decade, had originally appeared in three different forms in three different publications. They all had a common theme, however—actor, stuntman and friend Glenn Strange, who played the Frankenstein Monster on numerous occasions, including three Universal motion pictures (*House of Frankenstein* in 1944, *House of Dracula* in 1945 and *Abbott and Costello Meet Frankenstein* in 1948), various television shows and in personal appearances.

The first of these articles to see print was an interview conducted by film historian, collector and actor Bob Burns and myself in Bob's home on June 16, 1965. The original version of this interview included much information about Glenn's non–Frankenstein appearances in Westerns, serials, in rodeos, etc., which I did not feel appropriate given the theme of this book and also that of the present piece. It appeared under the title "Special Interview: Glenn Strange" in the fourth issue of *Modern Monsters* (October-November 1966), a monster-movie magazine I was editing at the time for Prestige Publications.

The second article was actually an "add-on" to "The Lone Stranger," written by Forrest J Ackerman and first published in an earlier issue of his magazine *Famous Monsters of Filmland*. This new material was published in "*FM*" number 105 (March 1974) as a memorial to Glenn, who had died in 1973.

The penultimate piece, published subsequent to the "*FM*" article, was originally titled "Glenn Strange Frankenstein: Monster of Dodge City." It was my obituary of Glenn appearing in Marvel Publication's black and white comic magazine *Monsters Unleashed!* number 4 (April 1974).

The last piece was simply a "monster-movie memory" I was asked to write by Dennis Druktenis for his *Castle of Frankenstein* (2002) magazine recounting my first experience with seeing the movie *Abbott and Costello Meet Frankenstein*.

The challenge in re-presenting this material here was, like Victor Frankenstein himself trying to create a human being, cutting and revising and rearranging the original materials to make a new and hopefully better "whole."

❊    ❊    ❊

On September 20, 1973, death claimed another performer associated with the portrayal of Frankenstein's Monster, 74-year-old character actor Glenn Strange, who passed away due to cancer just two brief months following the death of another veteran actor known for playing the Monster, Lon Chaney, Jr.

Boris Karloff, who created the first enduring screen image of Frankenstein's Monster in *Frankenstein* (1931), had died in 1969; but Glenn Strange remains, arguably, the most exploited and recognizable movie Frankenstein Monster of them all. For it was his familiar, craggy-lined face, usually in the make-up created for him by Bud Westmore's team in Universal-International's comedy-horror classic *Abbott and Costello Meet Frankenstein* (1948), that became the template for a seemingly endless output of masks, dart boards, games, puzzles, model kits, decks of cards, transfers, iron-ons, movie viewers, paint-by-numbers sets, loose-leaf binders, statues, swizzle sticks, candy and yet more paraphernalia. Unfortunately, Glenn Strange never enjoyed a dime in royalties over the sales of such myriad items, although his face sold barrels of the merchandise over the years. (Universal, however, enjoyed the handsome royalty revenues supplied by these Strange-related items.)

Glenn Strange was born in 1911 in Weed, New Mexico. The young Irish-Cherokee began work as a real-life cowboy, moonlighted as a heavyweight wrestler, became a riding and roping star with cowboy hero Hoot Gibson's rodeo, and eventually entered talking pictures during the early

1930s as a stuntman (he very visibly doubles John Wayne in some of the "Duke's" first oaters). He would go on to make about 325 movies altogether, most of which were Westerns. But to fans of horror movies Glenn Strange was no cowboy but a bonafide *horror star*—a portrayer of the classic Frankenstein Monster, his name flashing upon the screen in the company of such respected genre names as Boris Karloff, Bela Lugosi, Lon Chaney, Jr., John Carradine and George Zucco.

Glenn Strange had been familiar with the creature made and given life by Frankenstein long before he ever donned the world-famous Monster getup.

"Like my brother and I, when we saw the Frankenstein Monster in El Paso, Texas," Glenn Strange told Bob Burns and me when we interviewed him in 1965, "neither of us knew a thing about make-up, but we knew that people couldn't just dig somebody up out of a grave, a piece here and there, and make a man out of it. And he said, 'You know they can't build a guy up like that and make him breathe again. But where the hell did they ever find a guy that looked like that?' This was the first Karloff *Frankenstein.* I never dreamed I'd be playing the part myself someday."

Glenn Strange's initial stint as the Monster was in Universal's 1944 multi-monster picture *House of Frankenstein.*

"*House of Frankenstein* was the first time I played the Monster.... It's kind of a funny thing, in a way. [Universal Pictures head make-up artist] Jack Pierce was making me up for an Yvonne De Carlo [movie] and I had to wear a big scar. I was laying in the chair—now I didn't know this, but they had been testing guys for the Monster, guys like [Western movie actor] Lane Chandler. But I didn't know it. I didn't know Jack; this was the first time I ever met him. He said, 'Just a minute,' and went over to the phone and called Paul Malvern. Well, I knew Paul very well. I'd made a lot of Westerns for him. Paul was on the lot and was going to produce [*House of Frankenstein*]. He came down and Jack said, 'Here's the contour we've been looking for. Right here.' And Paul said, 'That's fine with me. Do you want to put [the make-up] on him and try it out?' So when I was through with the De Carlo show, they put me on it. I went out and did a few little walk-throughs in the Monster get-up and they said, 'okay.' And that was it. That's the way I became the Frankenstein Monster."

Having the desired look, Strange then had to master the walk and mannerisms of the well-established character. To accomplish that, he went to the best and most immediate source available, the star of *House of Frankenstein.*

"Nobody ever helped anybody as much as Boris Karloff helped me,"

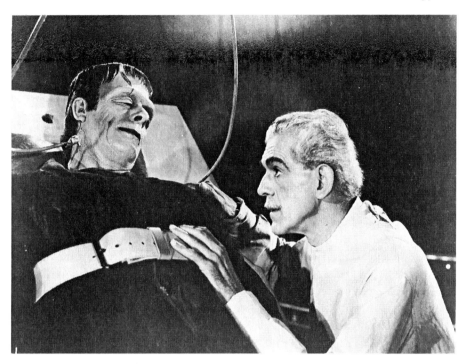

Glenn Strange, an actor best known for roles in Western movies, in *House of Frankenstein* (1944), his first stint at portraying the Frankenstein Monster. Strange was coached on set in the part by none other than the studio's original Frankenstein Monster, Boris Karloff, seen here in his role as "Mad Scientist" Dr. Gustav Niemann. (Courtesy Dennis Druktenis, *The Journal of Frankenstein* and *Castle of Frankenstein* magazines.)

said Strange. "I'll never forget that. I asked him for advice because I wanted to do this thing as near as he did. He was very kind about it. He would stay on the set and coach me. I know when I was on tour with the [later] Abbott and Costello thing, he was in New York doing *Arsenic and Old Lace*. A lot of people came backstage and congratulated him on the Abbott and Costello thing. And in the Sunday paper in New York he had given them the story of not he doing it, but me doing it. The whole thing. So right after I read that story, when I'd finished [a personal appearance for the movie], I'd always come out for two or three minutes and talk to the audience. I would say, "If you folks liked me as the Monster in *Abbott and Costello Meet Frankenstein*, then I want to give most of the credit to the man who created it, and the man who helped me in the show that I did with him, where he did the doctor. And he coached me on the walk and the movements and so forth. And if I made a good Monster, the credit goes to one of the nicest guys I know, Boris Karloff.' Later on, somebody told him what I was doing. But it was the only thing to do. He was getting all the write-ups for the thing and naturally, even though the younger generation knows better today, would. But even today, you say to the older generation, 'Who's the Frankenstein Monster?,' and they'll say, 'Karloff.'"

Not all of Glenn Strange's memories of *House of Frankenstein* were as pleasant as his being coached by Boris Karloff, especially the scene in which the Frankenstein Monster carries Dr. Niemann into the swamp to evade a pursuing, torch-bearing mob.

"If you recall the picture, I had to come out of the castle where Karloff had brought me back to life. I had a big strap that went underneath my coat, with a ring or snap on it. [Karloff's] double wore a belt around himself, and I'd snap into the ring and then put mine around him, 'cause nobody can walk around with a guy hanging under your arm. And coming down those steps, besides. There must have been 30 or 40 of those steps. They were chasing me with these torches. Somebody whizzed one of these torches—they were big, with a long club, and all that burlap on them— and hit me right between the shoulders, and almost knocked me off one of those steps.

"Then we went down into the swamp thing, where we went into the quicksand. That's where they lined up this big ring of tumbleweeds, then a little clear spot, and then another ring. They were dousing this with some sort of chemical; I don't know what it was. I said to the special-effects man that I couldn't move very fast with those boots, and carrying this guy besides. And now he's really just out, and I had to carry his whole weight. He said I had plenty of time to get across there. But actually, I didn't. That was just one flash, and burning all around there. I went straight through it, kicking the stuff out of my way as I went. It singed [Karloff's double's] hair. I almost lost that camera, I got in the water so fast, carrying him with me."

In the logical follow-up movie, next year's *House of Dracula*, Glenn Strange's Frankenstein Monster character is discovered, along with the skeletal remains of Dr. Niemann, below the home of another scientist, the illustrious Dr. Edelmann (played by Onslow Stevens). Returning also from the previous entry in Universal's Frankenstein series was John Carradine as Count Dracula and Lon Chaney, Jr. as Lawrence Talbot, alias the Wolf Man.

"And another thing, if you recall. Remember when I was laying in the quicksand in *House of Dracula*, and the opening scene had me with the skeleton of Karloff in the quicksand? Well, I was in there all day long and that stuff was cold! They poured it down a chute and into this cave-like thing. And [Lon] Chaney came down with a fifth and I think I got most of it. He poured it down me and it warmed me up some. They finished shooting and I went up to the dressing room. Of course, they had a nice fire up there. They took the make-up off and by the time I got about half undressed I was so looped I could hardly get up. I got warm and then I got tight. But I think he just about saved my life that day. I was chilling. I was cold. Well, by golly he was nice to me, and always has been. I'd like to do another picture with him sometime. He's followed in the footsteps of his old Dad pretty well. He's a good horror man; you know that. I doubt if anyone could have done as good as Lon as

Glenn Strange repeated his role of the Frankenstein Monster in 1945's *House of Dracula*, although the character's involvement in the film was minimal (his climactic scenes intercut with stock footage from an earlier movie, *The Ghost of Frankenstein*). (Courtesy Dennis Druktenis, *The Journal of Frankenstein* and *Castle of Frankenstein* magazines.)

the Wolf Man. He did a good job. But I liked him better in those Inner Sanctum mysteries he did for Universal, because you have no chance to act if you're a Wolf Man.... But I liked those Inner Sanctums. He had a good chance to show dramatic stuff in them and he proved it."

Dr. Edelmann later goes mad and restores the giant to his full strength. The Monster's ignoble "death" at the end of this film is, unfortunately, mostly in the form of stock footage from Universal's earlier *The Ghost of Frankenstein*, starring Lon Chaney, Jr. as the Monster.

*Abbott and Costello Meet Frankenstein* (1948) was made by the new Universal-International. In addition to being arguably the best comedy film starring the team of Bud Abbott and Lou Costello, it is generally regarded as the best horror or monster spoof ever filmed. Once again it reunited three infamous creatures—the Frankenstein Monster (Strange),

The Monster's (Glenn Strange) make-up was revised in both look and color by the Bud Westmore team in the comedy-horror hit *Abbott and Costello Meet Frankenstein* (1948). It was also revised within the film. This more menacing-looking version of the make-up, seen in a studio publicity photograph, thickened Strange's lips and included the "beauty spot" on his right cheek, carry-overs from previous Universal movies. These details would mysteriously vanish following the early scenes featuring the character. (Courtesy Dennis Druktenis, *The Journal of Frankenstein* and *Castle of Frankenstein* magazines.)

Count Dracula (Bela Lugosi returning to the role he created in the 1931 film *Dracula*), and the Wolf Man (Chaney). More on-screen footage than ever before of the Monster turned up in *Abbott and Costello Meet Frankenstein*, to the delight of the character's many fans, with the climax of this film showing the giant consumed in the flames of a burning pier.

For the Abbott and Costello picture, changes were made in the characters' make-up, often exaggerating their features. In the Monster's case, such alterations included over-emphasizing the high forehead, raising the electrodes on the neck to almost the level of the earlobes, combing the hair back on the sides, changing the shape of the forehead scar, as well as other innovations.

"My make-up was a little lighter in the Abbott and Costello film than the Jack Pierce make-up [in *House of Frankenstein* and *House of Dracula*]," remembered Glenn Strange. "But Jack did this himself. He'd set you in there for four hours and that was that. But we had Jack Kevan and Emil Levine and, of course, Buddy Westmore in the Abbott and Costello thing. They did some things I liked very much. That is, they made the scars in pieces and kept them that way and put them on. Jack Pierce built them with cotton and dried it. I think by making the scars and putting them on it saved quite a bit of time. But actually, for the color of the make-up, it seemed to me like it was a little lighter [in *Abbott and Costello Meet Frankenstein*], with a somewhat silver base. Jack's was kind of an aluminum gray, like when aluminum gets kind of dark, not light. The hair was black."

Regarding the question of stunt doubles, Glenn related, "Lon [Chaney] doubled for me once, when I broke the bones in my foot. I was walking along in *Abbott and Costello Meet Frankenstein* with a girl, to throw her through the window. I stepped on a camera cable. And those boots, you know, don't have any counter in them. And it flopped over. We thought we'd lose about three days shooting. But when they put the walker on, what they did was—you know the soles of those boots were four inches thick. You don't see them, but they're built up inside. It's cork or something like it. And they cut a section out in there so this walker would sit down in it. Then they slit the boot so I could get it on and then laced it, and then taped it, so you couldn't see it. I don't know how much they weighed, but they were heavy. In the meantime, Lon wasn't working that day, so he came down. They put the make-up on him and he did the scene for me.

"Nobody doubled me in *Abbott and Costello Meet Frankenstein*, except when Chaney did that. There were, of course, stand-ins who would do things in long shot with a mask on. Walter DePaulma used to be Lon's stand-in. That was on *House of Dracula*. On *House of Frankenstein* it was Don.... I can't think of his last name. But all of his running, jumping over logs and stuff [as the Wolf Man], he did himself."

Many monster-movie fans are surprised to learn that Glenn Strange's career in fantastic films spanned a number of titles besides those three in which he played the Frankenstein Monster. His first such picture was a Mascot serial released in 1932 entitled *The Hurricane Express*. Glenn played a gangster working for a mysterious villain known as "The Wrecker," who, for a dozen chapters, disguised himself by wearing totally life-like masks in the images of the other key characters, including the young hero played by John Wayne.

Glenn Strange's first "monster" role has gone virtually unheralded by many film historians, primarily because of a lack of complete credits in the titles of numerous old films. In the 1936 Universal serial *Flash Gordon* Glenn portrayed one of Emperor Ming the Merciless' centurion-like soldiers. But he also wore the metal garb of a robot-like character, and also carried off the helpless hero Flash (Buster Crabbe) in a pincer-like claw playing a dinosaur-like reptilian behemoth (called a "Gocko" in Alex Raymond's original comic strip).

In 1939, the year Boris Karloff returned again as the Monster in the film *Son of Frankenstein*, Glenn Strange menaced heroic Robert Livingston in Republic Pictures' serial *The Lone Ranger Rides Again*. But it was not until two years later that he again assumed the guise of a movie monster. The ultra-cheap movie *The Mad Monster* (1941) featured Glenn Strange as a "Lennie" type of simpleton who is transformed into a killer werewolf by a mad scientist played by George Zucco. The film was made by "Poverty Row" studio PRC (Producers Releasing Corporation) and might not have slipped into obscurity had it not been eclipsed by its competition, the Universal Pictures classic of that same year, *The Wolf Man*, starring Lon Chaney, Jr.

Two more eerie movies made by PRC followed, the first being *The Black Raven*, again starring Zucco, which featured Glenn Strange as a superstitious handyman named Andy. Though not really a horror film, this picture was of the "old dark house" and "stormy night" variety of mysteries so popular on screen and stage during the 1920s, 1930s and 1940s. Glenn was back associating with mad scientists in *The Monster Maker* (PRC, 1944), portraying a "man in a white coat" to the title character of the film, portrayed by J. Carrol Naish. Naish played a mad doctor who produced in his victims the very real, features-distorting disease acromegaly, altering them into monstrous distortions of their normal-appearing selves. (That same year both Strange and Naish would tangle with each other in *House of Frankenstein* as, respectively, the Monster and the murderous hunchback Daniel, whom the Monster eventually kills.)

Shortly after his final Universal Frankenstein role, Glenn Strange played Atlas the Monster, a kind of prehistoric man (with make-up again by Jack Pierce) revived by Frankenstein-type laboratory apparatus, in *Master Minds* (1949), a quickie made by Monogram Pictures with the Bowery Boys. This was probably as an attempt to capitalize on Strange's name and the popularity of the recent *Abbott and Costello Meet Frankenstein*. A weird experiment transfers the "mind" and voice of Satch (Huntz Hall), one of the Boys, into poor Atlas' head, with Glenn doing an admirable job of mimicking the comic actor's mannerisms.

"I was supposed to originally play the Creature from the Black Lagoon, too," Glenn Strange stated, "but that was another underwater hazard. They told me how much water stuff there was and I said, 'No, I don't want to do it.' It turned out that they used a swimming double after all, Ricou Browning from Hawaii. Ricou and I did a live show with Sonja Henie, and Bud and Lou, at NBC. I did the Monster and he did the Creature. I also appeared as the Monster on CBS, the *Tex Williams Show*. I played the fiddle with the outfit on. I was really surprised that Universal let them do it, but they did."

Around that time, Glenn also donned the Frankenstein Monster guise for more television appearances on shows like *The Colgate Comedy Hour*, with Abbott and Costello and the Gillman. In the early 1960s, as a publicity stunt for a local Los Angeles television station, he sat atop a flagpole for several days while disguised as the Monster. Viewers were asked to send in their guesses as to who the creature really was, many of the votes going either to Boris Karloff or Lon Chaney until Strange finally unmasked.

During the 1960s, however, Glenn Strange became identified with a character other than Frankenstein's Monster, that of "Sam the Bartender" on television's hit series *Gunsmoke*. It was in this role that the actor became familiar to and loved by thousands of home viewers who knew or cared little about monsters and horror movies. Yet Glenn would often receive fan mail, sent in care of CBS-TV (which produced and aired the show), asking about his old creature movies. The actor once told me of a particular letter that struck him as being rather amusing. "Dear Sam," the letter began, "please send me a picture of the Frankenstein Monster."

The present writer's first encounter with Glenn Strange's Frankenstein Monster—not in a spooky castle, but in a darkened movie theatre—was in August 1956. *House of Frankenstein* was the first "Frankenstein" movie I ever experienced. I saw it as part of a "triple horror show" that month and year at the Modé, a tiny (and nostalgically sleazy) theatre on Chicago's Northeast Side, with *House of Dracula* (actually also a "Frankenstein" movie, although I didn't know it when I bought my 25¢ ticket) and *The Mummy* (starring Boris Karloff). I had heard of Dracula before, but the Wolf Man character was entirely new to me, although just weeks before I had seen a similar character in the first-run neighborhood release of *The Werewolf* (on a terrific double-bill with *Earth vs. the Flying Saucers*). And, until that afternoon, I'd believed that the Monster was named "Frankenstein" and that Boris Karloff was the only actor to have played the character in the movies. I walked out of the Modé that day with a newly born passion for the Frankenstein Monster, Count Dracula and the Wolf Man. My only reservation about those films was the relatively small amount of time those characters—especially the Monster and Wolf Man—had on screen.

Within the months following, I also managed to catch *Frankenstein Meets the Wolf Man* (on a triple-bill with *The Atomic* [aka *Man Made*] *Monster* and *The Beast from 20,000 Fathoms* at the Biograph Theatre, outside of which John Dillinger had been shot) and, at the Modé again, *The*

*Ghost of Frankenstein* on the same program as James Whale's *Green Hell*, with not Strange but Bela Lugosi and Lon Chaney, Jr., respectively, filling the Monster's high black boots. After seeing those films, I knew one thing: The actor who had played the Monster in the two *House* movies (having paid little attention to the cast credits in those films, I still did not know the actor's name) looked better, stronger and more menacing, and did a better performance, in my opinion, than the actors in either *Meets* or *Ghost*. (All of these "Frankenstein" movies had been reissued to theatres by Realart in a kind of "sepia" tone, no doubt to squeeze out their last theatrical mileage before their release, in 1957 and 1958, to television as part of Screen Gems' "Shock" and "Son of Shock" film packages.)

As I began to talk about those films with my young friends, some of them began to link the horror characters with Bud Abbott and Lou Costello, referring to the comedy team's encounters with the Frankenstein Monster on TV's *Colgate Comedy Hour*, and in some weird hybrid movie in which the comedians tangled with all three classic horrors. Some of my friends' recollections were even of specific gags and bits form this "alleged" comedy/horror film. I thought about this a lot: Imagine, Bud and Lou, two of my favorite funnymen (right up there with the Three Stooges and Laurel and Hardy), versus three of my favorite horrors (up there with King Kong and the Creature from the Black Lagoon). The very concept was mind-boggling and seemed impossible, yet wildly appealing, especially to a monster-conscious kid still in grammar school. One thing was certain: If that movie really did exist, I had to see it!

Then one day I saw a small advertisement in the *Chicago Sun-Times* movie section for something called *Abbott and Costello Meet Frankenstein*, the ad including a caricature of the Frankenstein Monster's face. Not doubting it any longer, I knew at last that the movie was certainly real. Better still, now was my chance to actually see it. It was on a double bill with some other movie, the title of which has been long erased from my memory. Accompanied by my friend (and fellow monster-movie fan) Victor Fabian and our respective mothers, I went, possibly that same night. And for about an hour and a half the four of us laughed and thrilled, although Vic and I were more enchanted by the three monsters than were our mothers.

What both Vic and I *really* liked about *Abbott and Costello Meet Frankenstein* was the fact that three of our favorite creatures were in that movie—on screen and performing just the way we liked them—*a lot*. There were more scenes of the Frankenstein Monster and Wolf Man, for example, than in all their combined footage from both "*House*" movies. Naturally,

I did have quibbles with a few things—Dracula becoming an obvious cartoon when transforming into a bat and also casting a mirror reflection—but everything else about the picture was right on target. Also, the Frankenstein Monster portrayed in this film by that same powerful—and menacing—looking actor who had portrayed the character before in *House of Frankenstein* and *House of Dracula*. This time I could not escape noting his name, Glenn Strange, as it appeared boldly along with an animated cartoon of the character in the film's opening credits.

I was just the right age, 12, when I first saw *House of Frankenstein* and *House of Dracula*, and about 13 when I caught up with *Abbott and Costello Meet Frankenstein*—the right age for Bud and Lou's brand of humor and also for the old Universal monsters. In the succeeding years I would

Glenn Strange peruses a copy of *Shazam*, issue number 3, a "fanzine" published by the author in 1963, while awaiting make-up on the set (his backyard) of the amateur movie serial *The Adventures of the Spirit*. When this picture was snapped the actor was still seriously offering to shave off his "Sam the Bartender"/*Gunsmoke* mustache in order to portray a clean-shaven Frankenstein Monster. (Photograph by Bob Burns.)

see the Abbott and Costello movie countless times—on the theatre screen again, on TV and, more recently, on home video and DVD. But nothing can quite top that experience of seeing it the first time that night in 1957.

But there was an even better experience in store for this writer, occurring more than half a decade later....

How does a 19-year-old monster-movie fan feel when he meets for the first time the towering actor who portrayed the Frankenstein Monster, only to discover that his nickname is ... "Peewee?" In 1963 I was visiting Hollywood on a six-week vacation from Chicago; at a July Fourth party at the home of Glenn's cousin, musician Billy Strange, I shook Glenn's hand, after which he offered me some beans, about which he told

As none of us "on set" could *really* expect Glenn Strange to shave off his mustache for just a few moments on screen in *The Adventures of the Spirit* (basically a glorified home movie), let alone endure the rigors of wearing the heavy Frankenstein Monster make-up under the hot summer sun, we (from left to right, the author, Lionel W. Comport and Mike Minor) were content to watch Bob Burns apply the gray greasepaint to the actor's hands, wrists and arms only. (Photograph by Kathy Burns.)

me, "Cooked 'em myself." The comic nickname, I later learned from Glenn himself, was long ago given him for a laugh by a rodeo announcer. (Within the next 10 years, in the course of interviewing numerous actors and stuntmen who performed with the actor in his many movies and serials, I learned that they also called him by that name—and unanimously described him as one of the nicest guys in the film business.)

I realized almost from the start that Glenn Strange was a *real* person, totally lacking any of the pretense or artificiality of many performers.

My most thrilling personal encounter with Glenn Strange was when, a few weeks after our first meeting, I actually got to *direct* him as he reprised his role of the Frankenstein Monster. With the great assistance of Glenn's close friend Bob Burns, I became involved in the making of an amateur movie, *The Adventures of the Spirit*, a five-chapter serial very loosely inspired by the masked comic-book hero created by Will Eisner. The fourth chapter was titled "Frankenstein's Fury," and, to my eternal delight and gratitude, Glenn consented to reenact his old role as Frankenstein's Monster.

At the time, Glenn was, of course, a regular on *Gunsmoke*, portraying the mustachioed bartender. Graciously, he offered to shave off his mustache (and also tear the sleeves of his jacket) to play the part for me, something I could not in my heart allow. Instead, in the stifling heat of a California summer sun, he slipped on a Don Post rubber Frankenstein head mask, vintage 1948. But even hidden beneath the silver-gray false face, Glenn's size and mannerisms made him readily identifiable.

The Spirit (the author) is attacked by the Frankenstein Monster (Glenn Strange) at the climax of "Frankenstein's Fury," the penultimate episode of *The Adventures of the Spirit*, an amateur chapterplay filmed mostly in Southern California (this scene shot in Strange's Glendale backyard) with major help, support and guidance by good friend Bob Burns. Rather than spend time in the make-up chair being made up as the Monster, Strange instead wore this silver-gray mask, made in 1948 by Don Post for the actor's personal appearances as the character. (Photograph by Bob Burns.)

"Frankenstein's Fury" opens with a shot of a "human" Glenn Strange raising a placard identifying him as the portrayer in that episode of the Monster. Then he peers over the top of the sign, leering fiendishly. The episode then progresses with the Spirit, having already survived attacks by various other horror characters (most of them played by Bob Burns), wandering about the grounds of Castle Frankenstein. There Dr. Frankenstein (played by CBS-TV make-up artist Billy Knaggs) brings the Monster (in these scenes "doubled" by me) to life.

The Monster (Glenn Strange) stalks out of the building and confronts the Spirit. The masked hero fires silver pistols at the giant, not even slowing him down. The two big gray hands seek the Spirit's neck and begin to squeeze, ending the penultimate episode.

In the fifth and last chapter, "Human Targets," the Spirit is saved as Superman (Bob) flies down to the rescue, the climactic and more strenuous battle featuring Bob's friend Lionel W. Comport doubling Glenn.

My exhilaration during the making of this film was threefold: Not only had I directed the scenes with Glenn Strange, my legs and feet had in one shot "doubled" for him; I had also played the Spirit, and it was my neck that was encircled by Glenn's big gray-painted hands.

How fortunate I am to have known (and worked with) Glenn Strange. I am sure that everyone who knew him misses him.

# A FORGOTTEN
# FRANKENSTEIN?

Ever since the middle 1960s, when I first began to make friends with a number of Hollywood stuntmen, I have been interested in knowing which stunt performers doubled the actors who were getting the star billings in the credits of their respective motion pictures. At first it was somewhat disappointing to find out that the hero or villain performing all those dangerous feats on the screen was not the person listed in the cast. After a while, identifying the real person hiding behind the face of someone else, performing the leaps and falls and fighting, became both a challenge and a satisfying exercise.

I remember myself and my friend Victor Fabian being puzzled when we first saw the 1943 motion picture *Frankenstein Meets the Wolf Man* at Chicago's Biograph Theatre back in 1956 or '57 (on a triple bill with *The Atomic Monster*, the Realart re-release title for the, in some ways, Frankenstein-like *Man Made Monster*; and *The Beast from 20,000 Fathoms*). Although we had read the name of Bela Lugosi on both the film's opening credits and on the posters outside the theater, we did not know which character in the movie the Hungarian actor actually played. Furthermore, for some reason that neither Vic nor I could figure out, the Frankenstein Monster in that film sometimes looked "different," though the make-up remained consistent, from one shot to the next. In some scenes the Monster appeared quite powerful and menacing; in others, rather weak and non-threatening. (At that time I was not yet knowledgeable regarding Hollywood's use of stunt doubles.)

As I would later learn via the premiere issue of *Famous Monsters of Filmland* magazine, actor Bela Lugosi, who had turned down the role ultimately played by Boris Karloff in the original *Frankenstein* (1931), portrayed the Monster in *Frankenstein Meets the Wolf Man*. And clearly his distinctive "Dracula-like" features were visible through Jack Pierce's heavy Frankenstein Monster make-up. Still, if that was Lugosi beneath that high forehead and sporting those neck electrodes, why did he sometimes look, well ... different? To compound the puzzle, that same issue of "*FM*" also ran a photograph of that much more powerful looking Monster from *Frankenstein Meets the Wolf Man* holding actress Ilona Massey; curiously, Lugosi's name was not mentioned in the caption.

The mystery was eventually solved when I purchased the second issue (April 1959) of one of the lesser monster-movie magazines of the "*Shock Theater* era," *Monsters and Things* from Magnum Publications. In the article "The Story of Frankenstein," author Marie Oliveri stated the following: "It's also interesting to know that in 'Frankenstein Meets the Wolfman [*sic*],' an unnamed stuntman filled in for Lugosi in every heavy scene, including the famous fight scene between the two creatures of the title. Lugosi came in as the Monster only for the close-ups to growl a few times! Since he was 58 years old at the time, however, you can't really blame him!"

So, although the above quotation is not entirely true (Lugosi did far more than just performing the close-up growls), it did introduce me to the use of doubles in the Frankenstein Movies. Later I would learn that two stuntmen—Eddie Parker and Gil Perkins—donned the Monster garb in *Frankenstein Meets the Wolf Man*, and that other stuntmen would also step into the character's raised black boots from one movie to the next.

Stuntman and sometimes character actor Dale Van Sickel did the horror honors in a comedy film made by Universal Pictures in 1941. I was the writer who discovered the name of this previously unidentified Frankenstein Monster. When I informed *Famous Monsters of Filmland* editor Forrest J Ackerman of Van Sickel's death in 1956, he asked me to write an obituary for the stuntman for the magazine. The original article—then somewhat inaccurately titled "Farewell, Frankenstein: Last of His Line"—was published in "*FM*" number 136 (August 1977).

✳  ✳  ✳

The Frankenstein Monster. Universal Pictures. The names are almost synonymous because of the series of movies about that character that Universal made during the 1930s and 1940s.

Of course there were other Frankenstein films before Universal shot its classic *Frankenstein* in 1931. Thomas Edison's film company made the first *Frankenstein* in 1910, starring Charles Ogle as a Quasimodo-like Monster. In 1915 the Ocean Film Corporation released an adaptation of the Frankenstein story titled *Life Without Soul*, featuring Percy Darrell Standing, sans horrific make-up, as the artificially created "Brute Man." And in 1920 the Italian company Albertini Film made *Il Mostro di Frankenstein*, with the popular Umberto Guarracino as a burly "mostro."

But the Universal series is the only group of such movies generally considered to be the "canon" or authentic presentations based upon Mary Shelley's undying Monster.

The first "authentic" Frankenstein Monster to die was Bela Lugosi in 1956, followed over a decade later by Boris Karloff (1969), then Lon Chaney, Jr. and Glenn Strange (both 1973).

The stuntmen who sat in make-up maestro Jack Pierce's regulation barber chair to become transformed into the Frankenstein Monster in order to "double" for the above actors have also died:

Bud Wolfe, who filled in for Karloff in the more strenuous scenes in *Son of Frankenstein*, passed away in 1960. Eddie (or Edwin) Parker, who seemingly doubled for Chaney, Jr. in *The Ghost of Frankenstein* and positively for Lugosi in *Frankenstein Meets the Wolf Man*, died that same year.

George DeNormand, who apparently doubled for Karloff in *Bride of Frankenstein*, passed on in late 1976.

And in 1999, stuntman and actor Gil Perkins, who had alternated with Parker in doubling Bela Lugosi in *Frankenstein Meets the Wolf Man*, died also.

On January 25, 1976, following a long period of illness, another actor died whose identity in the role of the Frankenstein Monster was for many years unknown to fans of the character. An actor as well as a stuntman, he was 69 years old when he died. His name, a very familiar one to fans of the old-time movie serials and Western films, was Dale Van Sickel.

Van Sickel donned the Jack Pierce make-up and black padded suit only once to play the Frankenstein Monster. He played the part in a Universal comedy movie that was released in 1941, one year before *The Ghost of Frankenstein*. For the moment, however, the title of that film will remain a secret.

Born in 1907, Dale Van Sickel would become one of the all-time greats in the pantheon of Hollywood's foremost stuntmen. A former All-American football star, he—along with such famous stunt aces as Tom Steele, David Sharpe, Eddie Parker, Bud Geary, Duke Green and Kenneth Terrell—raised the field of movie action to an art form. Van Sickel's expert stunt driving can be seen in such motion pictures as the science-fiction classic *On the Beach*, released in 1959; in the Steve McQueen crime drama *Bullitt* (1968); and in Steven Spielberg's television thriller *Duel* (1971). Keen-eyed viewers might also recognize the muscular stuntman as he was "crushed" beneath the same toppling wall in the science-fiction movies *Earth vs. the Flying Saucers* (1956) and *20 Million Miles to Earth* (1957). He was also one of the unfortunate "victims" of an intoxicated giant gorilla in *Mighty Joe Young* (1949). His stunting abilities were put to good use in countless horror, science-fiction and fantasy movies and television shows during the 1940s through the 1960s.

The serials—films shown one chapter per week, usually pitting some noble hero against a dastardly villain—proved to be Dale Van Sickel's real movie "home" during the 1940s and '50s. Besides being one of the best of the movie daredevils, Van Sickel was also a capable actor and often played one or more villains (getting killed off and then returning several chapters later, sometimes "disguised" with a mustache), while also doubling the hero or lead villain. Working with his friend and fellow stuntman Tom Steele, Dale Van Sickel created many memorable action scenes lensed by the directors of the Republic, Columbia and Universal chapterplays. At Republic Pictures, Dale and Tom carefully worked out the "choreography" of myriad incredible fight sequences. A favorite stunt "gag" in many of these fights was for either Dale or Tom to toss the other over his shoulder and, turning him upside down, onto a bookcase or fireplace mantel. Dale Van Sickel was also famous for literally launching himself off a wall, then "flying" directly at Tom in the middle of one of their brilliantly staged and executed serial brawls.

It was at Republic Pictures that Dale Van Sickel performed most of his stunts, including some of his best. As both gangster type and a stunt double, he worked in such fantastic Republic cliffhangers as *The Masked Marvel* (1943), *Haunted Harbor, Zorro's Black Whip* (both 1944), *Manhunt of Mystery Island* (1945), *The Crimson Ghost* (1946), *The Black Widow* (1947), *G-Men Never Forget* (1948), *Federal Agents vs. Underworld Inc., Ghost of Zorro* (both 1949), *Radar Patrol vs. Spy King, The Invisible Monster* (both 1950), *Flying Disc Man from Mars, Don Daredevil Rides Again* (both 1951), *Jungle Drums of Africa, Canadian Mounties vs. Atomic Invaders* (both 1953) and *Man with the Steel Whip* (1954), all containing elements of special interest to fans of celluloid horror, science fiction and fantasy.

In 1944 Dale Van Sickel appeared in the 15-episode movie serial *Captain America*, based on the Timely (now Marvel Comics) super-hero, a chapterplay which included a subplot in which a scientist, using Frankenstein-like gadgetry, brings a criminal back from the dead (in chapter eleven, "The Dead Man Returns"). Van Sickel's work in this production proved to be particularly thrilling. Captain America was "officially" played on screen by Dick Purcel, a B-movie actor who was perhaps a bit too old and overweight to be absolutely convincing as the famous Star-Spangled hero. But once "Cap" stopped talking and started fighting or leaping into action, he suddenly shed those unsightly extra pounds, acquired some muscles and literally became the character from the comic books. Padded only at the elbows and knees to avoid injury, Van Sickel, as Captain America, punched and rolled and kicked his way through some of the most frantic and beautifully choreographed fight sequences in movie-serial history.

One particular sequence in chapter four ("Preview of Murder") of *Captain America* has the patriotically garbed super-hero riding a motorcycle in pursuit of a robot-controlled truck. "Cap," or rather Van Sickel, then dumps the motorcycle and rushes to a hilltop, from which he leaps onto the truck as it speeds along the road below. Clutching the roof of the truck as its skids and squeals along the winding mountain road, Captain America manages to get inside—just before the driverless vehicle crashes into a building and explodes in a blinding flare of fire and smoke!

Naturally, Captain America (like all good Republic heroes) escapes from the truck before the collision and explosion, surviving to fight through the remaining chapters. Van Sickel climaxed the final episode, "The Toll of Doom," with another spectacular display of fisticuffs and acrobatics, this time battling one-on-one against the master villain calling himself the Scarab (played by Universal Frankenstein-movies veteran Lionel Atwill, doubled in this long fight scene by stuntman Duke Green). As the two men grappled, Captain America's lovely girlfriend Gail Richards (Lorna Gray) remained in danger of being transformed into a mummy!

Dale Van Sickel wore the leather jacket, bullet-shaped helmet and jet-pack—the now near legendary "rocket suit" of Republic Pictures—in three different serials. In *King of the Rocket Men* (1949) he, along with David Sharpe and Tom Steele, doubled for star Tris Coffin in the latter's role of flying Jeff King. (Mae Clarke, who played Elizabeth in the 1931 version of *Frankenstein*, also starred in this serial.) Rocket Man King was able to zoom through the sky courtesy of some fantastic, thoroughly convincing special effects created by the brother team of Howard and Theodore Lydecker, who sent a life-sized dummy soaring along wires from one hill-top to another. On the ground, however, the character was brought to life via the stuntwork of Van Sickel, Sharpe and Steele. The Rocket Man character proved popular enough for Republic to revive him, albeit under different names. In *Radar Men from the Moon* (1952) Commando Cody (played by actor George Wallace) wore the flying suit, and in *Zombies of the Stratosphere* (also 1952) it was the more mundanely named Larry Martin (Judd Holdren). In each of these series, and also in the *Commando Cody* (1953) series that followed, first in theaters and then on television, the character was doubled many times by Dale Van Sickel.

But what of Dale Van Sickel's role as the Frankenstein Monster?

Actually, Van Sickel was the first actor to succeed Boris Karloff as the Monster in a Universal film.

The movie was shot in 1941 and released the following year under the title *Hellzapoppin'*. It starred the popular comedy team of Ole Olsen and Chic Johnson, who created an incredible conglomeration of zany visuals for this production, based on their earlier live stage show. In one scene co-star Martha Raye's character trips on the floor of a nightclub while Olsen and Johnson's crazy show is underway. We hear a voice from off-screen ask if she needs any assistance. When she looks up she sees the giant form of the Frankenstein Monster looming over her. The Monster then proceeds to pick her up and (aided by "invisible" wires) toss her onto the stage.

The scene was a brief one and the first in which the Monster spoke since 1935, when Karloff dramatically stated, "We belong dead!" at the climax of *Bride of Frankenstein*.

We might add here that the Frankenstein Monster was also written into the script of another Olsen and Johnson comedy movie made at Universal, *Crazy House*, which the studio released in 1944. Whether or not the Monster's scenes were actually *filmed* (as was Basil Rathbone's, who

Stuntman Dale Van Sickel, impersonating the Frankenstein Monster, gives the stunt double for comedienne Martha Raye a superhumanly strong assist in the zany Ole Olsen and Chic Johnson comedy *Hellzapoppin'* (1942). For many years this Universal film has been out of official release, apparently due to ownership entanglements associated with the original material first presented by Olsen and Johnson as a stage extravaganza.

had starred in *Son of Frankenstein*, comedy cameo as his trademark character Sherlock Holmes) is not known. Nevertheless, the Monster does not appear in the final cut of this motion picture.

For many years it had just been assumed that Eddie Parker, who would play so many monsters at Universal during the 1940s and 1950s, played the Frankenstein Monster in *Hellzapoppin'*. This conclusion seemed reasonable enough in view of Parker's other such performances. In addition to the stuntman's later stints as the Frankenstein Monster, presumably in *The Ghost of Frankenstein* and without question in *Frankenstein Meets the Wolf Man*, he most likely doubled Lon Chaney, Jr. as Kharis in Universal's "Mummy" series, and certainly played horror characters in such movies from that studio as *Abbott and Costello Meet Dr. Jekyll and Mr. Hyde* (1953), *Abbott and Costello Meet the Mummy* (1955), *Tarantula* (1955), *The Mole People* (1956) and others. Yet Parker's face, despite the heavy make-ups the man was made to wear, is often recognizable under all of the putty and latex.

When this writer had an opportunity to see this movie for the first time projected on a screen, it was clearly *not* Eddie Parker's face showing through the Frankenstein Monster make-up.

Somehow the Monster's face reminded me of someone else I had often seen in serials and other action shows. The facial structure reminded me, in fact, of Dale Van Sickel. Another clue that perhaps Van Sickel was under that make-up was that the stuntman appeared as himself in another scene in *Hellzapoppin'*, doing a comic plunge into a swimming pool at a swank Hollywood party. I knew that studios often tried to get the most for their money when it came to using specialty performers like stuntmen. Also, it was often a courtesy on the studio's part to let a stunt double, who spends most of his time filling in for the leading man, also do a cameo *sans* disguise. It seemed to me both logical and a nice thing to do for Universal to assign Van Sickel to both roles. As he was almost unrecognizable (except to those audience members who knew stuntmen) under the Frankenstein Monster make-up, there was no reason to bring another stunt person on board to do the swimming pool "gag."

Logically, Dale Van Sickel *could* have played both the Frankenstein Monster and fallen into the pool as himself in *Hellzapoppin'*. Eddie Parker, then, could have begun his career as a Universal monster the following year, starting with *The Ghost of Frankenstein*. Still, however, I only had my own speculation to go by; and I wanted *absolute proof* that Dale Van Sickel indeed was *that* Frankenstein Monster.

Unfortunately, neither the end credits for *Hellzapoppin'* nor the movie's cast sheets gave credit to the person who played its Frankenstein Monster. And so, one afternoon during the late 1960s, I turned to the stuntman/actor himself. Luckily I was, at the time, a friend of Dale's friend and colleague Tom Steele. Acquiring Dale's phone number from Tom and using the latter's name as an introduction, I rang him up and simply asked him if he had done that role.

"That was a long time ago," Dale Van Sickel told me. "I'd almost forgotten about it."

And with that reply, a long-standing mystery was cleared up, one that had perplexed fans of Universal Pictures' Frankenstein Monster for many years.

# IV

# PETER CUSHING:
# "DR. FRANKENSTEIN,
# I PRESUME"

Two of my Big Regrets of Life are that I never met Boris
Karloff or Peter Cushing. Although I *almost* met Karloff on
several occasions, and got a *message* to Cushing through a
friend who worked at the BBC (because of a Frankenstein-
related television show with which both Cushing and I were
associated), and though I did get their autographs while both of
these English actors were still alive, I never had an in-person
meeting with either of them.

Just as Boris Karloff's named had become so strongly
associated with that of the Frankenstein Monster, ever since his
first appearance as that character on the screen in the 1931
movie *Frankenstein*, so was Peter Cushing's name linked
forever with Baron Victor Frankenstein, the character he
established in *The Curse of Frankenstein* in 1957.

The following article about Peter Cushing and his role as
Baron (and Dr.) Frankenstein, then titled "Dr. Frankenstein, I
Presume," was assigned to me by my friend Jim Harmon for
publication in the eighth issue (August 1975) of *Monsters of the
Movies*, a magazine put out by the same company that
produced the Marvel Comics titles. Much of the content of that
particular issue was devoted to that great British actor. The
article would subsequently be reprinted as "Peter Cushing—Dr.

Frankenstein, I Presume?" in *The Frankenstein File* (New English Library, 1977), a book edited by Peter Haining.

\* \* \*

To a great number of people—not necessarily "in the know" film buffs, but nevertheless quite intelligent, even learned human beings—the name "Frankenstein" is instantly identified with a certain shambling flat-headed Monster with metal electrodes on its neck ... and for that mis-identification we have, in part at least, Universal Pictures to blame.

When Universal made its original series of films based upon Mary Shelley's classic novel *Frankenstein; or, The Modern Prometheus* back in the 1930s and 1940s, it was basically the adventures of the Monster that were being chronicled from one movie entry to the next. The various Dr. Frankensteins at that studio, more and more so as the series continued to progress, continued to change and be replaced. Colin Clive, the best of these Frankenstein "doctors," only managed to survive two of the films, *Frankenstein* (1931) and its direct sequel *Bride of Frankenstein* (1935), both of which were directed by the same man, James Whale. Yet Henry Frank-enstein's (as Clive's character was named) creation continued to endure, in spite of the various explosions, sulfur baths, fires and floods to which he was subjected in the series. Whether this approach was intended from the onset, it was certainly intensified by superb make-up and the casting of a brilliant, relatively unknown actor, Boris Karloff, as the Frankenstein Monster. We can wonder what might have befallen the series if this same "new" actor had played the scientist rather than his misshapen cre-ation.

Largely it was because Universal legally owned their own visual actu-alization of the Frankenstein Monster that Hammer Films went off in its own direction when producing *The Curse of Frankenstein* in 1957, the color motion picture that arguably gave birth to the "modern" horror movie. Then again, maybe the film's director, Terence Fisher, felt restricted in placing emphasis upon such a limited character as the Monster. What-ever the reasons (and there may have been more), the Hammer Franken-stein series would shift the emphasis away from the lumbering Monster and bring his unorthodox creator into the laboratory spotlight—a deci-sion that would prove to be most satisfactory.

Except for the exuberantly crazed Colin Clive in the first two Uni-versal Frankenstein movies, the actors who played the infamous doctor (and his human offspring) were to many filmgoers disappointing. In *Son of Frankenstein* (1939), Basil Rathbone, as son Wolf, overacted to the point of providing unintentional humor. Sir Cedric Hardwick, as "second son" Ludwig in *The Ghost of Frankenstein* (1942), was his usual stuffy and, to many, dull self, hardly a character to steal any attention away from the Monster (Lon Chaney, Jr.).

It is an interesting coincidence that the actor who would, some decades later, be chosen by *Curse of Frankenstein* producer Anthony Hinds to immortalize this previously less popular character had already worked with James Whale, when the latter directed the 1939 costume drama *The Man in the Iron Mask*.

That actor was Peter Cushing.

Cushing had been, like Boris Karloff, playing character parts in motion pictures for many years, beginning during the 1930s. But, like that other British actor, it took a Frankenstein movie to bring Cushing to worldwide recognition. And, just as Karloff would be eternally identified with the role of the pathetic Frankenstein Monster, so would Cushing make the Monster's *maker* role his own.

In *The Curse of Frankenstein* the Baron was not portrayed as merely a dedicated or overly enthusiastic scientist as in the Universal films, obsessed with the creation of human life from the organs and tissues of the dead. Times and movies had changed since the Thirties and Forties. This film marked the advent of a new era in horror movies, where blood and eroticism, replacing the old Gothic tools of shadow and suggestion, were offered on the screen in vivid (and often dripping) color. Hammer Films' Baron Frankenstein had as great a love of living as he had for creating life. He enjoyed good wine and a better woman as much as he did instilling life into something he has created from dead matter. Perhaps the Baron reasoned that to create life, one must first experience life to its fullest. Thus, in *The Curse of Frankenstein*, the handsome, distinguished Baron enjoyed an affair with his voluptuous servant Justine (Valerie Gaunt), while simultaneously awaiting his marriage to his beautiful fiancée Elizabeth (Hazel Court).

Nevertheless, Cushing's Victor Frankenstein was truly dedicated to his grisly profession—perhaps, in some ways, even more than any other movie Dr. Frankenstein had been before him. While Colin Clive, interpreting the Frankenstein character more in the tradition established by Mary Shelley's book, was content seeking his human "raw materials" in graveyards, off gallows and in the charnel houses, Cushing's Baron was less patient. He opted not to soil his impeccably clean attire by digging in

"THE CURSE OF FRANKENSTEIN"
In Eastman Colour                              Cert 'X'
starring  PETER CUSHING with
HAZEL COURT    ·    ROBERT URQUHART
and CHRISTOPHER LEE as the CREATURE

A determined Baron Victor Frankenstein (Peter Cushing) sets off to save his beloved bride Elizabeth from the clutches of the Creature that he created in *The Curse of Frankenstein* (1957), the first major, feature-length Frankenstein movie to be released in color. This movie, from Hammer Films, with its *grand guignol* style supplanting the black and white Gothic look of the old Universal series, changed forever the "look" of horror films.

cemeteries, when a simple murder was far more practical, clean and offered an infinitely superior selection of organs. After all, as Frankenstein might say, what mattered a few insignificant lives in the interest of scientific progress?

Peter Cushing, in real life an easygoing, pleasant-natured gentleman, played this intense incarnation of Baron Frankenstein superbly. In addition to being brilliant and dedicated, Cushing's Baron was also cynical and sarcastic, often cutting as deeply with his words as with the blade of his sharpest scalpel. But, like Karloff before him, the inner warmth of the off-screen Peter Cushing usually had a way of making itself apparent, regardless of the monstrous crimes his screen character was committing. The result was a fiend the audiences could love as much as hate and fear.

*The Curse of Frankenstein* was Hammer's first version of the original story, although it retained little from either the Shelley novel or the first Karloff movie. Rather than send out some servant to steal the preserved brain of a human being, the Baron himself pushed old Professor Bernstein (Paul Hardtmuth), a distinguished scientist and colleague, to his death. Later the scientist's brain awaited new life within the skull of the dormant Creature (played by Christopher Lee in his first real "monster" role).

The Creature (as the being was called in the Hammer version as opposed to Monster) attained its artificial life with the usual electrical paraphernalia, here displayed with a quaint look to coincide with the movie's 19th century setting. Eventually Baron Frankenstein would learn that Justine was carrying his baby, and to prevent an embarrassing revelation, especially in lieu of his upcoming marriage, he sent the pregnant woman to be killed by the chained Creature.

A unique aspect of *The Curse of Frankenstein* is that it was framed by scenes of Victor in a jail cell awaiting execution by the guillotine. In a last effort to save his own life, the Baron revealed his story to a parson, describing the creation of the fiend responsible for a number of deaths, and of its inevitable destruction in a vat of acid. But regardless of what the Creature actually did, Frankenstein's own confession would have condemned him. For within the flashback that constituted the bulk of the story of *The Curse of Frankenstein*, Victor was clearly shown sending two people — Professor Bernstein and Justine — to their deaths.

When the present writer first saw *The Curse of Frankenstein* (at its premiere afternoon at a downtown Chicago theater, co-billed with Hammer's *X the Unknown*), I was much impressed — not so much by the putty-like white make-up worn by Christopher Lee (I was still too accustomed to the Universal version), but rather by the color, the sense of the baroque achieved (albeit on, unknown to me, a small budget) through impressive sets and excellent photography, and the performance of Peter Cushing (although I was not yet aware of this actor's name). I did not see the film again until it played, in a heavily censored version, during the early 1970s as the CBS-television late-night movie. Again, its most outstanding feature was Peter Cushing's performance, it being even more impressive than I had remembered it.

Hammer Films' executives must also have perceived the charisma of the Peter Cushing–Baron Frankenstein combination (as powerful in its own right as the Christopher Lee–Count Dracula image that would be established the following year in the studio's *Horror of Dracula*) and proceeded to star him in a follow-up movie entitled *The Revenge of Frankenstein* (1958). The original Creature, of course, had been totally dissolved in the first film by acid. It was impossible to revive him, *á la* Universal Pictures, for the sequel. Yet, since the Baron had emerged from *The Curse of Frankenstein* as a more powerful character than the Creature anyway, that hardly mattered.

Baron Victor Frankenstein was now the focal character of what was becoming the Hammer Frankenstein series, and, to many film buffs and Frankenstein fans, it was a welcome change of pace. In *The Revenge of Frankenstein* the Baron escaped his execution and resurfaced incognito as Dr. Victor Stein. But the man's name was all that had changed. Victor was still in the monster-building business, this time finally succeeding in creating what at first seemed to be a perfect human being. Only when subjected to severe physical violence did this creature, named Karl (an oddly ubiquitous name in later Hammer movies, this Karl played by Michael Gwynn), revert to a twisted and cannibalistic monster.

Hammer Films had taken the old Frankenstein theme, shifted the emphasis from the Monster to its maker, and thereby found themselves with a winning series.

Peter Cushing returned again as the Baron to star in the Hammer sequel *The Evil of Frankenstein* (a 1964 entry that played rather loosely with the continuity established by *Curse* and *Revenge*), with a Monster (Kiwi Kingston) somewhat resembling that of the old Universal movies (Universal released *Evil* and, therefore, allowed Hammer to adapt their copyrighted make-up) and a plot—including a nefarious hypnotist who gets control of the Monster and uses the being for his own criminal purposes—in some ways similar to some of those used by Dick Briefer in his old *Frankenstein* comic-book series of the early 1950s. From there Cushing returned in *Frankenstein Created Woman* (1966) and, as his most ruthless Baron of all, in *Frankenstein Must Be Destroyed* (1969). That same year Cushing and Christopher Lee did comedy cameos, as Baron Frankenstein and Count Dracula, respectively, in the United Artists comedy *One More Time*, starring Peter Lawford and Sammy Davis, Jr.

The *One More Time* appearance almost seemed to be the end of the Baron Frankenstein character, at least as far as Hammer was concerned. Hammer studio executives must have felt that the venerable (and still enormously popular) actor had grown too old for the role he had made his own, and that younger audiences wished to see someone closer to their own ages playing Victor Frankenstein.

*The Horror of Frankenstein* rolled before Hammer's cameras in 1970.

Baron Frankenstein (Peter Cushing) bears the fruits of his latest experiment—the reconstructed (both physically and spiritually) Christina, played by former *Playboy* magazine "centerfold" Susan Denberg, in *Frankenstein Created Woman*, a 1966 film whose title was inspired by director Roger Vadim's earlier... *And God Created Woman*, starring Brigitte Bardot. Alas, this and other still shots of Denberg in her "lab bikini" were for publicity purposes only; they do *not* appear in the movie.

The "horror" to many Hammer fans was that the movie was being made *sans* Peter Cushing. To aficionados of the series, excluding Cushing constituted a major sin. To the powers-that-be at Hammer, however, this was the beginning of a great new run of Frankenstein movies.

*The Horror of Frankenstein* was both a remake and a send-up of *The Curse of Frankenstein*. Ralph Bates, a long-haired young actor that Hammer was grooming as their new horror sensation (considered for the Dracula role too, among other parts), was the new Baron Victor Frankenstein, while British muscleman Dave Prowse was the new Monster. Bates portrayed the Baron as a cold and near-perverse hedonist who loved and killed as it suited him, smirking and making snide comments all along the way. Unfortunately, Bates, though a good-looking and capable actor, made the young Baron (as opposed to Cushing's interpretation of the character) difficult to actually *like*. Somehow, despite his talents, Ralph Bates simply was *not* Baron Frankenstein, although he might have come off well enough as the Cushing character's son. Hammer's attempt at infusing new life and energy into the character proved more of a disaster than any of Victor Frankenstein's ill-fated early experiments. Maybe Bates just lacked the experience or the cynicism or the warmth of Hammer's original Baron.

Whatever Bates lacked, Peter Cushing still had it, and *The Horror of Frankenstein* certainly missed the charismatic presence of the older performer.

Not very surprising, then, was Hammer's wise decision to resume their Frankenstein film series by continuing where they had left off before retiring their original Baron. *Frankenstein and the Monster from Hell*, released in 1972, featured a noticeably older, yet able as ever, Peter Cushing back in the role he created for the screen 15 years earlier.

The horror movies made by Hammer Film have often been denigrated by "serious" students of the genre, who label *The Curse of Frankenstein* and its successors as exploitative exercises in gore and sex. Whatever the individual's opinion of these films, one must remember an important fact. Hammer was able to take an apparently moribund film subject—the Frankenstein theme—and revive it, especially during an era more attuned to such science-fictional themes as mutant monsters created through the misuse of atomic power. The success of *The Curse of Frankenstein* spawned a new age of Gothic horror films, creating an arena in which those old-style monsters, the creations of Frankenstein, the vampires and the zombies, could stalk again in films more geared to a modern-day audience. Also to be considered is the fact that Hammer did what Universal could not do, or at least did not believe could be done—make *seven* Frankenstein motion pictures without having to resort to teaming up their Creature or Baron with Dracula, the werewolf or any other member of their pantheon of horrors.

Moreover, also to be remembered is the fact that *The Curse of Frankenstein* made a star of Peter Cushing, a fine actor who, until 1957, had been used to little advantage on the motion-picture screen. Because of *Curse*, its sequels and the many other movies he subsequently appeared in, Cushing became immortalized in the memories of film buffs as Baron Frankenstein, an identification as endearing and enduring as Basil Rathbone's Sherlock Holmes, Johnny Weissmuller's Tarzan, Sean Connery's James Bond, and, of course, Boris Karloff's Frankenstein Monster.

Hammer never announced a sequel to *Frankenstein and the Monster from Hell*. If they ever had, I would presume to speculate that the star of that film would have been Peter Cushing, hard at work in the business of creation and revival of the dead. For many of us there was only *one* Baron Victor Frankenstein.

# V

# *YOUNG FRANKENSTEIN—* CLASSIC IN THE MAKING

The first time I had ever heard of the motion picture *Young Frankenstein* was after the telephone rang, waking me up in bed one morning early in 1974. Bob Greenberg, a close friend since we were both teenagers living in Chicago, rang me up and asked if I'd care to visit the 20th Century–Fox sets of this new comedy film, which was co-written and being directed by Mel Brooks of recent *Blazing Saddles* success. Bob's main "in" at the studio was his long-time personal friendship with actor Peter Boyle, who was cast as the Monster in *Young Frankenstein*. Bob said that we could spend the morning and afternoon at 20th, hobnobbing with Brooks and also the movie's stars.

Naturally, I got up and began getting dressed.

The following article is the result of that set visit.

Before writing the original article, I was torn, regarding loyalty, as to where I should have it published. At the time I was a freelance assistant editor and writer, working steadily under the editorship of friend Jim Harmon at *Monsters of the Movies*. I also happened to be a good friend of Forrest J Ackerman, then the editor of *Monsters of the Movies*' original inspiration, the legendary *Famous Monsters of Filmland* magazine. Both of these "monster movie" magazines wanted my article. A telephone call from *Famous Monsters*' publisher James Warren subsequently helped me settle the matter and, for reasons both personal and monetary, I opted for Forry Ackerman's periodical. (I did, however, contribute a very short piece under the title "Frankenscope: Young Frankenstein"—alas, no byline included—to the second issue [August 1974] of *Monsters of the Movies*. Because of the short length of that article, and also due to repetition of material, the "*MoM*" article is not included in this collection, although some portions of it have been incorporated into the piece that follows.)

The original piece appeared in the 111th issue (October 1974) of *Famous Monsters of Filmland* under the optimistic title "Young Frankenstein—A Return to Greatness." To my knowledge it was the first real article written and published about the movie.

Around the time the "*FM*" article first saw print, I received an invitation from Mel Brooks to attend a screening of the "rough cut" of *Young Frankenstein* at a 20th Century–Fox studio screening auditorium. Brooks and star Gene Wilder (who co-wrote the screenplay for the film and starred as Frederick Frankenstein) addressed the audience in the crowded auditorium. Brooks stated that what we were about to see was a two-hour turkey from which a 90-minute comedy masterpiece must be extracted. We, the audience members, were encouraged to evaluate the movie in its present overly long form, and then send in our suggestions for scenes and shots to be deleted. Brooks did not promise to follow any of our suggestions. One of the things that was jettisoned, however, was the recognizable voice of actor John Carradine heard over the first laboratory scene in that much longer version. (Some of the deleted footage is now included on the DVD and special-edition videotape releases of *Young Frankenstein*.)

In my case, at least, that was certainly true. I later received a letter from Brooks thanking me for my editorial suggestions, but also noting that the cuts would not be the one I would have preferred to have been made. Nevertheless, *Young Frankenstein*— decades after its first-run release—has earned itself the deserved reputation of a modern-day classic. In this writer's subjective opinion, it is Mel Brooks' best motion picture and one that works on several levels. It is also one of the last great films of any genre to be shot in black and white, utilizing actual black and white (as opposed to color, later to be dropped out) film stock.

Thanks, Mel Brooks, Peter Boyle and, of course, the late Bob Greenberg for a truly wonderful day.

❋   ❋   ❋

The Frankenstein Monster, clad in a loose-fitting, leopard-print sports shirt, was walking briskly (*walking*, mind you, not shuffling, shambling or stalking) along the streets of New York as they existed during the 1890s. The creature's pale green skin appeared eerie in the also pale light from the overcast sky. Contributing to this rather incongruous imagery was the expression on the fabled being's face. Somehow it suggested the familiar countenance of Marlon Brando.

Accompanying the green-faced giant on his casual stroll through Gotham was a small entourage of "human beings," one of which was actor Rob Reiner, better known as Michael (aka "Meathead") on the hit television series *All in the Family*. A less familiar face belonged to filmmaker Bob Greenberg, co-animator (with John Lange) on the award-winning cartoon *Joshua and the Blob*, and also the creator of many of the exciting optical effects in the science-fiction cult film *Dark Star*. Last among this small band was the present writer, a Frankenstein buff of many years, who found a particular kind of significance in parading about "New York" with this new incarnation of Frankenstein's Monster.

The Monster, in this situation, was portrayed by actor Peter Boyle in the new 20th Century–Fox horror satire *Young Frankenstein*. This was the final day of shooting for the film, and the people involved in the production, like the Monster in Frankenstein's laboratory, were electrified that their epic was on the verge of completion. I had telephoned *Famous Monsters of Filmland*'s editor Forrest J Ackerman to drive down to the studio in Century City, California, to join Bob and myself in witnessing the final scenes of *Young Frankenstein* as they unfolded before the cameras. Unfortunately, to Forry's regret, *FM* deadlines superseded professional pleasure, which is the reason the present writer had the privilege of writing about what promised to be the most brilliant Frankenstein movie since the classic days of Boris Karloff.

*Young Frankenstein* was directed by comedy legend Mel Brooks, twice an Academy Award winner (for the short film *The Critic* and the feature-length film *The Producers*) and the writer/director of, among other movies, the Western fantasy *Blazing Saddles*, a truly wild motion picture. Fans of Brooks and his distinctive brand of humor also remembered his work on the old *Your Show of Shows* comedy program of the early 1950s, starring Sid Caesar and Imogene Coca, and on the "2000 Year Old Man" record albums done with Carl Reiner (Rob's father).

Mel Brooks had always harbored a love for the "old style" horror movies of the 1930s—the early Frankensteins and Draculas produced at Universal Pictures, films that relied upon story, characterization, fine acting and Gothic atmosphere rather than gratuitous violence and gore. Consequently, in *Young Frankenstein*, Brooks took the most extreme care to recreate the look, mood and "feel" of those much-revered classics. It was the director's goal to ensure that *Young Frankenstein*, although poking fun at those old Universal movies, would be made with integrity, affection and care.

For the sakes of authenticity and tradition, Brooks wisely chose to have his film shot in black and white (as were the old Universal movies). To recapture that old monochromatic look, Brooks enlisted the considerable talents of Jerry Hirschfield, a true master of black and white cinematography, with titles including *Diary of a Mad Housewife* (color), *The Incident* and *Goodbye, Columbus* (color) numbering among his other film credits. Also, the story and characters in *Young Frankenstein* reflected Mel Brooks' appreciation for and love of those Frankenstein movies of an earlier and, in some ways, more imaginative era; *Young Frankenstein* was designed to arouse in fans of those films feelings of nostalgia.

Before continuing, it would be wise to explain why the Monster character in *Young Frankenstein* was wearing a leopard-print shirt and strutting along the sidewalks of Manhattan.

It was Bob Greenberg who first opened to me the creaky doors to the Frankenstein castle—at least to the indoor set built to represent that old Gothic structure on the 20th Century–Fox lot. Bob was a good friend of Peter Boyle, the husky, six feet, two inches tall character actor who portrayed the Monster in *Young Frankenstein*. Today was Bob's second visit to the *Young Frankenstein* set and, luckily for the present writer, on *this* excursion he was allowed to bring along a friend.

As Bob had already informed me, "Uhnnnnn!" was *the* word on the *Young Frankenstein* set, which told me that the atmosphere I was about to experience was the correct one. Everyone, according to my friend, said this protracted grunt to each other—including actors, cameramen and grips. "Uhnnnnn!" I liked the sound of that "word."

Bob and I drove onto the 20th Century–Fox lot and strode across the giant standing New York exterior sets that had been built some years ago for the film *Hello, Dolly!* Briefly we stopped at one of the indoor sets where

*Young Frankenstein* (1975) director and co-writer Mel Brooks (center) coaches actor Peter Boyle, as the Monster, in the correct delivery of the line, "Uhnnnnn!"

the "brain stealing" scene was about to roll. Peter Boyle, someone informed us, was still in his make-up trailer, which was parked on one of the *Hello, Dolly!* streets.

We found Boyle's trailer quickly enough, and what transpired therein proved to be an experience in itself. Peter Boyle was seated in a chair while a familiar-looking make-up artist applied the pale green greasepaint to his face. The make-up maestro was none other than William Tuttle, certainly no stranger to the world of fantastic movies. Immediately visions of some of Tuttle's previous monster creations were conjured up in my imagination, including the bestial Morlocks of *The Time Machine* and the shaggy lycanthrope of *Moon of the Wolf.* Other imagery also came to mind, such as the various characterizations of actor Tony Randall in *The 7 Faces of Dr. Loa,* that triumph winning Tuttle the first Oscar ever given out for screen make-up.

Boyle had never before portrayed a monster for the cameras and did not anticipate becoming identified with horror pictures or roles. Before *Young Frankenstein* he had enacted a variety of character parts, both on the stage and also in such movies as *The Candidate, Steelyard Blues* and, perhaps most notably, as the titled middle–American bigot in *Joe*. The actor also had the distinction of bearing a more than slight resemblance to Marlon Brando, and being able to do a commendable impersonation of Brando's voice and mannerisms.

At that moment, however, Peter Boyle was gradually being transformed by Tuttle into a creature assembled from dead bodies.

The make-up for this latest version of the classic Frankenstein Monster character was kept relatively simple. William Tuttle's intent was to allow for the Monster's ferocity and his ability to arouse terror, but also for the character to convey such emotions as sadness and love. Like Boris Karloff more than 40 years earlier, Boyle's pliable and expressive face had to reveal the Monster's feelings and moods, so Tuttle eschewed the more traditional and obvious array of scars and stitches.

Tuttle added darker shading to Boyle's cheeks, giving them a more sunken appearance. To the actor's forehead Tuttle affixed a rubber appliance affording him a sloping, Neandertal-like brow. On either side of the brow was added a small, rather unobtrusive "stitched" gash. Reddish coloring was applied to the actor's lips. For comedic visual effect, a metal *zipper* graced the right side of Boyle's neck.

When Tuttle's make-up work was eventually finished, Peter Boyle would don the familiar dark, padded suit and a pair of heavy boots enhanced with five-inch souls. In that moment, a new conception of the Frankenstein Monster—immediately recognizable as such—had been created.

As William Tuttle completed his latest creation, the make-up trailer became a bit cramped. Among the people crowding inside the small space were Rob Reiner and his then wife, Penny Marshall, and, shortly thereafter, the actor who had played the leader of the flying monkeys in MGM's classic musical fantasy *The Wizard of Oz*.

To this eclectic group of visitors, while Tuttle finished powdering down the greenish face, Boyle remarked, "Hey, I've just got to show you Stage 5. That's where they've got the big castle set."

The make-up at last finished, Peter Boyle slipped on his leopard-spotted shirt supplied him by the studio, and then led the small group of Greenberg, Glut, Reiner and Marshall outside for a brief trek through Dolly's New York. Then we all piled into Reiner's rented car and drove across the studio lot to the fabled Stage 5.

There have been countless science-fiction tales of people being transported through time and space. But how frequently do such phenomena occur in the real world? For this writer, the experience on Stage 5 was the closest I had ever had to traveling back through time. In stepping onto

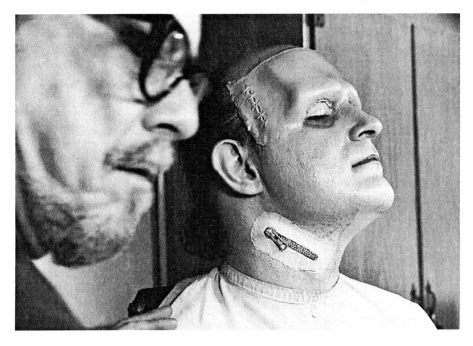

Make-up master William Tuttle transforms actor Peter Boyle into a new Monster, replacing the traditional neck electrodes with a zipper, for the 1975 comedy classic *Young Frankenstein.*

the vast interior sets of *Young Frankenstein,* I felt that I had been whisked back to another studio at another time—Universal Pictures back in 1931—or to some gloomy village in the wilds of Transylvania (where *Young Frankenstein* is set).

Dale Hennessy created the fantastic sets for *Young Frankenstein,* sets, in this writer's opinion, definitely of Academy Awards quality. (Hennessy also created the futuristic sets for the Woody Allen science-fiction comedy film *Sleeper,* and *did* win an Oscar for his inspired depiction of "inner space" in the movie *Fantastic Voyage.*) Sparing not the slightest detail, Hennessy designed and then had built a full-sized castle set that was so authentic in appearance that only the set backings, the motion-picture equipment and the materials for the later cast and crew party reminded us that we were, in reality, on a movie set.

Following the made-up Peter Boyle, who came off as the Frankenstein Monster moonlighting as a studio tour guide, we explored the incredibly realistic Castle Frankenstein, discovering the following:

The village courtyard, with its curved archways, its cobblestone street and the logo "Frankenstein" emblazoned in letters of raised stone over the entranceway to the castle.

Victor Frankenstein's library, crammed to capacity with authentic old books on medicine and surgery.

Frankenstein's bedroom, including more jam-packed bookshelves, one of which also doubled as a "secret door" leading to the laboratory.

The dungeons, with their heavily barred doors, capable of keeping in (or out) a real Monster.

Room upon room upon room. And every one so meticulously detailed that they never ceased conveying the illusion of reality.

Of all the sets constructed for *Young Frankenstein*, two of them were the most outstanding. The first of these was the facsimile of the Castle Frankenstein rooftop, with its ancient turrets and parapets standing out starkly against a moonlit sky. Our group climbed the steps that led us to that rooftop, the set where some of the film's climactic scenes would take place. From this high vantage point we could see arguably the most spectacular set of all—the laboratory of Victor Frankenstein.

The laboratory set was alive with electrical apparatus that appeared as if it could really bring life to something created from death!

There were enormous coils and transformers, terminals from which jagged fingers of electricity jumped at the mere throw of a switch, wheels that spun and gave off hot nimbuses of crackling power.

To one side was a silvery, horizontal platform large enough to support a giant human form, complete with metallic bands to strap down that being.

Directly overhead, a transom could be opened to receive the platform as it ascended toward the dark heavens, and subject the creature strapped to it to the raw, primal forces of a studio-created electrical storm.

The laboratory equipment looked familiar, as well it should. For this was the very same machinery built by electrical wizard Kenneth Strickfaden in 1931 for the original Boris Karloff classic movie *Frankenstein* and also its sequels.

We explored virtually every inch of that laboratory set. Admittedly, I had to fight the compulsion to climb upon that inviting platform, so similar to the one that Karloff himself had lain supine upon 43 years earlier.

But it was already approaching noon. If we were to observe any of the final *Young Frankenstein* scenes being shot, we could expend no more valuable time basking in the darkly atmospheric sets of Mel Brooks' version of Castle Frankenstein.

Fortunately, the scene that we did see shot paralleled one familiar to fans of the 1931 Karloff classic. The scene was set in a university "brain depository," a room adorned with bottled brains and a door equipped with a slot for slipping through brains "after hours." The prop brains on that set looked unpleasantly authentic. And when Bob Greenberg and I noticed the "reserve" supply of "props" being kept cool in a tray of ice, we immediately knew the reason why!

Acting in this scene was Igor (pronounced "eye-gore" in the movie), played by bug-eyed British comedian Marty Feldman. (This was Feldman's second movie meeting with the Frankenstein Monster. His first was in the 1970 comedy film *Every Home Should Have One*, in which, during a fantasy sequence, the funnyman became Count Dracula and encountered a Frankenstein Monster resembling Glenn Strange's version of that character.)

Igor had some of the greatest brains in the world to choose from for his master's, Frederick Frankenstein, experiment in life and death. A close inspection of the containers revealed labels identifying their occupants as having once belonged to Albertus Magnus and Cornelius Agrippa (real life "heroes" of Percy Bysshe Shelley, future husband of Mary Godwin, who wrote the original novel of *Frankenstein; or, the Modern Prometheus*).

There were also brains with labels punning the names of currently living celebrities.

Our group watched the scene commence as Igor—mimicking Dwight Frye as the hunchbacked Fritz in the 1931 movie—dropped one of the good brains. He paused to look at the camera and very seriously deliver the line [which would be deleted from the final edit of the movie], "I know, I know. But how *else* is one supposed to create a monster?"

Gene Wilder played the part of Dr. Frederick Frankenstein (pronounced "Fronk-en-steen" during the first half of the movie, as his character was trying to separate himself from the stigma of his family's infamous name), a wide-eyed innocent young man who was more confounded by creating human life than diabolically inspired by it. In the recent years preceding *Young Frankenstein*, Wilder amassed an impressively large fan following as the result of his performances in such films as Mel Brooks' *Blazing Saddles* and also the gentle fantasy fable *The Little Prince*. Unknown to many of Wilder's fans, however, the actor himself once portrayed an artificially made man brought to life, only this time by magic instead of science. Wilder played the title role in *The Scarecrow*, a play written by Percy MacKaye (and the basis for the 1923 silent film *Puritan Passions*). He was a field scarecrow given life by a vengeful witch, a pathetic creature who, upon tasting this supernatural gift, strove to become a real human being. The videotaped play was presented over UHF television channels during the early 1970s and was occasionally rerun.

Madeline Kahn, nominated for an Oscar for her role in the film *Paper Moon*, was cast as Elizabeth, Dr. Frankenstein's socialite fiancée. Cloris Leachman became Frau Blucher, Frankenstein's housekeeper (and Victor Frankenstein's former "girlfriend"), who happened to have a weird affinity for monsters. Inga, Dr. Frankenstein's blonde assistant, was played by beautiful Terri Garr, while Kenneth Mars outdid Lionel Atwill, exploring every comical possibility in his role of the wooden-armed police Inspector Kemp.

The costumes worn by the actors in *Young Frankenstein* were designed by Dorothy Jeakins, a three-time Oscar winner for the movies *Samson and Delilah, Joan of Arc* and *Night of the Iguana*.

The original story of *Young Frankenstein,* scribed by both director Mel Brooks and star Gene Wilder, was an expert blend of horror, Gothic atmosphere and satire: The old Dr. Beaufort von Frankenstein dies, leaving a rather peculiar last will and testament. All of his fortune is to be divided equally among the members of his family—*unless* some "young Frankenstein" deems to pursue the study of medicine [this plot element was excised from the final cut of the movie]. Beaufort's grandson, Frederick Frankenstein, has ventured into a medical career. But Frederick has also rejected everything connected with mad experiments and even madder monsters. Furthermore, he insists that his name is not pronounced as the familiar "Frankenstein," but rather "Fronk-en-steen," hoping to remove himself further from the lingering notoriety of the work done by his grandfather Victor Frankenstein, creator of the original Monster.

Nevertheless, Frederick journeys to Transylvania (this locale having been "borrowed" from Count Dracula) to claim the ancestral Frankenstein estate and fortune. There, at least for a while, he maintains his disinterest in the artificial creation of human life. But Frederick's lack of concern for such traditional Frankenstein activities comes to an abrupt end when Frau Blucher plays him an ancient Transylvanian lullaby on her violin. There is an old adage about music soothing the savage breast. In this case music has the opposite effect, rousing the young Dr. Frankenstein's long-suppressed desires, enflaming him with the compulsion to create his own living man.

Inadvertently discovering that his bedroom bookcase doubles as a secret door, Frederick finds the hidden staircase that leads down into the laboratory formerly used by his grandfather to energize the Frankenstein Monster. The laboratory is loaded with bizarre electrical devices. And at

Dr. Frederick Frankenstein (Gene Wilder) attempts to give life to his Monster (Peter Boyle) amid some of the electrical apparatus designed and built by Kenneth Strickfaden for the 1931 *Frankenstein* in director Mel Brooks' comedy classic *Young Frankenstein* (1975). Some film buffs have speculated that Wilder's blond-haired character is intended to represent—albeit all grown up—young Peter Frankenstein, played by Donnie Dunagan in the 1939 Universal movie *Son of Frankenstein.*

its top is a large transom, ideal for raising the long horizontal platform into the furies of a lightning storm.

Before long, the hump-backed, twisted-limbed and black-cowled Igor is dispatched to purloin the brain intended to go into the skull of Frederick's own new version of the Frankenstein Monster.

Frederick's Monster completed, the young medical man dons protective glasses, switches on his predecessor's laboratory apparatus and, riding along with it, raises his still-lifeless creation to the transom. Atop the roof, Igor waits with the kite that will attract the electrical might of the storm. (Unlike the huge kites used in the 1935 movie *Bride of Frankenstein*, those seen in *Young Frankenstein* are the standard kind sold in any toy or "ten-cent" store.)

The Monster's dormant form receives the full power of the electricity, both God- and man-made. Then it and Frederick are lowered back into the laboratory, where the young scientist almost goes insane contemplating his success.

As in the original Boris Karloff Frankenstein movies, the new Monster inevitably escapes from the laboratory, roaming about and terrorizing the countryside. In a parody of a classic scene from the initial Karloff film, the Monster has a brief encounter with a little girl. No, this being a comedy, he does not drown the child; for this creature, though most people fear him, is actually quite lovable.

Eventually the Monster stumbles upon the hut of a blind hermit (played *sans* billing by Gene Hackman). Grunting (*á la* Karloff) with delight, the Monster enjoys the hermit's music, but then becomes the inad-

Peter Boyle as the Monster and Gene Hackman (uncredited) as the blind hermit in one of *Young Frankenstein*'s many comedic homages to the old Universal movies, this scene more than just inspired by one in that studio's *Bride of Frankenstein*.

vertent victim of the sightless man's hospitality. Recall the touching scenes of the Monster and blind hermit in *Bride of Frankenstein*? Mel Brooks shatters them in *Young Frankenstein*. Brooks' hermit offers the Monster a bowl, then proceeds to pour him a ladle of steaming hot soup. But unable to see what he is doing, the blind man accidentally misses the bowl, pouring the near-scalding liquid into the giant's lap! When the hermit offers the Monster a smoke, he succeeds only in setting his green thumb on fire!

The Monster then continues on his escapades away from the castle, displaying a liking for music. Thus it is with that old Transylvanian lullaby that Frederick, Igor and Inga eventually lure the creature back to Castle Frankenstein.

This was one of the scenes that Bob Greenberg and I had the privilege of viewing—in the form of "dailies" or "rushes"—in a private screening room on the 20th Century–Fox lot, along with Mel Brooks, Gene Wilder, Peter Boyle, Marty Feldman, Terri Garr and the technical crew of *Young Frankenstein*.

First, Igor sits atop one of the Gothic parapets of the castle, like some human gargoyle, sounding a horn intended to attract the Monster from wherever he is. Igor blows the horn several times, then slowly swings into a jazz arrangement of "You Made Me Love You," ending with the "I didn't wanna do it" music. When this fails to bring back the Monster, Frederick takes another tack [these scenes also being removed before the final version of the film was edited].

On the rooftop of Castle Frankenstein, Frederick sets up a couple of music stands and an old stand-up microphone that would be familiar to fans of Bing Crosby–type crooners and the big bands that dominated popular music long before the advent of rock 'n' roll. The scientist and his hump-backed assistant then play a duet—yes, that same Transylvanian lullaby—until Inga spots a giant, green-skinned form approaching the castle.

Infatuated by the music, the Monster staggers across the castle's courtyard, grunting, arms outstretched. Then, clutching the vines that grow up along the castle wall, the creature begins to climb.

Inga reaches out to help the struggling Monster.

"No!" commands the emotionally charged Frederick Frankenstein. Then, in a parody of a line from a 1960s television commercial, he adds, "Can't you see? He wants to do it himself."

Groaning, snarling, grimacing, the Monster finally pulls himself safely atop the castle roof to join Frankenstein, Igor and Inga.

Those were but a sample of the scenes—take by take, and in some cases snicker by snicker—we were treated to in that screening room. I, for one, wondered how, with such zany goings-on, even such professional performers as Wilder, Feldman, Garr and Boyle could get through them while maintaining their straight faces.

As the story progresses toward its end, Dr. Frankenstein realizes that there is only one way to save his creation from the angry villagers—perform another experiment, one that will impart upon the Monster some portion of his own intelligence and personality. Again the giant is strapped to the great platform in the laboratory. But this time Frederick also takes his place on a second such platform. A metal skullcap is placed over each of their heads. Again the laboratory devices crackle and spark with white-hot life and the mind-transference experiment progresses with apparent success.

Now a true bond exists between creator and created. They are, in a sense, "brothers" under the skull cap. Possessing some of his maker's mentality, the Monster's own personality undergoes a very noticeable change. Yet there are some unexpected "after effects"....

There are genuine homages to the old Universal Frankenstein Movies scattered throughout the comic madness of *Young Frankenstein*. For example, in a scene reminiscent of one in *Son of Frankenstein*, the Inspector, checking out rumors that the Monster walks again, plays darts with Dr. Frankenstein—with wild results. Another scene depicts the Monster chained in a police station, as in *Bride of Frankenstein*. The "mind transference" scene, with both Frederick and the Monster strapped to platforms amid zapping electrical apparatus, suggests a similar scene in *Frankenstein Meets the Wolf Man*. Yet another follows a mob of irate villagers, wielding clubs and blazing torches, searching the mist-shrouded woods for the Monster, a scene ubiquitous to just about all of the old Universal movies. And so on and so forth.

Mel Brooks had personally requested that the various surprises at the end of the film (and also a special sequence in which young Dr. Frankenstein exhibits his creation to the public) remain secret until the film's premiere. Nevertheless, the climax of *Young Frankenstein* proved to be unlike that of any other Frankenstein motion picture yet produced. The character of Elizabeth, influenced by Elsa Lanchester's monstrous role in *Bride of Frankenstein*, must have been more surprised than anyone else.

Bob Greenberg and I joined Mel Brooks, Gene Wilder, Peter Boyle, Terri Garr and motion-picture music composer Quincy Jones for lunch in the studio commissary. Browsing through a copy of my book *The Frankenstein Legend: A Tribute to Mary Shelley and Boris Karloff*, Brooks and Wilder revealed to us a legitimate interest, not only in the old Universal Frankenstein movies, but also in Mary Shelley's novel of *Frankenstein*. Both of them, along with most everyone else at that table, expressed their dislike of such graphically gory productions as the recent 3D film *Flesh for Frankenstein* (also known as *Andy Warhol's Frankenstein*). They preferred the less bloody product of the 1930s and 1940s. And it is just that kind of a product that is also *Young Frankenstein*.

When Mary Shelley first incorporated the suggestion of immortality in *Frankenstein*, she could in no way have imagined just how immortal her Monster character would become. A number of movies involving the Frankenstein Monster had already been released in the 1970s, these including the Spanish/West German *El hombre que vino de Ummo* (1970), the "blaxploitation" entry *Blackenstein* (1972), the French *Les experiences erotiques de Frankenstein* (1972), the Italian *La figlia di Frankenstein* (1972), the Mexican *Chabelo y Pepito contra los Monstruos* (1973), the Spanish *El espiritu' de la colmena* (1973) and the aforementioned *Flesh for Frankenstein* (1974), to name some of them.

But we can ignore most if not all of the above titles. Mel Brooks' *Young Frankenstein* was *the* Frankenstein movie of that half decade—arguably of *any* year since the original Universal series. Greatness had been restored to the immortal Frankenstein Monster. *Young Frankenstein* possessed all the right component parts to be the best spoof of the genre since the excellent *Abbott and Costello Meet Frankenstein* back in 1948.

*Young Frankenstein* was scheduled for a Christmas, 1974, release by Brooks and producer Michael Gruskoff (who also produced the Universal science-fiction movie *Silent Running*). Judging from what this writer had observed, both on set and also in the screening room, I knew that horror-film fans bemoaning the passing of the old classics into the realms of history and nostalgia could not ask for a better Christmas present.

Surely it was mere coincidence that the Karloff *Frankenstein* of 1931 also premiered in December. Still, I would like to believe that the opening of Mel Brooks' *Young Frankenstein* that same month, though 43 years later, was more than that. I would say that it was appropriate.

Bob Greenberg and I left the 20th Century–Fox lot feeling good that day, somehow forgetting that the sky was cloudy and presaged rain, and that there was a sharp chill in the breezy air. Before we returned to the car, once more to drive through the artificial streets of Gay '90s New York City, we made one final visit to Castle Frankenstein. Although this wonderful set would soon be "struck," the victim of the workmen's hammers and saws, the place would exist forever on celluloid and in our memories.

# VI

# SUPER-HEROES VS. FRANKENSTEIN (AND COMPANY)

When Jim Harmon began editing *Monsters of the Movies* magazine, it was always a challenge for him, and also for those of us on his editorial staff, to come up with new and fresh ideas for articles. Whenever possible we strove not to run stories on the same "tried and true" topics—*e.g.*, a history of Universal Pictures' Frankenstein movie series, a biography of Boris Karloff or a detailed plot synopsis of one of the Frankenstein movies made at Hammer Films—that, in our opinions, had been "done to death" over the years in all of the other monster-movie magazines.

Having long been a fan of so-called "super-heroes," whether on the screen or in some other medium, I suggested to Jim an article in which such do-gooders battled Frankenstein's Monster and other unnatural horrors, in addition to the usual megalomaniacs and gangsters. A fan of such heroes himself, especially those in the old radio shows and movie serials, Jim gave me the go-ahead. The article, in its original (and much shorter) form, first saw print in "*MoM*" number 4 (December 1974), then entitled "Superheroes vs. the Monsters in Distant Lands."

✳    ✳    ✳

Frankenstein's Monster, Count Dracula, the Mummy and other horror characters have frequently been foes, on the motion-picture screen, of super-heroes, those stalwart champions of right and justice, sometimes disguised under masks or gaudy costumes, and occasionally aided in their heroic activities by their possession of great powers. From the earliest days of motion pictures through the 1960s, such heroes and their monster foes have fought each other on movie screens. Although these battles have been shown in American theaters and, via television release, in American living rooms, the origins of the majority of these action-packed encounters have generally been on foreign soil.

A formally clad, cloaked Count Dracula made one of his many screen appearances in such a movie. The vampire had been imprisoned in a barred cell within the throne room of his undead wife. He could only observe as the blood-hungry Countess commanded her army of powerfully built henchmen and shapely, batwing-adorned vampiresses. Suddenly a new addition to this bizarre array of characters stood before the evil vampire queen. He was powerfully built and wore tights, trunks and a glittery jacket. His features were concealed behind an ornate, tight-fitting mask that covered his entire head, exposing only his eyes, nose and mouth.

In this instance, Count Dracula was portrayed by veteran character actor John Carradine, who had already played Count Dracula in various motion pictures, on the legitimate stage and on television.

The masked super-hero, who would soon be battling the undead warriors, was known only as Mil Mascaras, which translates from Spanish as "Thousand Masks," so named because of the seemingly endless array of disguises this professional wrestler cum crimefighter has worn during his long ring and screen careers. As for the true identity of Mil Mascaras (actually wrestler Aaron Rodriguez), that remained a secret to the people working in front of and behind the cameras of this 1969 movie, *Las vampiras* ("The [Female] Vampires"), only one of virtually countless movies made in Mexico combining super-heroes and horror.

Certainly in the tradition of the comic-book super-heroes are these masked wrestling stars from Mexico who, like Mil Mascaras, have for many years moonlighted in the screen adventures as authentic costumed crimefighters. Inarguably the greatest of all of these South-of-the-Border mystery men was El Santo (his name meaning "the Saint" and often subtitled with "El Enmascarado de Plata," or "the silver-masked man"), a real-life champion wrestler who for decades seemed to be as ageless as the fictional Phantom, or "Ghost Who Walks," of newspaper comic-strip fame. Santo (real "secret identity": Rodolfo Guzman Huerta) had been appearing in

Spanish-language movies since 1958 (*Cerebro del mal,* or "Brain of Evil") and, during his long run of titles, virtually no one ever viewed his unmasked face. (Santo would continue to make movies, fighting monsters and other evil-doers, for more than 30 years, his last being the 1982 action picture *La furia de las Karatecas* ["The Fury of the Karate Experts"], after which other performers using his name, most notably his son, would continue to appear on the screen.) Santo's popularity would become so great over the years that he would be awarded his own comic-book series, published in Mexico, with art adapted from actual photographs, with Santo battling more monsters and villains whose activities were not affected by the low budgets of the silver-masked man's movies. There was also Santo merchandise for sale to his fans, elevating him to the same media status as some of his American super-hero counterparts like Batman and Superman.

Much of Santo's extensive body of filmed exploits was merely an imitation of the old movie serials made in the United States from the 1930s through the mid-1950s, filled with chases and fistfights and scowling, dark-suited crooks. Yet a number of them also mimicked the horror films made during the 1930s and 1940s by Universal and Columbia, combining monsters and deep shadows with the cliffhanger-style action. *Invasion of the Zombies* (1961) [note: throughout this article the author has used the English-language titles when a film has been given a United States release; otherwise the original foreign-language titles are generally used] was Santo's first encounter with supernatural monsters, in this case the so-called walking dead. When a band of zombies, controlled by a hooded mastermind, went on a spree of robbery and death, Santo was called in to end their reign of terror. Santo's great strength and fighting skills destroyed these living dead men; he also unmasked their leader, a person who had been posing as a blind man.

The next year Santo was fighting the caped undead in *El Santo contra las mujeres vampiras* (seen on United States television under the misleading title of *Samson vs. the Vampire Women*), one of his most popular movie adventures. When a coven of lovely female vampires attempted to make a young innocent their new queen, the masked wrestler again leaped into serial-style action. In one unintentionally amusing scene, staged in a wrestling arena (most of Santo's movies had their main action interrupted by lengthy wrestling matches), the vampires substituted one of their own kind for Santo's also masked opponent. For a while it appeared as if Santo had been defeated by his super-strong adversary (he was "using Karate!" Santo explained as they grappled in the English-dubbed version of the

A motionless Frankenstein Monster (actually a dummy) seems to stand guard in the background as Mexican wrestling champion turned movie super-hero Santo ("El Enmascarado de Plata") battles some unsavory monsters in *Santo en el museo de cera* (1961; seen on American TV as *Samson in the Wax Museum*).

film). Finally Santo unmasked him, revealing the hairy face of a snarling werewolf! When the irate spectators converged upon the beast-man (as if this revelation was not giving them their pesos' worth), the werewolf transformed into a vampire bat and flew away. In the climax of this movie, our hero finally tracked the vampires to their nest and set a torch to their undead bodies.

In 1961's *Santo en el museo de cera* (seen on television in the United States with its title changed to the misleading *Samson in the Wax Museum*), the masked hero had his first meeting with the Frankenstein Monster—in a way. The Universal-style Monster was one of many exhibits populating a private wax museum's chamber of horrors, accompanied by figures of such infamous characters as the Phantom of the Opera and Quasimodo, the Hunchback of Notre Dame. Among the other monstrous exhibits were several shaggy werewolf-like characters. At least some of these figures,

Santo eventually learned, were not made of wax, but were actually real human beings transformed into hideous monsters by the mad museum proprietor (played by the distinguished international actor Claudio Brook) and kept by him in a state of suspended animation. In the end these figures were revived to battle the silver-masked super-hero, who dispatched them with a vat of boiling wax.

Whether or not the Frankenstein Monster figure was one of these transformed human beings, or was, in fact, just made of wax, was never explained in the Santo movie. However, in real life, this *was* just a lifeless dummy and one of many props that eventually found their way into other movies shot in Mexico. Among the other films in which this same motion-less Frankenstein Monster made "guest appearances," scaring non-heroic characters, were *La Señora Muerte* ("Madame Death," 1968) and *Dona Macabra* ("Macabre Gift," 1978).

Santo's movie adventures continued to vary over the years between standard crime stories and tales based in science fiction and the super-natural. In 1963 again, in *Santo contra el estrangulador* ("Santo vs. the Strangler"), a direct sequel to *El espectro del estrangulador* ("The Spectre of the Strangler"), the hero fought and defeated a mysterious strangler inspired by the Phantom of the Opera. The following year Santo became involved with the supernatural in *El poder Satanico* ("The Satanic Power") and *Atacan las brujas* ("The Witches Attack").

Santo physically battled a Dracula-style vampire (played by Fernando Osés) in *El Baron Brakola* (1965), and then met the original Count him-self (Aldo Monti) in *Santo en el tesoro de Dracula* ("Santo in the Treasure of Dracula," 1968, also known as *Vampiro y el sexo* because of the movie's more adult content). In the latter movie, a young woman was regressed to a previous incarnation (*á la* the well-publicized "Bridey Murphy" case) where, in an earlier century, she was victimized by the vampire Count. Santo observed her previous experiences over a time-television of his own invention, seeing Dracula discovered when his body cast no mirror reflection, and then summarily staked. In the present, Santo tracked down Dracula's grave and removed his priceless ring (the "treasure" of the film's title). After gangsters extracted the stake from Dracula's heart, restoring him to life, the vampire fought the masked wrestling hero, only to be staked once again.

By the late 1960s "El Santo" was teaming up with other Mexican masked wrestling heroes, most notably the second most popular performer in this genre, Blue Demon (real name apparently never disclosed, even after the man's death and burial in his blue mask). Blue Demon had fought a werewolf in his first motion picture, *El Demonio Azul,* entitled after the blue-masked hero. Together Santo and Blue Demon crossed paths with a veritable team of unearthly creatures—the Wolf Man (Vicente Lara), a Dracula-like vampire (David Alvizu), the Mummy (Fernando Rosales), the Cyclops (Gerardo Zepeda, who also played a zombie in the movie), a number of zombies, plus the monster "Franquestain," the latter played by tall Mañuel Leal wearing a Don Post Frankenstein Monster "custom mask" to which had been affixed a mustache and goatee—in the 1969 film *Santo y Blue Demon contra los monstruos* (the translated titled being obvious). Mad scientist Bruno Calder (Carlos Ancira) was revived from the dead to continue his diabolical activities. Almost immediately Calder proceeded to unleash upon the world some of its worst horrors, creating an evil duplicate of the Blue Demon in the process. There was much unintended humor in this very shoddy production, especially in a sequence in which, while Santo takes time off to fight in yet another wrestling match, "Franquestain" and the other *monstruos* invade the arena and join in. Equally amusing was a scene in which the mustachioed and bearded "Franquestain" drove away in a car. Defeating the bogus Blue Demon, Santo and his masked partner then fought off the monsters with fire, inevitably setting off a series of laboratory explosions that destroyed all of them.

In 1970 Santo enjoyed a rematch of sorts with some of his old undead foes in *La venganza de las mujeres vampiro* ("The Vengeance of the Vampire Women"), followed that same year with encounters with walking dead men in *Santo en la venganza de la momia* ("Santo in the Vengeance of the Mummy") and *Las momias de Guanajuatao* ("The Mummies of Guanajuato"). The latter movie, also starring Blue Demon and Mil Mascaras, was based upon an actual tourist attraction in Guanajuato, Mexico, where disinterred mummified corpses—the "rent" for their graves having "expired"—are displayed in a gallery. Blue Demon once complained in a television interview that he and Mil Mascaras did most of the actual "work" in this movie by wearing down the mummies, after which Santo showed up to administer the *coup de gras* (and also enjoy most of the glory).

Santo's career again crossed over into the realm of Mary Shelley's Monster, this time retaining the (near) correct spelling of the name, in the 1971 movie *Santo contra la hija de Frankestein* [note spelling] ("Santo vs. the Daughter of Frankenstein"), wherein the silver-masked hero tangled with two different monstrous beings. Dr. Frieda "Frankestein" (played by Gina Romand) maintained her youth in vampire fashion by taking into her body the blood of other humans. Among her more traditional

"Franquestain" (actually actor Mañuel Leal wearing a Don Post "custom" Frankenstein Monster mask to which whiskers have been attached) carries off a victim in *Santo y Blue Demon contra los monstrous* (1968).

experiments were the creation of a gorilla-man named Truxton (Gerarado Zepeda, who played the Cyclops when Santo and Blue Demon met *"los monstruos"*) and also a new Frankenstein type monster named Ursus (also played by Zepeda). Forced to combat the apeman, Santo beat him to death with chains, after which the masked wrestler fought Ursus, impaling the monster on a cross-shaped grave marker. Tending to Ursus' wounds and befriending the creature, Santo teamed up with the brute to save the wrestler's girlfriend from "Señorita Frankestein's" latest experiment. After killing his creator, Ursus stumbled into some laboratory apparatus, setting off yet another inevitable horror-movie explosion.

Blue Demon teamed up with real-life escape-artist-turned-movie-super-hero Zovek in the 1972 movie *La invasion de los muertos* (*The Invasion of the Dead*), featuring a horde of science-spawned zombies apparently inspired by the success of the recent American film *Night of the Living Dead*. When Zovek unfortunately died during production of this film, Blue Demon had to defeat the walking dead single-handedly.

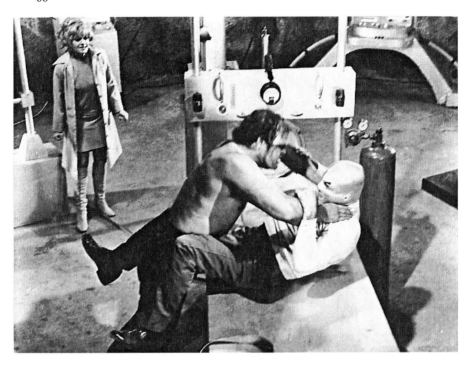

Ursus (Gerarado Zepeda) attacks Santo, as the monster's creator, Dr. Frieda Frankestein (Gina Romand), watches approvingly, in the 1971 Mexican action-horror movie *Santo contra la hia de Frankestein* (note spelling of the name).

Santo and Blue Demon once more combined their masks and wrestling abilities for the 1973-released movie *Santo y Blue Demon contra Dracula y el Hombre Lobo* ("Santo and Blue Demon vs. Dracula and the Wolf Man"). Both Dracula (played by Aldo Monti) and the Wolf Man (not the Lawrence Talbot character of Universal Pictures fame, but Rufus Rex, played by Agustín Martínez Solares, Sr.) were revived from their coffins. Once alive again, Dracula used Rufus to seduce a lovelorn young woman. The highlight of this movie was a climactic battle scene, with Santo and Blue Demon fighting for their lives in an underground chamber against an entire pack of human werewolves.

That same year both super-heroes again joined forces in *Santo y Blue Demon contra el Dr. Frankenstein* (the name, at last, spelled correctly). In this film 113-year-old (but youngish looking) Dr. Irving Frankenstein (Jorge Russek) was up to the usual experiments associated with his family's name, transplanting human brains and bringing life back to the dead in his secret laboratory. His main creation, however, was Golem, a black zombie-like man sporting a scar around his cranium who was controlled via an electronic gadget in his brain. Dr. Frankenstein's biggest mistake, however, was trying to create a less awkward being by using Santo's brain, posing as a wrestling promoter to carry out his mad plan. After Santo eventually defeated Golem in the ring, he and Blue Demon pursued the monster and his creator along the catwalks high above the wrestling arena, with the monster and his maker finally falling to their deaths.

In addition to Santo, Blue Demon and Mil Mascaras, there were other colorfully garbed super-heroes who fought monsters below the border. These included a 1959 entry in Mexico's popular "Momia Azteca" series, *La maldicion de la momia* (seen on television in the United States as *The Curse of the Aztec Mummy*). A character from the previous Aztec Mummy film donned a white super-hero outfit, complete with Santo-like mask and cape, to fight the Mummy and the evil human mastermind seeking to control it, and called himself the Angel.

There was also a series of movies featuring the heroic Neutron (played by muscular actor Wolf Ruvinski) who, although not a wrestler like Santo and his colleagues, resembled one in his black, lightning-bolt adorned mask and costuming. In the 1962 entry *Los automatas de la muerta* (seen on American TV as *Neutron Against the Death Robots*), the ebony-masked super-doer fought a band of mindless, Frankenstein Monster–like human automatons controlled by a giant, blood-nourished composite brain created from the individual brains of three scientists).

Readers of comic books had thrilled to the exploits of costumed and super-powered heroes and their encounters with various inhuman creatures, like vampires and the Frankenstein Monster, since the beginning of the medium back in the 1930s. Yet considerably earlier than the inception of the comic book, super-heroes on the screen were pitting their might and wits against all manner of hideous monsters.

Less earthly and often immortal super-heroes have also tangled with monsters in their motion-picture adventures, some of these movies having been made during the infancy of the medium. French science-fiction, fantasy and horror film pioneer Georges Méliès included super-powered mythological champions in some of his short films made during the early 1900s, such productions affording this former stage magician a chance to experiment with creating some of the movie screen's earliest examples of special visual effects. For example, in *Jupiter's Thunder Bolts* (1903) the god-hero commanded the elements and produced thunder and lightning. Jupiter remained in his heavenly domain in this film. It would actually be the task of Jupiter's son Hercules to come down to the Earth of mortals and pit his superhuman strength against the numerous monsters living there in ancient times.

Hercules, the man-deity offspring of Jupiter and a mortal mother, fought movie monsters as early as 1910, the same year that the first version of *Frankenstein* premiered on American movie screens. This French film, bearing the quite unspectacular title of *Hercules and the Big Stick*, thrust the mythological hero into combat—armed with a big stick, presumably— against the hydra, a legendary multi-headed monster.

It was not in France, however, but in Italy that the mighty Hercules achieved his greatest fame on the screen. *Hercules*, released in the United States by film entrepreneur Joseph E. Levine's Embassy Pictures in 1957, not only introduced the famed man-god to American movie audiences, it also made an international star of Steve Reeves, who had previously won the titles of "Mr. America," "Mr. World" and, ultimately, "Mr. Universe" (and who would become the favorite film star of Dr. Frank N. Furter" in the 1975 Frankenstein-movie spoof *The Rocky Horror Picture Show*). *Hercules* was not only the story of the titled hero himself, but also included in its plot the tale of Jason and his Argonauts. In this version, the dragon that Jason defeated to possess the fabled Golden Fleece was replaced by a bipedal dinosaur-type monster in the *Tyrannosaurus* mold. But the stiffly moving reptilian monster (actually an unbilled extra wearing a Godzilla-like costume) offered little opposition to Hercules' team of heroes. The success of *Hercules* spawned such a rash of sequels and imitations during the 1960s that the reader, if wanting to know the titles of most of them, should consult film researcher Walt Lee's comprehensive index, *Reference Guide to Fantastic Films* (1972–74).

Italian motion-picture producers have unleashed so many of these so-called "sword and sandal" epics that they seemed to be competing in sheer numbers with the American Western movies. Quite often they pitted their mythology-based super-heroes against monsters of their ancient ages. In 1960 Hercules struggled against and eventually defeated a fire-breathing reptile in an opus that was released in the United States as *Goliath and the Dragon*. This film, like so many others of its genre—and for a number of reasons had its title changed for American distribution. Mark Forest played Hercules, or "Goliath," pitting his great strength against such horrors as an enormous bat and a three-headed dog. The promised dragon of the title was, unfortunately, mostly an unconvincing full-sized prop. The highlights of the movie were a modicum of shots wherein the dragon was actually a stop-motion puppet animated by the United States company Project Unlimited. The creature was given life via the artistry of future Oscar nominee Jim Danforth in the young animator's first professional stop-motion job.

Arguably the best of these motion pictures was *Hercules in the Haunted World* (1961). Expertly photographed by director Mario Bava (among his other credits are the horror films *Black Sabbath* and *Black Sunday*), the movie revealed the world of the dead, a cavernous realm composed of weird rock formations and populated by all manners of monstrous beings. Overlording the vast "Haunted World" was the vampire Lico, played by the Dracula of Hammer Films, Christopher Lee. To save the life of his beloved princess, Hercules (Reg Park) had to descend into Hell itself and secure a mystic plant. If the hero did not acquire the plant in time, her blood would feed Lico, affording him eternal life. Among the hellish creatures faced by Hercules was a monstrous, man-like thing of living rock. Naturally the noble hero vanquished the man of stone, then continued to pursue Lico. After defeating a number of flying, wispy vampire creatures that emerged from their ancient crypts, Hercules battled the superhumanly strong Lico himself, finally pinning him under a huge boulder where he was incinerated by the mystic power of a lunar eclipse.

Hercules (Dan Vadis) fought another dragon in *Hercules the Invincible*, and (as played by Kirk Morris) an enormous sea serpent in *Hercules, Samson and Ulysses* (both 1962). In 1964 the mythological super-hero (again played by Dan Vadis) encountered 10 Frankenstein-like warriors of bronze in *Hercules vs. the Giant Warriors*, and (now with Reg Park in the title role) not only met another giant monster, but also a pack of werewolves in *Hercules, Prisoner of Evil*.

Fans of the "true" Hercules films might have been offended by an American parody released by Columbia Pictures in 1962. *The Three Stooges Meet Hercules* was a black and white spoof of the color "sword and sandal" genre, in which Stooges Moe, Larry and Curly, along with puny time machine inventor Schuyler Davis, were zapped back to the era of Hercules. There and then the Stooges not only met such fantastic creatures as the hydra (now sporting *nine* heads) and the Wild Ox of Thessaly, but also a rather villainous Hercules (played by the appropriately name Samson Burke). After days of pulling the heavy oars on a slave ship, Schuyler built up his muscles until he was able to physically overpower the shaggy Siamese Cyclops (two actors joined by a big fur coat) and be mistaken for Hercules himself. The inevitable encounter between the two musclemen followed, with the expected results.

Most American monster-movie buffs, who were not particularly enchanted by the grunting and sweating performances by Italy's mythological supermen, preferred yet another adventure fantasy featuring Hercules. *Jason and the Argonauts* (Columbia, 1963) was stop-motion animation maestro Ray Harryhausen's British-made version of the myth of Jason and the Golden Fleece. As in the original Greek tale, Hercules was portrayed as one of Jason's crew as they all set sail on the young hero's ship, the *Argo*. This time Hercules was depicted as an older and noticeably leaner character by British actor Nigel Green who, though less beefy than Steve Reeves and his body-builder cronies, made up for his relative lack of brawn with his superior acting talent. Hercules accompanied Jason and his Argonauts to an island dominated by Talos, a towering bronze statue. Jason warned Hercules not to take anything on the island. When the demigod purloined a giant brooch for use as a javelin, however, the metal Talos—like some gigantic metallic Frankenstein's Monster or Golem—stiffly came to life, preventing the *Argo* from departing the harbor and upsetting her crew. This time it was Jason and not the bigger and stronger Hercules who resolved the problem. Spotting a plug in the giant's metal heel, Jason tugged with all of his might, loosening it to release a stream of sizzling molten bronze. Talos, like Achilles of legend, was defeated through his heel. Cracks appearing (via frame-by-frame animation) in his metal hide, the giant crashed against the ground into a heap of bronze shards. Ray Harryhausen went to great lengths to achieve the somewhat "jerky" effect of Talos moving, in order to impart the feeling that this was indeed a creature of ambulating bronze.

Hercules did not (as he did in the Steve Reeves *Hercules* movie) accompany Jason any further on his quest for the Golden Fleece. If he had, the demigod would have met some of Harryhausen's finest creations, including the bat-winged harpies, the multi-headed hydra that guarded the fleece, and, ultimately, a squad of sword-wielding skeletons grown from the hydra's teeth.

There were other offshoots of the Hercules movies, including the Italian *Son of Hercules in the Land of Fire*, a 1963 epic starring former "Mr. America" Ed Fury as the title character (actually named Ursus), this hero fighting and defeating a very inhuman-appearing Medusa.

And when speaking of the Italian Hercules films, the character Maciste should not be overlooked. Maciste was an Italian strongman of near Herculean strength and virtue. (Apparently he would also turn out to be an immortal of sorts, whose adventures would be set during any time era his writers deemed appropriate.) The hero first appeared (this first time out portrayed as a black man) in the 1914 silent Italian costume epic *Cabiria*; and his as-yet-unstated immortality kept him perspiring and slaying monsters ever since. Even as early as 1926, in the Italian silent opus *Maciste in Hell*, the now forever–Caucasian muscleman (here played by Umberto Guarracino, the barrel-chested actor who played the Monster in the 1920 Italian silent movie *Il mostro di Frankenstein*) was kept busy fighting the devils and demons of Pluto in the fiery realm of the damned.

Maciste encountered his greatest cast of monsters during the 1960s, the era in which Hercules was enjoying the peak of his own screen popularity. *The Witch's Curse* (1960) again brought Maciste (Kirk Morris) to Hell in order to lift an old hag's curse from a Scottish village. The expected Gustave Dore–inspired torments of the damned souls abounded, including a grisly scene in which a vulture eternally picked at the entrails of a condemned sinner. The following year Maciste was again groaning and fighting monsters that would have crushed a lesser hero. *Maciste e la regina de Samar* ("Maciste and the Queen of Samar") pitted the hero (now played by Alan Steel) against a horde of stone men from another world. *Maciste in the Land of the Cyclops* (seen on television as *Atlas Against the Cyclops*) brought the strongman (Gordon Mitchell) to a cave inhabited by the man-eating, one-eyed monster. *Maciste contro il vampiro* (known in the United States as *Goliath and the Vampires*) had Maciste/Goliath (played by former movie Tarzan Gordon Scott) go to a vast cavern to vanquish a tyrannical vampire and his faceless human automatons.

By 1962 even the Italian productions were spoofing their own product. *Hercules vs. Maciste in the Vale of Woe* was the story of two fight promoters who traveled via time machine into the distant past in hopes of staging a boxing match between the heroes Hercules (Frank Gordon) and Maciste (Kirk Morris). Many of the laughs in this movie were unintentional as the two conmen met the heroes of the film's title. The evil sorceress Circe was also present, adding a number of werewolves to her menagerie of human animals. Maciste's monstrous foes also came from a new source altogether in 1964's *Maciste contro gli domini della Luna*, a movie seen in North America with the Americanized and more commercial title *Hercules Against the Moon Men*. Once again the non-aging hero found himself struggling against minions made of living stone.

Perhaps the most spectacular Hercules-type epic of them all was the Russian spectacle *The Sword and the Dragon* (1956), the tale of the legendary Ilya Mouromets (Boris Andreyev), the 11th century super-hero. Not only was Ilya a *big* man, capable of uprooting a full-sized tree with his bare hands, he was also armed with a magic sword that could withstand any attack. The hero's encounters with a giant and a demon that could cause great winds with each exhalation of his balloon-like cheeks were always victorious. At the climax of this movie Ilya faced a flying three-headed dragon. Yet even so formidable a creature could not overpower the Russian hero's strength and sword.

Perhaps the ultimate in monster-crushing super-heroes was Ultra Man, one of many such characters originating in Japan. The super-hero began his career on *Ultraman*, a television series made during the 1960s by Tsuburaya Productions, the company responsible for the special visual effects in the original series of Godzilla and related monster movies made by Toho International. The gigantic super-hero's adventures originally aired on a weekly basis on television; later they were combined to make a number of feature-length movies, after which Tsuburaya continued to feature spin-offs of the character in new TV series and original motion pictures. Perhaps Ultraman's creation was inevitable. There had to be *some* titanic and super-heroic force capable of combating and then vanquishing the seemingly endless parade of gigantic reptiles, insects, crustaceans and alien threats that relentlessly menaced Japan.

The original Ultraman was an Earthman who, whenever a monster threatened Japan (or any other place on the planet), transformed into a more-than-skyscraping silver alien, big and strong enough to vanquish anything that walked, crawled or flew (one of his abilities was flight). Week after week Ultraman fought menace after menace spawned in Frankenstein-like laboratories, under the sea, beneath the ground or anywhere. These monsters were all rather hastily slapped together by the Tsuburaya creature makers. And when new creations could not be produced in time, some familiar creatures from the Toho giant-monster movies—including Godzilla, the so-called "King of the Monsters," and Baragon, the prehistoric reptile introduced in *Furankenshutain tai Baragon* (released in the United States as *Frankenstein Conquers the World*)—were brought out of retirement, disguised by new frills and horns. The typical Tsuburaya spectacle, albeit on a less grand scale, graced every *Ultraman* episode, even when the monster proved to be sillier than some of those also appearing in the theatrical films. Arguably the series' main fault was its repetition. Ultraman would be battling some menace when suddenly a light began flashing on his chest. The show's announcer would alert us that this was Ultraman's warning signal: If it stopped flashing before he regained his human form, Ultraman would never rise again. But the super-hero always triumphed at the last moment and always did rise again, on both the small living room and large theater screens.

American super-heroes have also fought monsters on the screens, most of them in the old chapterplay adventures made decades ago by

Republic Pictures and Columbia Pictures. For example, two of the most famous comic-book super-heroes of all, Batman and Robin (played by Lewis Wilson and Douglas Croft), in the 1943 *Batman* serial, spent 15 episodes grappling with a squad of science-created zombies controlled by the nefarious Japanese villain Dr. Daka (J. Carrol Naish). Masked and costumed, the titled jungle-based heroes of such serials as *The Phantom* (1943) and *Adventures of Captain Africa* (1955), both from Columbia, included episodes wherein the hero (Tom Tyler playing the Phantom and John Hart the very similar Captain Africa) battled bare-handedly a monstrous gorilla. Adversaries in more of the Frankenstein Monster mold— actually mechanical, seemingly indestructible manlike robots controlled by evil villains—menaced several chapterplay super-heroes, all courtesy of Republic Pictures.

In 1940's *Mysterious Dr. Satan*, the masked crimefighter Copperhead (played by Robert Wilcox, although his spectacular fight sequences and other heroics were courtesy of stuntman David Sharpe) fought a clanking robot controlled by the character after which this 15-episode serial was named (played by Eduardo Cianelli). This "man of steel" was not new to the screen in 1940, nor would that year see its last appearance. The robot suit had been recycled from an earlier Republic chapterplay, *Undersea Kingdom* (1936), in which the mechanical creature (then called a "Volkite") was given orders by future movie Frankenstein Monster Lon Chaney, Jr. The same robot—or at least the same silvery costume—returned yet again in the 1952 serial *Zombies of the Stratosphere*, and in the 1953 *Commando Cody* film (and subsequent TV) series. Then under the control of an extraterrestrial villain, the robot fought and was conquered by two of Republic's resident rocket-suited flying super-heroes, named Larry Martin in *Zombies* and Commando Cody, Sky Marshall of the Universe in the follow-up. In all of its performances the Republic robot was played by the appropriately named stuntman Tom Steele.

Frankenstein Monsters, vampires, werewolves, robots and other monsters; sometimes it required more than torches, wooden stakes, silver bullets and other traditional methods to put these creatures to rest. Sometimes it required the super-heroic efforts of someone wearing a mask or cape. Sometimes it took a super-hero to do the job right.

# VII

# "What's Up, Doc Frankenstein (Jekyll and Fu Manchu)?"

Ever since I was a very young child I have loved animated cartoons. I recall, upon entering a movie theater when I was a child during the late 1940s and early 1950s, asking the usher or ticket taker if there was going to be a cartoon that evening, and becoming quite depressed if his answer was in the negative. (Three hours or so sitting through a couple of movies without an animated color short was simply too grueling an experience even to contemplate.)

As I grew older and developed a fondness for fantastic movies, I think the cartoons I loved the most were the ones having horror or science-fiction themes, particularly those featuring such familiar fantastic characters as the Frankenstein Monster, Dr. Jekyll and Mr. Hyde, Dracula, King Kong and others of their ilk. When Bugs Bunny altered his furry body into the shape of Dr. Frankenstein's Monster, or Mighty Mouse tangled with Dr. Jekyll's cat, it was always a very special event for me.

One day in 1974 I approached *Monsters of the Movies* editor Jim Harmon with an idea for an article I wanted to write about Frankenstein's Monster and other such characters as they appeared in animated cartoons. Jim liked the idea and gave me the go ahead. When, in writing the article, I discovered that the subject matter covered more territory than would fit into a single article, I asked Jim if I could expand the feature into a second part. Again he agreed to the idea. As scheduling would have it, almost a year would separate the two installments.

The article appeared in its original two-part form—under the title "What's Up, Doc Frankenstein?"—in *Monsters of the Movies* number 3 (October 1974) and number 9 (September 1975). Much additional material appears in the piece that follows.

✻  ✻  ✻

Count Dracula and a future Frankenstein Monster, all rolled into one persona, visited the Walt Disney studios during the late 1930s to contribute to the production of what would be later hailed as a masterpiece of cartoon animation, the feature-length film *Fantasia* (1940). Actually, this was the Count's second stint on the Disney payroll, the first being as a drawn cartoon character, animated one frame at a time, in the black and white *Mickey's Gala Premiere* (1933, also known in later years as *Movie Star Mickey*). In that short subject Dracula shared a scene with Frankenstein's Monster and Dr. Jekyll's alter ego Mr. Hyde, who chortle heartily as Mickey wins an award for his acting ability.

In *Fantasia*, however, Dracula was not to appear as an animated character—at least not exactly. He had, in fact, been hired to *act* before the live-action cameras, providing footage that would inspire the movements of yet another cartoon figure.

All right, I have been deliberately misleading.

It was not *really* Count Dracula (or Frankenstein's Monster) who lent their talents to *Fantasia*, but rather the actor whose name is virtually synonymous with that of the King of Vampires—Bela Lugosi. The Hungarian actor was chosen by Walt Disney to emote with all of his broad, theatrical gestures and expressions (as he had done in his role of the bloodthirsty Transylvanian) as a model for Chernobog, the fabulous devil of Bald Mountain, in one of the segments of *Fantasia*. The film presented visual interpretations of great and familiar pieces of classical music in a perfect blend of sound and sight. One of the most memorable segments of this motion picture would be the one in which Lugosi was slated to perform, Mussorgsky's "Night on Bald Mountain."

The intent was that the Disney artists and animators, primarily

Vladimir (Bill) Tytla, would use Lugosi's theatrical, Dracula-like actions as the basis for the horrifying demon of Bald Mountain. However, when Lugosi's movements later proved not to be what the animator was looking for in his devil, the segment's director, Wilfred Jackson, enacted the scene himself to Tytla's satisfaction.

First glimpsed as seemingly a part of Bald Mountain itself, Chernobog slowly unfolds his bat-like wings, stretches his sinewy limbs in the black of night, then proceeds to threaten the town in the valley below with an assortment of werewolves, vampires and other supernatural horrors. Only the first light of dawn compels the demon to shield himself with his wings and return to a state of dormancy. "Night on Bald Mountain," with its supremely powerful devil performing in accordance with Mussorgsky's music, remains one of the classic sequences of animated terror on the screen.

Other sequences in *Fantasia* also had elements related to the supernatural and monsters. "The Sorcerer's Apprentice," from the musical piece by Paul Dukas, which was based in turn upon Goethe's *Der Zauberlehrling*, featured Mickey Mouse as a wizard's helper who gives "life" to inanimate objects with disastrous results, a theme not unlike that in both Mary Shelley's *Frankenstein* and the legend of the Golem.

"The Rite of Spring," another episode of *Fantasia*, based on music by Igor Stravinsky, traversed time to present the Earth as it "was" (or at least as Disney and his artists would have us believe it was) millions of years before the coming of man. We are shown the world taking physical form amid a series of geologic events. Life originates in the seas, microscopic organisms that grow and divide and evolve. Eventually the Earth is populated by all shapes and sizes of reptilian life—all this to Stravinsky's music. Scientifically speaking, this episode of *Fantasia* is replete with errors. Many of the dinosaurs and other prehistoric fauna depicted therein never existed together, neither at the same time nor in the same place. The lumbering plated dinosaur *Stegosaurus* is too large; and the carnivorous *Tyrannosaurus*, which lived many millions of years after the last *Stegosaurus* perished, only had two (not three, as the film depicted) fingers on each tiny hand. These and many other paleontological mistakes became even more apparent when the sequence was edited down into an educational short subject, complete with documentary-style voice-over narration, titled *A World Is Born*. Nevertheless, to animation and movie buffs such errors are overshadowed and even obliterated by the sheer magnificence of the segment, so all that matters is the life-and-death struggle between these wondrous creatures and their inexorable and tragic extinction.

Walt Disney contended that with laughter there must also be tears. Often those Disney-inspired tears went right along with chilled spines and shrieks of terror. *Fantasia*, one of Disney's masterpieces of animation, was but one of his feature-length offerings which unleashed horrendous monsters into the cartoon world.

When Disney created the animated full-length feature motion picture, he and his staff of artists and craftsmen brought to the screen some of the most formidable fiends and villains ever to ice the backbones of young audiences. The first feature-length cartoon was Disney's *Snow White and the Seven Dwarfs* (1937). What child ever seeing the film's Wicked Queen demanding that her henchmen fetch the heart of the innocent Snow White and return with it in a box can ever forget the horror the scene suggests, even though the man never carries out his mission to his mistress' specifications? That was extremely heavy horror for its time, equal to or even surpassing that served out at the time by studios like Universal Pictures in their *adult* horror films. The Wicked Queen was Disney's answer to Shakespeare's Lady Macbeth. When the Queen uses a mystic spell to transform herself into a cackling hag, her metamorphosis rivals that of Dr. Jekyll into Mr. Hyde. Arguably, the Wicked Queen's only real rival in the classic witchery department is the Wicked Witch of the West played by Margaret Hamilton in *The Wizard of Oz*.

In *Pinocchio*, released the same year as *Fantasia*, Walt Disney gave us—if we extend our imaginations a bit—another variation on both the Frankenstein and Golem themes, with a lifeless humanoid figure achieving life through some external agency (in this case, the supernatural power of the Blue Fairy). Disney's employees ran the entire gamut of their art in this masterpiece of animation, bringing to the story of a living puppet who wants to be a real boy humor, warmth and characterization, as well as some of the finest cartoon animation ever put on film, with music to match. But there was also terror in *Pinocchio*. The scene set on Pleasure Island wherein the bad boys transform, like werewolves, into donkeys is rightly considered by many film buffs to be one of the most effective horror scenes ever filmed. Disney certainly understood the psychology of children and knew what could truly *scare* the younger members of his audience. For a child to see another youth (albeit a "bad boy") crying for his mother, then hear that plea segue into the braying of a beast (coupled with a visual transformation into a human animal) was surely a vivid lesson in behaving. As a credit to Disney's genius, this scene, which could have been objectionable if handled by someone less caring, was executed with understanding and good taste.

*Pinocchio* also boasted the dreaded Monstro, the most monstrous whale ever to crash and splash about the screen. Even the various movie Moby Dicks appeared to be like smiling "Flippers" by comparison, as Monstro's cave-like mouth opened to its maximum, swallowing even whole boats.

Walt Disney, along with his staff of writers, artists, animators and technicians, continued over the years to create monsters and fiends for their animated features. *The Reluctant Dragon* (1941), for example, was an amusing film about a dragon who would rather enjoy a peaceful life in the country than battle courageous knights. The dragon in *Sleeping Beauty* (1959), on the contrary, was more of the traditional sort. It was a monster in the strictest sense of that term, the transformed evil witch Maleficent, who required the size and power of a reptilian, winged and fire-breathing dragon to attack Prince Charming.

Although Walt Disney brought his monsters to animated perfection within the color frames of his feature-length movies, he was actually creating cartoon horror on the screen much earlier, in black and white short subjects starring the unsinkable Mickey Mouse.

Mickey encountered his own version of King Kong in a 1933 cartoon entitled *The Pet Shop* (also known as *Mickey the Gorilla Tamer*). For some reason, perhaps fathomable only to the mind of a mouse, Mickey keeps a gorilla caged in the pet shop where he works. When the big ape casts an amorous look at Mickey's girlfriend Minnie Mouse (as if Kong falling in love with a *human* woman was not bizarre enough), it bends the bars of its cage and escapes, clutching the female rodent in a hairy paw. Coincidentally, our hero has left a book in the shop conveniently picturing King Kong atop the Empire State Building. Mimicking that scene, the gorilla piles up boxes and caps them with a bird cage (suggesting the old dirigible mooring mast topping what was once the world's tallest skyscraper), then climbs to the summit with Minnie held dearly. Mickey requires the help of the pet shop birds, imitating the biplanes from the climax of *King Kong*, to cut the big-thinking simian down to size.

The year 1933 was a good one for monster fans but a bad one for Mickey. That year he also encountered an assortment of infamous human fiends. Besides tackling the gorilla in *The Pet Shop* and meeting Frankenstein's Monster and cohorts in *Mickey's Gala Premiere*, the world's most famous mouse also met the diabolical Dr. XXX. *The Mad Doctor* spoofed, to some extent, First National's *Dr. X*, made the previous year, and also Universal's *Frankenstein*, released the year before that. In truth *The Mad Doctor* is a mini–horror movie shot via drawings instead of live actors and containing some truly gruesome images. Mickey sees his dog Pluto abducted by a mysterious cloaked figure and secreted away to an ominous-appearing castle. Going in pursuit of his pet, Mickey discovers the mystery man to be the sinister Dr. XXX. This leering, mad fiend subjects both Pluto and his master to the monstrous devices in a laboratory that either Drs. Frankenstein or Jekyll would be proud to call home. Luckily, just as he is about to be divided by the madman's descending buzz saw, Mickey awakens from his bad dream (not an uncommon ending for cartoons of this period).

A more ambitious *King Kong* satire was made the same year as *The Pet Shop*. Since the "Eighth Wonder of the World" was energized upon the screen via puppet animation in 1933, it may have been logical that the same year would see a similar character stomping through the medium of the animated cartoon. *King Klunk* was a Walter Lantz cartoon starring Pooch the Pup, one of the seemingly countless anthropomorphic animals of that period. Pooch ventures to a prehistoric world where he meets a native girl named Gooma-Gooma. But Pooch's affections for the girl with the exotic name are rivaled by those of the enormous gorilla King Klunk, who first battles an amphibious *Tyrannosaurus*-like dinosaur, then chases Gooma-Gooma through a modern city. Finally the King is *klunked* off the Empire State Building by an airborne Pooch the Pup.

In 1934 Walter Lantz had a toy Frankenstein Monster resembling Boris Karloff come to life in a department store in the cameo-filled color cartoon *Toyland Premiere.* Years later, Lantz subjected his classic creation Woody Woodpecker to various terrors inspired by the old horror movies, like *Frankenstein* and *The Invisible Man*, made by Universal Pictures (the same studio where the Woody cartoons were made and released). *Operation Meatball* (later retitled *Invisible Woody*), for one, released in 1951, had the red-topped character vanish in a supermarket. *Franken-Stymied* (1961) pitted Woody against a mechanical chicken plucker made in the image of Frankenstein's Monster, finally turning the creature against its mad-scientist maker. And *Monster of Ceremonies* (1966) featured another mad doctor, this one attempting to build a Frankenstein-type creature and transforming Woody into a monster robot.

Returning to the topic of cartoon dinosaurs, the very first classic animated cartoon character was just such an animal. *Gertie* (also known as *Gertie the Dinosaur*) was the creation of Winsor McCay, a cartoonist most famous for his *Little Nemo in Slumberland* newspaper strip, made in 1912. In a later version of the short film, McCay is shown in a live action prologue betting a group of friends (including cartoonist George McManus, of *Maggie and Jiggs* fame) that he can bring his dinosaur Gertie to life on screen. Utilizing a series of drawings, each one slightly different and photographed in sequence one frame at a time, McCay succeeds in "bringing to life" Gertie, an *Apatosaurus* (then commonly known as *Brontosaurus*). Gertie proved to be the progenitor of all future anthropomorphic cartoon animals. When originally presenting his cartoon in such venues as the music halls, McCay appeared on stage in front of a screen upon which the Gertie footage was projected. The cartoonist would interact with his character, prompting her to do tricks. Finally (by cleverly ducking behind the screen) McKay would appear to ride away on Gertie's back. *Gertie* was a sensation, so popular, in fact, that McCay made a sequel, *Gertie on Tour*, in 1917, while animator John Bray also made his own, similar (but less charming) version of *Gertie the Dinosaur*.

Warner Bros., the studio responsible for what many animation buffs regard as the funniest cartoons ever made—with it stellar line-up of animated stars, including Bugs Bunny, Porky Pig, Tweety and Sylvester, Daffy Duck and the Road Runner—was a potent force in keeping such infamous horrors as Frankenstein's Monster and Mr. Hyde before the eyes of the public. Warner's black and white cartoon *Hollywood Capers* (1936) featured a mechanical Frankenstein Monster that is zapped to "life" on a movie set, creating many problems before being lured into a powerful electric fan by hero Beans. The stuttering Porky Pig met a sabotaging Borax Karoff, a Frankenstein Monster look-alike, in the cameo-filled cartoon *Porky's Road Race* (1937). The musical cartoon *Have You Got Any Castles* (1938) had the Frankenstein Monster, Mr. Hyde, Dr. Fu Manchu and the Phantom of the Opera emerge from books about them and then dance together. In *Hare-Conditioned* (1945), Bugs Bunny impersonates a "horrible Frankincense Monster" to escape a pursuing department-store manager. That same year, Bugs imitated the Frankenstein Monster to chase his less threatening foe Elmer Fudd in *Hare Tonic*. *Dr. Devil and Mr. Hare* (1964) had crafty Bugs Bunny build his own Frankenstein Monster for the purpose of defeating the rowdy Tasmanian Devil.

Among the greatest of all Warner animators and cartoon directors (it is impossible to single out *one* of them as "best") was Robert Clampett, who was responsible for many of that studio's most memorable animated short subjects. Clampett's association with monsters at the Warner Bros. studios can be traced back to 1932 with the "Harmon-Ising" cartoon *Three's a Crowd*. In this cartoon Clampett recreated via animated drawings one of the most well known horror scenes of all. (It was Clampett, by the way, who "invented" the story formula of bringing advertising signs or, later, book covers to life in an earlier "Merrie Melodies" cartoon.) In *Three's a Crowd* the idea was changed from signs to book covers to show actor Fredric March's version of Dr. Jekyll spring to life off the cover of the Robert Louis Stevenson book and then transform, as he did in the 1931 movie classic *Dr. Jekyll and Mr. Hyde*, into his evil counterpart.

The same animation idea was applied the following year to *I Like Mountain Music*, a cartoon in which the pictures on magazine covers come to life, and for which Clampett originated the giant gorilla character Ping Pong. (Years later, Clampett's Ping Pong would live again, although in a different medium and within a concept that had its origins when Bob was still a child.)

In 1925 *The Lost World* premiered and young Bob Clampett, somewhat of a dinosaur buff, went to see the seemingly living prehistoric beasts that walked and fought one another on the silent-movie screen. The scenes of the "*Brontosaurus*" causing havoc in London, and then swimming back toward its anachronistic world, inspired Bob to create his own (albeit humorous) sea serpent. Traces of Clampett's original conception would be evident in many of his Warner cartoons. Yet the idea reached full-blown fruition after Clampett left the Warner Bros. studios in the late 1940s and pioneered early television with his classic puppet show *Time for Beany*, which later became an animated TV series called *Beany and Cecil*. (Remember that ending tune, sung by Cecil the Sea Sick Sea Serpent? "A Bob Clampett cartoo-*ooon!*")

Cecil was the end product of Bob Clampett's *Lost World* inspiration. His first series, *Time for Beany*, also became the new home for Ping Pong. The giant Kong Kong–inspired ape was impersonated on the live TV show by an actor wearing a gorilla costume and "assisted" by a live chimpanzee. In one spectacular *Time for Beany* story line, Pong helped Beany, Cecil and their puppet friends ward off an invasion of unidentified flying objects. Not surprisingly, Clampett incorporated scenes of flying saucers shooting out of a volcano crater and attacking a city, producing one of the first real spectacles on *live* television. Ping Pong would later be featured again on the *Beany and Cecil* cartoon show.

In 1933 Robert Clampett was one of the gag writers on the black and white cartoons *Bosko's Mechanical Man* and *Wake Up the Gypsy in Me*. In the former, Bosko, the screen's first African American animated hero, builds a monstrous robot out of junk and an automobile motor, then, *á la* Dr. Frankenstein, uses electricity to bring the metal creature to life. When the big mechanical man starts to move, Bosko shouts, "Frankensteeen!" and runs away from the thing in terror. Naturally the robot, in true Frankenstein style, causes much trouble for our little hero. *Wake Up the Gypsy in Me* spoofed the 1932 MGM costume drama *Rasputin and the Empress* by featuring the sinister Lionel Barrymore–inspired character Rice Puddin'.

Bob Clampett's *Lost World* influence was apparent in the 1936 cartoon *Buddy's Lost World*. Buddy sails to a prehistoric island where the "tree trunks" he walks beneath are actually the legs of a giant *Apatosaurus*. The long-necked dinosaur gives Buddy a wet "slurp kiss," a gag that would eventually become an integral part of Cecil's personality. In 1939 Clampett again brought dinosaurs to animated life, along with a nasty pitch-black sabertoothed cat, in the cartoon *Prehistoric Porky*.

The monsters were only beginning to run rampant in Bob Clampett's Warner Bros. cartoons. Porky Pig tackles and defeats the gorgon Medusa in *Porky's Hero Agency* (1937), then meets both the Invisible Man and a very cowardly Frankenstein Monster, the latter being subjected to a police "third degree," in *Porky's Movie Mystery* (1939). In *Hollywood Steps Out* (1941), a cartoon for which Clampett devised some of the gags, the Frankenstein Monster does a very stiff conga dance while, in another scene, a caricatured Boris Karloff makes an appearance as himself. Bug Bunny briefly alters his fuzzy form to that of a stiff-legged Frankenstein Monster in the Clampett-directed *What's Cookin', Doc?* (1944). And in Clampett's Daffy Duck cartoon *The Great Piggybank Robbery* (1946), Bob spoofed the famous comic-strip police detective Dick Tracy. Daffy, as "Duck Twacy," tangles with such monstrous villains as "Wolf Man," "Bat Man" and "Neon Noodle," a living neon sign in the shape of Frankenstein's Monster.

Unfortunately, one of the most promising (and, at the time, innovative) of the "serious" cartoons (in the sense that the Superman Paramount cartoons were serious; see below) died aborning. Bob Clampett, while still a writer/artist/director at the Warner Bros. cartoon department, was enlisted by Tarzan creator Edgar Rice Burroughs to make an entire series of animated color shorts based upon his popular science-fiction hero John Carter of Mars. The year was 1935, almost half a decade before the first of the Superman cartoons. The *John Carter of Mars* shorts, then, *could* have been the first animated films to deal with monsters and science fiction and also to depict an adventure hero with *realistic* animation.

For the actions of John Carter himself, Clampett used the "roto-scope" process, by which an animator can trace over the filmed movements of a human figure with quite realistic results. In this case, Clampett's animation followed the movements of an athlete who performed all the leaping and swinging of the Earthman who is transported to the planet Mars. Clampett designed realistic versions of the *Tharks*, the green men of *Barsoom* (the Martian's name for their own planet), and the eight-legged *thoats*, which the Barsoomians rode as transportation. He filmed scenes of Carter leaping about the great futuristic Martian cities, unfettered by gravity, and shots of great fleets of rocket ships blasting out of the crater of a Red Planet volcano.

What happened to this very promising series?

"The cartoons were to be released by MGM," Bob Clampett told this writer around 1973. "The MGM sales heads in Hollywood and New York

Bugs Bunny "morphs" into a "Karloffian" Frankenstein Monster in this scene from *What's Cookin', Doc?*, a 1944 Warner Bros. cartoon directed by Bob Clampett. Cameos of the Frankenstein Monster and other popular Hollywood characters and celebrities often turned up in animated shorts. (Courtesy the late Bob Clampett.)

were very excited over the idea. But the reaction from most of the exhibitors across the country, especially in the smaller towns, was negative. They said that the concept of an Earthman on Mars was entirely too farfetched for their "Corn Belt" and "Bible Belt" audiences.

"It's ironic," Clampett mused, "that the first *Flash Gordon* serial was released in late 1936 by Universal and did fantastic business. Maybe MGM felt that serials played only to children at Saturday matinees, while the John Carter color cartoons would have been seen by adult audiences in the evenings. At any rate, MGM decided against going ahead with *John Carter of Mars* and suggested instead that I do an animated series called *Tarzan and His Animals*—with the animals performing the kind of gags I was then writing for the Warner cartoons! A really awful premise. I would have done the best I could with it, but Warner Bros. made me a much better offer to stay with them. I gladly accepted."

For many years the ill-fated John Carter test footage, drawn and animated by Bob Clampett, was believed to be lost. Fortunately, however, Danton Burroughs, the grandson of John Carter's creator, located during the early 1970s some of the rare film tests in the storage vaults at Edgar Rice Burroughs, Inc., located in Tarzana, California. Anyone having seen this footage can attest to the loss that has been suffered by MGM's premature cancellation of the series. The sight of the Martian riding the thoat, with its perfectly coordinated eight legs moving in full gallop, is certainly magnificent. Indeed, it was a pity that the myopic exhibitors of 1936 deprived their potential audience of such fantastic adventure.

An interesting side note is that Bob Clampett, from 1943 to 1945, had also been developing a live-action comedy series idea for the then new medium of television. The project was called *The Monster Family*. The family consisted of the Frankenstein-like father, named Frankie Monster (the name intended to suggest that of crooner Frank Sinatra), his vampire wife and their equally monstrous son. As far as Frankie and his family were concerned, they were "just plain folks." Frankie could never quite grasp why other people did double takes or fainted when he and his brood walked by. Does this premise sound somewhat familiar?

The first episode of *The Monster Family* was to have the threesome go to the beach where they naturally cause a commotion. Years after *The Monster Family* idea was developed on paper, copies of Bob Clampett's drawings for this first episode, along with notes on the show's concept, were taken to a major studio for consideration. Clampett never again heard a word about his creation. But *The Munsters* would debut on network television in 1964, becoming a very popular series in its original two-year run, and remaining equally popular for decades to come in reruns. Justice, at times it seems, can be monstrous!

Through the 1930s and into the 1960s, familiar movie-monster imagery continued to turn up in cartoons. Betty Boop, perhaps the sexiest of all the old animated characters, also met her share of horrors. *Betty Boop, M.D.* depicted an astoundingly convincing metamorphosis of the Fredric March Dr. Henry Jekyll into Mr. Edward Hyde. In *Betty Boop's Penthouse*, Betty is menaced by a Frankenstein Monster created from a retort dripping chemicals. Betty's very sexual appeal stops the stalking brute in its giant tracks, changing him into an effeminate flower (also giving the older members of the theater audience something to contemplate and perhaps chuckle over on the way home). Both of these cartoons were released in 1933, just two years after Paramount's *Dr. Jekyll and Mr. Hyde* and Universal's *Frankenstein*.

The animal characters in 20th Century–Fox's Terrytoons frequently met Frankenstein's Monster, Count Dracula, Mr. Hyde and other horror characters. The black and white *Gandy Goose in G Man Jitters* (1939) had the titled fowl dream that he was being pursued by the Monster, Dracula and a lot of ghosts, with a clockwork mechanism *sproinging* from the Monster's chest as he drops. Some of the Monster's scenes from that cartoon, now in color, were later incorporated into the action of both *Gandy Goose in Fortune Hunters* (1946) and *Heckle and Jekyll in King Tut's Tomb* (1950).

Mighty Mouse, Terrytoons' most popular character, met his share of characters patterned after familiar monsters. Among the super-powered rodent's many 1940s and 1950s adventures with such creatures were *Mighty Mouse in Svengali's Cat* (1946), pitting the caped and flying hero against a powerful hypnotist; *Mighty Mouse in the Witch's Cat* (1948), wherein a feline gets hold of its mistress' potions; *Mighty Mouse in Prehistoric Perils* (1951), in which he fights dinosaurs; and *Mighty Mouse in Goons from the Moon* (1951), with our champion battling catlike alien invaders. In *Mighty Mouse Meets Jekyll and Hyde Cat* (1948), the Mouse encounters Dr. Jekyll's cat, the only remaining occupant of the scientist's old laboratory. When the cat mixes up its master's old transformation potion, only the super-rodent powers of the titled hero can save the nearby mice population from the evil feline version of Mr. Hyde.

Mighty Mouse had two adventures involving the Frankenstein Monster. In one of these, *Mighty Mouse in the Jail Break* (1946), the Frankenstein Monster and Dracula only make brief appearances as inmates at Alcatraz. The earlier *Mighty Mouse in Frankenstein's Cat* (1942), however, was fully devoted to the Frankenstein theme. In this one, the Frankenstein monster-cat becomes a real menace to the villagers (read: mice) living in the shadow of the Frankenstein castle. Amid scenes spoofing the then current Universal movies (including an irate mob of torch-bearing mice), Frankenstein's cat is finally sent running away by the super heroic Mighty Mouse.

In 1949, "Frankie Stein" menaced the character Bubble and his talking taxicab Squeaky in the British cartoon *Old Manor House*. Ten years later, a Peter Lorre type character, accompanied by the Frankenstein Monster, enter a ghost-ridden haunted house in the Paramount Pictures musical cartoon *Boos in the Night*.

It was during the 1960s that the near-sighted Mr. Magoo (voiced by actor Jim Backus) had two spooky yet comical encounters with the celebrated Frankenstein Monster. UPA's theatrical cartoon *Magoo Meets Frankenstein* (1960) brought the squinting hero to what he believes is a

Squinty-eyed Mr. Magoo enacts the part of a maniacal "Doctor Frankenstein" in that installment of UPA's *Famous Adventures of Mr. Magoo* animated series, first aired in 1965 over the NBC television network. Jim Backus, as always, provided the character's distinctive voice.

resort hotel. Actually, Magoo becomes the "guest" of Professor Frankenstein, who just happens to require a human mind to transfer to his Monster. Through his own inimitable luck, Magoo manages to turn the tables on the Professor, making him the Guinea Pig, exchanging Frankenstein's mind with that of a rooster. *Magoo Meets Frankenstein* was standard Mr. Magoo fare—which could *not* be said of the character's next association with the Frankenstein theme.

Mr. Magoo appeared as a quite fiendish Dr. Frankenstein in the UPA television series of 1965, *Famous Adventures of Mr. Magoo*. In the episode "Doctor Frankenstein," the unorthodox scientist plans to conquer the world with a veritable army of artificially created Frankenstein Monsters. Dr. Frankenstein raves and basks in his own delusions of grandeur as he plays with his electrical apparatus in his laboratory. Only the inevitable explosion ends the mad scientist's madder dreams. (This segment of the

The Monster appeared as a cartoon character in "Doctor Frankenstein," one of the *Famous Adventures of Mr. Magoo*. This time the creature was really a "good guy," while his creator was a megalomaniac out to conquer the world. (This episode was later included in the feature-length movie *Mr. Magoo, Man of Mystery*, released in 1967.)

series was later incorporated into a feature-length movie, *Mr. Magoo, Man of Mystery*, which occasionally plays on television.)

"Serious" cartoons have long been more a part of the world of horror and monster movies than most fans of the latter genres probably realize. The set of 17 "Superman" cartoons made in color by Paramount Pictures from 1941 through 1943 are generally regarded as simply expertly designed and animated short subjects depicting the super-heroic exploits of the famed Man of Steel. But Superman tangled with as many inhuman monsters as he did gangsters in this classic series. In *The Arctic Giant*, for example, the Man of Tomorrow battles an enormous *Tyrannosaurus*, its city-smashing rampage presaging Godzilla and its ilk by more than a decade. In *The Mechanical Monsters* Superman is nearly defeated by an army of super-powerful robots who move with stiff Frankenstein Monster–like movements and even fly. *Underworld World* brings the Man of Steel into conflict with a lost race of birdmen. In *The Mummy Strikes*, the hero from Krypton battles not the usual lone undead Egyptian, but a whole hoard of them, and each one a giant. And in *Terror on the Midway* Superman pits his titanic strength against that of a gorilla as big as Mighty Joe Young.

Over the years there have been many screen adaptations of Edgar Allan Poe's classic short story "The Tell-Tale Heart." Strangely, one of the most authentic (and terrifying) adaptations on celluloid happened to be a cartoon short made in 1954 by UPA. Furthermore, this animated film was photographed in three dimensions. James Mason narrated *The Tell-Tale Heart*, relating the story of a man killing another man after he becomes obsessed with the latter's haunting, vulture-like, pale blue eye. Through some unnerving, surrealistic graphics and Mason's chilling voice-over performance, the viewer virtually experiences the terror of the story's protagonist as he hears the telltale beating of his dead victim's heart. The animated *Tell-Tale Heart* remains an authentic excursion into terror as seen and heard through a demented mind.

Monsters of various sizes and shapes have also appeared in independently made cartoons, some of which have enjoyed releases in theaters or on television. The popular *Bambi Meets Godzilla* (1969), an extremely short black and white subject made by Marvin Newland, simply shows Bambi the deer eating peacefully, only to be squashed moments later under a gigantic reptilian foot. And *The Mad Baker* (1972), made by the Crunch Bird Company, follows a living chocolate cake, created by a Dracula-like mad doctor, causing havoc until being destroyed (mimicking the climax of Universal's *Frankenstein*) in a burning windmill, where it is vanquished vampire style by the rising sun. In *Frankenshoe* (1979), made by Rick Reed, a German scientist gives life to a mass of clay in an artist's studio.

One of the more impressive of this "new wave" of independent animated cartoons was *Joshua and the Blob* (begun in 1971 and released in 1972 as a companion short to the live-action motion picture *Son of Blob*). The cartoon was animated and directed by 21-year-old John Lange. The cartoon's assistant animator, Bob Greenberg, also created some of the spectacular animation effects in the science-fiction comedy movie *Dark Star*.

Joshua is a kind of Everyman, although a very weird-looking one, his reactions being more or less those of any of us. In appearance, Joshua is almost a monster himself, consisting mainly of a stout brown body (mostly belly) and a head, the latter mostly nose and an enormous tooth-filled mouth. However, the real "monster" of the cartoon is a pulsating pink blob that crawls into Joshua's mundane life.

Yet is this blob *really* a monster (like its live-action namesake)?

As any of us might do, Joshua at first attempts to reject this alien creature. Yet the more Joshua tries to shrug off the mysterious blob, the more tender, the more amorous the strange thing becomes. At last our Everyman can no longer resist the affections of the blob and the screen erupts with what can only be described as visualized happiness, an explosion of colorful imagery and joyous music. Joshua discovers that his new pink "friend" has metamorphosed into a pink lady. And to Joshua's eternal joy, she is a distaff counterpart of himself.

*Joshua and the Blob* received a number of awards, including the first prize in the category of animated films for children at the annual Animated Film Festival in Zagreb, Yugoslavia. (The previous year, John Lange's *Joshua in a Box* cartoon took first place.) The short was also a first-prize winner in animated film festivals held in London and Hollywood.

Monsters and horror are clearly a part of the world of the cartoon. This article has mentioned only a few of these animated gems. Virtually every animated cartoon character has had his, her or its share of horrific experiences over the course of the series.

And so remember, the next time our favorite floppy-eared bunny hero chomps that carrot and says his trademark line, "What's up, Doc?" we might take special note—for that "Doc" to whom Bugs is referring might very well boast the last name of Jekyl, Fu Manchu ... or Frankenstein.

# VIII

## THE BEATLES
## MEET FRANKENSTEIN

During the middle to late 1970s, my friend Ron Haydock was hired by publisher Edward Goldstein to edit a series of magazines grouped together as the E-Go Collectors Series (E-Go standing, of course, for Edward Goldstein). Ron produced a series of these magazines based upon such disparate topics as Sherlock Holmes, King Kong, John Wayne, Henry Winkler, Laurel and Hardy, Robert Blake and others, just to name some of them. I wrote articles for most of those magazines, often falling back upon the topic (when I could think of nothing else or really was not interested in the person or character upon which the issue was based) of "[insert subject] Meets the Monsters."

In 1977 Ron asked me if I could write something for his next E-Go collectors magazine, *The Beatles*. Having been a hard-core Beatles fan since I saw their first major American television appearance on the *Ed Sullivan Show* in 1963, and having identified in some ways with Beatle John Lennon, I immediately accepted the invitation. But at a loss for something to write about the famous foursome, I fell back on my old tried and true basic theme. Thus, *The Beatles* magazine, which came out in May 1977, featured my article originally titled "The Beatles Meet the Bogeymen."

✳ ✳ ✳

Frankenstein's Monster, King Kong and even a cloaked figure looking suspiciously like Hammer Films' version of Count Dracula....

Indeed it seems strange to find the names of such infamous menaces—and more—linked with the Beatles, the musical foursome that, in the early 1960s, changed forever—and worldwide—the face and sound of rock music. But Frankenstein's Monster and other fantastic characters have been a part of the Beatles' motion picture and television careers since the middle 1960s. For many years John Lennon, Paul McCartney, George Harrison and Ringo Starr have, either as a group or individually, been associated with various monsters and bogeymen of the large and small screens.

On the tube, *The Beatles* was a cartoon series produced by King Features Syndicate, playing on the ABC television network from September 25, 1965, to September 7, 1969. Paul Frees, among the upper echelon of voice-over actors, spoke the word for the cartoon John and George, while Lance Percival spoke for Paul and Ringo. The individual episodes comprised simple stories based upon two of the Beatles' recorded songs. And it was in this two-dimensional, drawn and animated medium that the Beatles were spooked by a number of sinister characters.

In the second half of episode number two of *The Beatles* cartoon show, in an adventure built around their song "If I Fell," the four "mop tops" from Liverpool meet a female made scientist who wants to bring to life a Frankenstein-type monster that she has created. All that the creature lacks is a brain, and its creator wants to give it that of a beetle (note spelling). Not surprisingly, the woman's bumbling assistant brings her John Lennon—"the brains of the Beatles"—instead of the lowly bug. John manages to escape while his band's music plays on the soundtrack.

In other episodes of *The Beatles*, our singing heroes are menaced in Transylvania by none other than Count Dracula, and, in Paris, by the hunchbacked Quasimodo, still ringing the bells at Notre Dame cathedral.

*The Beatles* was a popular series and held its own in the ratings at ABC for four years. It was defeated in 1969 when rival network CBS introduced its new line-up of cartoon shows, including Hanna-Barbera's *Frankenstein, Jr. and the Impossibles*. This mechanical flying super-hero version of the Frankenstein Monster proved to be too powerful an adversary for the Beatles to escape, even backed up by their fabulous music.

Fantasy was an important ingredient in the Beatles' live-action movies. Their second feature-length production, *Help!* (1965), was a spoof of the James Bond and other "super spy" films being made at the time. *Help!* relied heavily on such fantastic plot elements as paralyzing and shrinking rays, and even included a magic ring (worn by Ringo, of course) which is sought by a cult of weird fanatics. There were no monsters in this picture but plenty of strange events happening.

Two years later, the musical group took their fans on an even more strange—bizarre, actually—*Magical Mystery Tour*, a made-for-TV, surrealistic excursion into the psychedelic realm designed to please any fan of fantastic movies.

It was *Yellow Submarine* (1968), an elaborate feature-length cartoon, wherein the Beatles not only had another Frankenstein experience, but also encountered the giant gorilla King Kong. The British-made production was made by Subafilms and King Features Syndicate (the same company that released the TV cartoon series), and released to theaters by United Artists. It featured a new style of groundbreaking animation by Jack Stokes and Bob Balser, heavily influenced by the "psychedelic" era in which this movie was made.

In one of the early scenes, in which the individual Beatles are introduced, Ringo is shown in a laboratory in the role of a mad scientist. Strapped to a platform is the huge motionless figure of the Frankenstein Monster. Ringo manipulates the controls of his weird electrical apparatus, charging the giant figure with electrical power. The Monster comes to life, rises from the platform and literally transforms into the cartoon figure of John Lennon (this Beatle's second association with a Frankenstein character). In a later scene in the movie, the mighty Kong is shown peering through a window while, in a "Sea of Monsters," a number of giant dinosaurs can be seen through the portholes of the Beatles' Yellow Submarine. Other bizarre characters populating *Yellow Submarine* included the likable Nowhere Man and villainous Blue Meanies.

By 1968, Ringo Starr had launched himself into a more serious (and solo) acting career, in addition to his musical one and filmed appearances with the other Beatles. That was the year he was featured in author Terry Southern's *Candy*, a sexy comedy based on Southern's novel and released in the United States by Cinerama. The movie included in its cast of eccentric characters a strange and magical hunchback, while the title character is a beautiful being that descends to Earth from space.

Ringo's association with Southern continued into the following year's comedy *The Magic Christian*, again based upon the author's novel, an elaborate satire on man's greed that climaxed with a bizarre sequence of events engineered by fabulously rich Guy Grand (Peter Sellers) aboard the ship *Magic Christian*. These included a surprise guest appearance by Christopher Lee, the star of such British horror movies as *The Curse of*

*Frankenstein* and *Horror of Dracula*, decked out in vampire fangs and flowing cloak. Although indeed resembling the famed Count Dracula, who had been starring in a series of movies made by Hammer Films since 1958, Lee did not play that character in *The Magic Christian*, as he first appears in a woman's cabin, reflected in a mirror and baring his fangs, then later stalking through the ship's corridors in slow motion, cape billowing behind him. Rather, he was billed in the film's credits as the "Ship's Vampire." "I didn't wear the gray wig," Lee told this writer in 1972, referring to his Hammer Dracula guise. "And I wore a black tuxedo with a bow tie, if you remember. I didn't play Dracula." No, he was simply one of the actors hired by the eccentric Grand to haunt *The Magic Christian*.

In 1973, following the official break-up of the Beatles in December of 1970, Christopher Lee would appear as a photograph on the jacket of *Band on the Run*, an album recorded by Paul McCartney and his post–Beatles group Wings.

Ringo's association with Frankenstein's Monster and other fantastic characters was just beginning. In 1973 Ringo and pop-music star Harry Nilsson co-starred together in *Son of Dracula* (shot under the title *Count Down* and later reissued as *Young Dracula*), made by the British company Apple Films. Ringo (who also produced the film) played the magician Merlin, and Nilsson, who also wrote the music for the movie, was Count Down, Dracula's musician son. The cast included some faces familiar to buffs of earlier Frankenstein movies. Featured were such stalwarts of British horror films as Freddie Jones (the result of Baron Frankenstein's latest experiment in Hammer Films' *Frankenstein Must Be Destroyed*) and Dennis Price (a body snatcher in Hammer's *The Horror of Frankenstein*, then Dr. Frankenstein himself in the Spanish/French *Dracula contra el Dr. Frankenstein* and its follow-up movie *Les experiences erotiques de Frankenstein*). The movie was directed by Freddie Francis, who in 1973 had helmed the Hammer Frankenstein series entry *The Evil of Frankenstein*.

The plot has the vampire-born Count Down descending into the "Netherworld" to assume his rightful place as Overlord, where, as per his destiny, he will lord over such horror classic characters as Baron Frankenstein, the Frankenstein Monster, walking mummies, werewolves and other creatures of darkness. Baron Frankenstein (Jones) opposes the young vampire when, aided by his father's foe Van Helsing (Price), he seeks a cure for his vampiric condition and the destruction of all the monstrous beings inhabiting the Netherworld.

*Son of Dracula* flopped at the box office. The film's soundtrack, including incidental music written by Paul Buckmaster, was issued in 1974 on a 33-rpm album by Rapple Records (ABLI-0220). One of its songs, "Without You," became a hit record at the time of the album's release, most people hearing it having no idea that it sprang from a movie about such characters as Dracula and Frankenstein's Monster.

In 1981 Ringo Starr was again associated with movie monsters, this time of the prehistoric sort in the United Artists comedy film *Caveman.* Ringo played a likable Stone Age Everyman who encounters various dinosaurs (including an overweight, bumbling and eventually "stoned" *Tyrannosaurus rex*) and other ancient reptiles (brought to life on the screen via the stop-motion artistry of Jim Danforth and David Allen), as well as a kind of Abominable Snowman character (played by very tall actor Richard Moll, who would, in later years, play Frankenstein Monsters on various television shows).

During the 1980s, Ringo Starr would have yet two more involvements with Frankenstein's Monster. In a music video based on Starr's 1972 song "Back Off Boogaloo," a peace-loving, flower-toting Frankenstein Monster lumbers out of his tomb and meets a bearded and black-clad Ringo in the cemetery. The two become instant friends, embracing and dancing with each other, even enjoying a picnic together in a series of parodies of various romantic-movie scenes, before the picture and the music finally fade away.

In a music video based upon Ringo's song "Whack My Brain," Ringo goes through a haunted house where he plays a game of poker utilizing Tarot cards with images of the Frankenstein Monster, Dracula and a human skeleton. Starr encounters a man wearing a straight jacket and a huge dinosaur topiary before the video ends.

One last musical notation: Sometime in the 1960s, during the height of the Beatles' popularity as a singing group, a promotional novelty record was issued under the title "Frankenstein Meets the Beetles" (DCP 1126; again, note spelling). But this item, unlike the real Beatles themselves, seems to have slipped away into obscurity.

On both the motion-picture and TV screens the Beatles have often been associated with a number of fantastic characters, creatures and situations. Yet perhaps none of these were as fantastic as the group's own popularity, which endures to this day.

# IX

# A Score of Frankenstein Misconceptions

In 1974 Jim Harmon was hired by Magazine Management to the new magazine *Monsters of the Movies*. He almost immediately brought me on board this project as an associate editor. When Jim asked me to write another Frankenstein-related article for the second issue (August 1974) of *Monsters of the Movies*, I was not, at first, overly excited.

That issue was to be mostly devoted to the Frankenstein Monster and, being the Frankenstein buff that I was, I certainly wanted to be included. However, I had already written so much about the Monster and his history in various articles, not to mention some lengthy books, that I really didn't know where to begin. I was not particularly interested in writing yet another article on the history of the Universal Pictures Frankenstein movie series or how Mary Shelley originally got the idea for her novel *Frankenstein; or, the Modern Prometheus*.

Finally, after mulling over some ideas in my mind and rejecting all of them, I came up with the idea of doing an article based upon various misconceptions about the Frankenstein Monster and his world. Jim liked the idea and it appeared in that issue of *Monsters of the Movies* under the title "The Myths of Frankenstein." Purposely I would avoid some of the more obvious errors, such as the popular use of the name "Frankenstein" when referring to the nameless Monster.

Unfortunately, thanks to various problems originating at the New York offices of Marvel, Ron Haydock's name appeared in the byline, an error finally corrected herein.

Ironically, the original version of the piece actually perpetuated some myths of its own, misconceptions also corrected in this revised version.

\* \* \*

There seem to be more myths and misconceptions concerning Victor Frankenstein and the Monster he created than, perhaps, the number of parts that went into the latter's artificial construction. I suppose that is understandable when one considers the myriad novels, short stories, theatrical plays, motion pictures, radio and television programs, comic books and strips, not to mention merchandise, that have been based on the character and theme Mary Wollstonecraft Shelley first presented in 1818. Some of the more common misconceptions follow, and the truth regarding them will be subsequently told.

To begin:

1. The scene in Universal Pictures' original *Frankenstein* movie in which the Monster (Boris Karloff) drowns the child Maria (Marilyn Harris) in the lake was never shown in prints released theatrically in the United States.

For decades, every true Frankenstein-movie fan has most likely been familiar with the story of this classic scene's deletion from the final cut of the movie. Boris Karloff has often been quoted stating that he had requested that the film's director James Whale excise the scene because, in the actor's opinion, it made the Monster appear to be too brutal. Listening to an audiotape in my collection, made from the original soundtrack transcriptions for the premiere release of *Frankenstein*, I found the questionable scene to be missing, as in the standard version of the movie that had been playing on television since 1957 (when Screen Gems first released its "Shock" package of old Universal horror movies to TV). Curiously, that recording *did* preserve another generally removed scene, Henry Frankenstein, at the moment of the Monster's creation, exclaiming, "In the name of God, now I know what it feels like to *be* God!"

Over the years there had been rumors that "complete" versions of the film—dating as far back as 1931—exist, probably in British-release prints.

That legend seemed to be resolved when horror and science fiction author Robert Bloch and monster-movie authority Forrest J Ackerman attended a screening of *Frankenstein* in Southern California during the 1940s and, to their mutual shock and delight, actually *saw* little Maria thrown into the lake by the Monster. (A still from the movie, showing the *splash* Maria made as the Monster tossed her into the water, had often been printed in various publications.)

During the 1990s, the British material did surface and was reinstated into newly released videotapes of *Frankenstein*. By the time the film came out on the new DVD format, the missing line exclaimed by Henry Frankenstein, provided by the present writer and professionally dubbed from my own tape of the soundtrack, thanks to David J. Skal, was also back where it belonged.

2. Boris Karloff made good his vow, stated in 1939, that the movie *Son of Frankenstein* would be his swansong appearance as Frankenstein's Monster.

The British actor's vow to let the Monster rest in peace, at least regarding his own portrayal of the character, was noble enough. To Karloff, the Frankenstein Monster had nowhere else to go dramatically—nowhere except *down*. However, the actor did, in fact, break his own promise on at least three subsequent occasions.

In 1940 Karloff donned the familiar outfit of Frankenstein's Monster (with make-up by Jack Pierce, the creator of the original guise) for an all-celebrity baseball game (leading men versus comedians) played at Los Angeles' Gilmore Stadium. Karloff shared the field with such film stars as Buster Keaton (who, among other celebrities, "fainted" in his presence), Jane Russell and the Three Stooges. Part of the action, in which the Frankenstein Monster hit a home run and lumbered the bases, was recorded in a home movie by comedian Ken Murray and included in his film, sometimes aired on television, *Hollywood, My Home Town*.

Next, in 1958, when the revitalized original (though rebuilt) Monster's face is unwrapped at the climax of Allied Artists' low-budget movie *Frankenstein 1970*, the character's face is revealed to be that of Karloff. *Technically* this constitutes yet another appearance of Boris as the Frankenstein Monster, albeit a very brief one.

And finally, in 1962 Boris Karloff surprisingly allowed himself to be made-up (by Abe Haberman, using photographs from *Son of Frankenstein* for reference) in the uncomfortable Frankenstein Monster get-up for an appearance—with fellow horror actors Lon Chaney, Jr. as the Wolf Man

Boris Karloff, in make-up by his old friend Jack Pierce, appears again as the Frankenstein Monster for an all-star baseball game held at Hollywood's Gilmore Stadium in 1940. The man "fainting" in the Monster's presence is silent-movie comic genius Buster Keaton. (UPI photograph.)

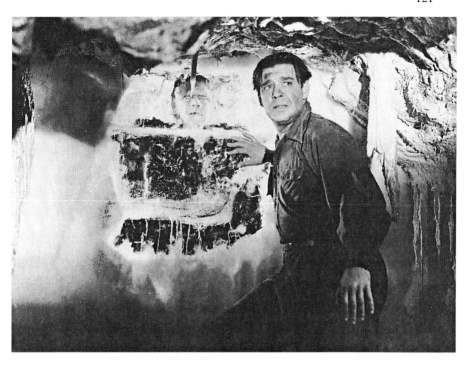

Bela Lugosi as the Monster can plainly be identified behind the studio artificial ice as the character is discovered by Lawrence Talbot (Lon Chaney, Jr.) in *Frankenstein Meets the Wolf Man* (1943). In the actual movie, however, the Monster in the ice was played by a stuntman.

and Peter Lorre as a sinister Edgar Allan Poe–type character—on television's *Route 66* series, especially surprising given the actor's advanced years and poor health.

3. That terrific initial close-up of the Monster, with the powerful neck muscles, in the ice in the movie *Frankenstein Meets the Wolf Man* (Universal, 1943) was the made-up face of Bela Lugosi, the actor billed as the Monster in that film.

Bela Lugosi was neither in good health nor of a relatively young age when he played the Monster for the first and only time in *Frankenstein Meets the Wolf Man*. Perhaps executives at Universal felt that Lugosi's face lacked the necessary physical strength to convey with enough impact that first impression of the Monster's visage to the movie's audience. Or possibly Lugosi simply refused to get inside that grotto of artificial ice for any sizable length of time, either because of his ego or because it was difficult to stand so rigidly before the camera to get the scene (although a still photograph does exist clearly showing Lugosi behind the ice wall that Wolf Man Lawrence Talbot, played by Lon Chaney, Jr., discovers in the ruins beneath Frankenstein's castle). Maybe Lugosi was not otherwise scheduled to be on the set that day.

Whatever the real reason, that fantastic first appearance was not Lugosi, but appears recognizable as Gil Perkins, one of two stuntmen who doubled for him in that movie (see below). The other stuntman, Eddie Parker, is recognizable as the Monster in other scenes in *Frankenstein Meets the Wolf Man*.

4. Depending upon what country you were in when you saw the British movie, *The Curse of Frankenstein* presented its Creature with one, two, three or even *four* eyes.

This fallacy has appeared in print repeatedly since the original release of this Hammer Film in 1957. In truth, there was only *one* make-up (by Phil Leakey and Roy Ashton) for the Creature, although it seems to be true that different edits of the film, exported to other countries, were more grisly in some scenes than the versions released in the United Kingdom and United States. Apparently this misconception originated with a widely published photograph of actor Christopher Lee as the Creature, a "glob" of make-up on one cheek, due in part to the lighting in the picture, suggesting a third eye. The fact that the alleged variety of make-ups for the Creature may also have been a product of Hammer's publicity department was verified to me by Christopher Lee, who should know, having had to endure being made-up as the character.

As Lee informed me in 1972, "There is no truth whatsoever to the rumor that I wore a different make-up in *The Curse of Frankenstein* for supposedly different versions of the film. At no time did the Creature have three eyes. Only two, one of which was diseased and ultimately became an eye-socket alone because of receiving a bullet in the face.... The make-up I wore took three and a half hours to get on. I could hardly move my head, or eat, or do anything. I had all sorts of things glued to my face—undertaker's wax, plastic, all sorts of horrid things. I felt embalmed. It was most unpleasant. But I just took refuge behind my face and tried to forget it all."

5. Mary Godwin (later Shelley), in selecting the name of her protagonist in *Frankenstein; or, the Modern Prometheus*, recalled the authentic German castle "The Frankenstein" and its legend about a Knight named George slaying a man-eating monster during the 13th century.

**"THE CURSE OF FRANKENSTEIN" WILL HAUNT YOU FOREVER!**

in WARNERCOLOR Presented by WARNER BROS.

Rumors persisted in monster-movie magazines during the late 1950s that the make-up, designed by Phil Leakey and Roy Ashton and worn by Christopher Lee as the Creature, in the 1957 Hammer production of *The Curse of Frankenstein* had a different number of orbs depending upon the country in which you viewed the film. However, there was no truth to those reports.

Although there has been much speculation that Mary was aware of and even visited this castle in Darmstadt, Germany, there is no concrete proof of this. To understand what may be Mary's real motivation for selecting the name of Frankenstein, one should first realize that Mary Godwin (as was her name when she wrote her story) virtually worshipped her lover and future husband, the poet Percy Bysshe Shelley. Mary incorporated much of Shelley's philosophies and beliefs into *Frankenstein*, and probably went to him, at least in part, for her lead character. The "Franken" may have been adapted from inventor Benjamin Franklin, whom Shelley regarded as a "modern Prometheus" for bringing down the lightning from the heavens and giving it to mankind. (Shelley had written *Prometheus Unbound*, and the full title of Mary's novel is *Frankenstein; or, the Modern Prometheus*.) The "stein" conceivably came from the character of Wolfstein in Shelley's *St. Irvine.* Wolfstein, like Shelley himself, sought the secret of immortality. As for the "Victor" of Victor Frankenstein, that (according to Christopher Small in his book *Mary Shelley's Frankenstein: Tracing the Myth*) was a pen name often used by Percy Shelley.

6. Eddie Parker was the only stuntman or actor to "double" as the Monster in the Universal Frankenstein movies.

In an article I wrote long ago ("Monster Man for All Occasions," in *Modern Monsters* number 3, August 1966), under the pen name "Don Grant," I erroneously attributed too many such appearances as the Frankenstein Monster to big utility stuntman Eddie (also known as Edwin and simply Ed) Parker. Humbly I now stand corrected, as subsequent research has demonstrated that many people appeared on camera in the Monster's guise other than Boris Karloff, Lon Chaney, Jr., Bela Lugosi, Glenn Strange … and Parker.

As early as the first *Frankenstein,* the Monster seems to have had his "doubles." One still photograph from that film, in which Henry Frankenstein (Colin Clive) and Professor Waldman (Edward Van Sloan) stand over the drugged Monster, reveals someone, lying almost face down on the floor, who is clearly not Boris Karloff. The identity of this stand-in remains unknown (although future cowboy star Robert Livingston can be viewed doubling Colin Clive—who was no longer available at the time—lying in bed in the last scene of the movie, shot as an afterthought). This unidentified man is most likely also on screen when the Monster's unconscious hulk is dragged away and back to Henry's laboratory.

Stuntman George DeNormand described to *Monsters of the Movies* (second issue, August 1974) editor Jim Harmon being made-up as the Monster by Jack Pierce and smashing up the laboratory for the film *Bride of Frankenstein* (1935). Close examination of this film reveals that the only scenes in which Boris Karloff may have had a stunt double were those where, seen from behind, he is bound to a pole by villagers and thrust down into a wagon, and then (as per DeNormand's description) the long shots in the laboratory where the Monster, rejected by his intended "Bride," goes on a rampage. (A stunt dummy, used also as a stand-in and seen in some of the film's production photographs, also seems to have been used during the actual explosion in the laboratory.) Universal studio records state only that George DeNormand doubled actor Reginald Barlow as Hans, the father of the little girl drowned in the previous movie, who falls into the water beneath the ruins of the burnt windmill and is then drowned by the burned and angry Monster. As close examination reveals that

In this scene from Universal Pictures' 1931 *Frankenstein*, Victor Moritz (John Boles), Henry Frankenstein (Colin Clive) and Professor Waldman (Edward Van Sloane) stand over the Monster, who has been rendered unconscious by a potent injection. The person wearing the Monster's make-up and clothes in this photograph, however, does *not* appear to be Karloff.

Karloff had no double in this sequence, perhaps DeNormand's personal recollections to Harmon as doing the Monster's role therein were distorted by time.

Stuntman Bud Wolfe (who also played Bela Lugosi's giant robot, a kind of mechanical Frankenstein Monster, in the 1939 Universal serial *The Phantom Creeps*) doubled for Boris Karloff in the next sequel, *Son of Frankenstein* (1939). The rather appropriately named Wolfe is easily spotted as Karloff's stunt double when actor Basil Rathbone, as Wolf von Frankenstein (in this scene also played by a stuntman), swings down and kicks the Monster into a bubbling pit of sulfur (see the author's book *The Frankenstein Legend: A Tribute to Mary Shelley and Boris Karloff* [Scarecrow Press, 1973] for a photograph of Wolfe filling in for Karloff).

And it was stuntman Dale Van Sickel doing the honors as the Monster in the zany comedy *Hellzapoppin'* (1942), wherein he tosses actress Martha Raye into an orchestra pit.

Stuntman Eddie (or Edwin) Parker, doubling for Bela Lugosi as the Frankenstein Monster, holds Ilona Massey (as Baroness Elsa Frankenstein) near the climax of the 1943 movie *Frankenstein Meets the Wolf Man*, the first entry in the
popular Universal series to pair up two of its famous monsters.

Eddie Parker's first doubling of the Monster seems to have been in
*The Ghost of Frankenstein* (1941), substituting in various scenes for star
Lon Chaney, Jr. Parker is probably the person seen in long shot (and seemingly wearing a slightly oversized rubber mask made in Chaney's image,
visible in some still photographs from the movie) on the roof when the
Monster retrieves little Cloestine's (Janet Ann Gallow) ball, kicked there
by a boy played by a very young William Smith. Parker also seems to be
the person (his shape, general build and also walking style matching his
scenes in the later *Frankenstein Meets the Wolf Man*) stumbling blindly
through the burning laboratory, clearly keeping his back toward camera,
sometimes blocking his face with his arms so as not to reveal that the
Monster in those scenes is not played by Chaney. If that is Parker doubling for Chaney, then it most likely is also him (again in the apparent
mask) falling beneath the burning timbers at the movie's climax, which
was later recycled for the ending of 1945's *House of Dracula*.

*Two* stuntmen doubled Bela Lugosi in *Frankenstein Meets the Wolf Man* (1943), Parker and a young Australian named Gil Perkins. As already stated, it is plainly Perkins whom Chaney as Larry Talbot extricates from the ice. Either Parker or Perkins could be the Monster kicking the barrels off the back of the wagon as Talbot escapes with the giant down the Vasaria street. During the scene in which the Monster and Talbot, strapped to platforms, are being energized by laboratory apparatus, both Parker and Chaney can be recognized; and, on just the final shot of this sequence, wherein pyrotechnics were involved, Perkins can be identified substituting for Chaney. Close examination of the battle between the Frankenstein Monster and the Wolf Man, however, reveals both Parker and Perkins at work. In most master or long shots, especially those in which the Monster and werewolf appear in full-body view together, and beginning with the one in which the Wolf Man attacks the Monster from behind and pulls him back and down the steps, Parker is identifiable as the Monster. In the other and generally closer shots (*e.g.*, the Monster grabbing Elsa Frankenstein [Ilona Massey] and struggling on the floor with the Wolf Man), it is Perkins, with Parker presumably doubling for Chaney. In the final long shot of the two characters, with the Monster appearing shorter than the Wolf Man and sporting regular shoes instead of the familiar raised black boots, it appears to be Perkins who steps back to be drenched by the incoming dam waters. Among the possible reasons (*e.g.*, availability) for utilizing two different stuntmen to double the same character in the same scene, one seems to this writer to be the most reasonable. Perkins was not a very tall man, while Parker reportedly stood six feet four inches tall *sans* the high-soled Monster boots. Maybe it was deemed more appropriate that the taller Parker appear in shots including the Wolf Man to give the Monster the required stature, while Perkins, seen in the tighter shots, was considered to have the better face for wearing the make-up.

Glenn Strange required no real stunt double for his three-picture stint as the Frankenstein Monster, except for the brief scene in *Abbott and Costello Meet Frankenstein* (1948) wherein Strange, having broken his foot in a previously filmed shot, let his friend Lon Chaney come in and substitute for him. Strange admitted to this writer that "doubles" and "stand-ins" sometimes appeared as the creatures in this movie wearing rubber masks. Photographs exist of Strange, in Monster make-up, posing with one of these masks. The actor's mention of such "doubles" and "stand-ins" also might explain why one shot near the end of *Abbott and Costello Meet Frankenstein*, wherein the Monster, on the burning pier, turns away from the camera and walks toward the flames—and getting precariously *close to* them (a potentially dangerous fire "gag"), does not look exactly like Glenn Strange, and more (to this writer at least), seems to resemble Eddie Parker.

7. The plot of the novel *Frankenstein; or, the Modern Prometheus* was set during the 19th century.

This is a very common misconception, probably fostered because the book was written during the 1800s. However, in the book, Captain Robert Walton's opening letter is dated "Dec. 11, 17—." It should be further noted that this date was written down *after* the bulk of the story—told in flashback—occurred.

8. The coloring of the Frankenstein Monster in the black and white Universal movies was always green.

Wrong!

This misbelief regarding the Monster's skin tone was the result of mask-maker Don Post manufacturing in 1948 a licensed rubber mask of the character for retail sale. Post told me that, rather than make his masks the true color of the movie character's complexion, he attempted to make them more commercial by choosing the eerie green. Thus, green was established as the Monster's "official" color as far as the public was concerned.

Actually the Frankenstein Monster had a gray, almost bluish-gray skin tone in all but three movies in the Universal suite of films. This color was selected by make-up artist Jack Pierce because it photographed as dead flesh on black and white motion picture film. Possibly tradition was also involved in the Monster's coloring, as the character was usually described as blue-skinned in many of the Frankenstein stage plays written and performed from the early 19th through early 20th centuries.

Some of the evidence:

I was told in person by a number of people who either wore or saw first-hand the Monster make-up that the coloring was gray. The list includes Glenn Strange, who wore the make-up more than once; actress Elsa Lanchester, who starred opposite Boris Karloff in *Bride of Frankenstein*; actor William Smith, who played the little boy who kicked the ball onto the roof in *The Ghost of Frankenstein* (and who played the Monster during the early 1980s on an episode of television's *Fantasy Island* series); electrical wizard Kenneth Strickfaden, who created the wild laboratory apparatus for the Universal Frankenstein movies; and others. Also, color photographs of Karloff in the Monster make-up on *Route 66* show him with a bluish-gray face (a color perhaps suggested to the make-up artist by the actor?). Furthermore, in Universal's television series *The Munsters* (1964–1966), shot in black and white and featuring Fred Gwynne's humorous Frankenstein character Herman Munster, Bud Westmore's make-up team again used the bluish-gray color for the character's basic skin tone.

One extra bit of circumstantial evidence:

In 1935 Metro-Goldwyn-Mayer made and released a musical short subject called *Two Hearts in Wax Time*, shot in Technicolor and including in its cast of famous villains—figures in a department-store window display that come alive—none other than the Universal Pictures version of Frankenstein's Monster. Indeed, this incarnation of the character was not like so many others which, over the years, were meant to *suggest* the character without infringing on Universal's copyright on their established

The Frankenstein Monster was portrayed by an unidentified actor wearing *gray* make-up—inspired directly by that created by Jack Pierce for Boris Karloff in *Bride of Frankenstein*—in the color MGM musical short *Two Hearts in Wax Time* (1935), accompanied by the pirate Captain Kidd, Dr. Fu Manchu and wife-murderer Bluebeard. Although the opportunity was certainly there, the makers of this film chose *not* to show the character with green skin.

make-up. No, the Monster in this short looked *exactly* like the character as he had appeared in the recently released *Bride of Frankenstein,* right down to the fire-singed hair and the dust on the black coat. Was this identical version of the make-up perhaps officially allowed, even sanctioned by Universal; and might the headpiece and costuming have actually been copied directly from the one made by Jack Pierce at that studio? With the make-up and clothing the same, was the Monster's skin tone also copied from Karloff's coloring in that role? The Monster, by the way, has *gray*—not green—skin in *Two Hearts in Wax Time.* Moreover, in one striking close-up the lighting makes the flesh take on a *bluish*-gray tone.

Universal deviated only twice from its standard gray coloration for the Frankenstein Monster. Color home-movie footage of Boris Karloff and Jack Pierce clowning around the make-up room during production of *Son of Frankenstein* reveals a green-faced Monster. However, *Son of*

There was but one entry in Universal Pictures' Frankenstein-movie series in which the Monster's (Boris Karloff) skin was *green,* the 1939 film *Son of Frankenstein,* which the studio originally intended to shoot in color. Note how the character's skin tone in *Son* differs significantly from that in the series' other entries. This previously unpublished photograph is from the private collection of the film's art director, Jack Otterson.

*Frankenstein* was the only film in the series intended to have been shot in color. (After a test reel was made and evaluated, the make-up not photographing as well as intended, the project went back to black and white. This test reel, according to rumors, surfaced within the last ten years, only to be subsequently lost or stolen.) And in *Abbott and Costello Meet Frankenstein* the Westmore team lightened the Monster's make-up to a more silvery gray (which they also seem to have done in the 1953 comedy *Abbott and Costello Meet Dr. Jekyll and Mr. Hyde*).

9. There was but one silent-movie version of *Frankenstein* before the Boris Karloff classic, made by Thomas Edison's film company in 1910.

There were actually *three* silent filmed versions of the Mary Shelley story. Edison's, with Charles Ogle as the bushy-haired Monster, was the first. But Ocean Film Corporation made a version titled *Life Without Soul* five years later, starring Percy Darrell Standing as the "Brute Man." And in 1920, Italy's Albertini Film–UCI made another, *Il mostro di Frankenstein*, with muscular Umberto Guarracino as "il mostro." That actor also starred in the 1926 Italian fantasy epic *Machiste all' Inferno* (*Machiste in Hell*).

Although the Edison version, long thought to have been lost forever, turned up again a couple of decades ago, the other two silent versions remain to be found.

10. Boris Karloff, Bela Lugosi and Lon Chaney, Jr. never appeared together in the same film.

That statement was at least partially true—but not entirely. For there are stock-footage clips of Karloff as the Monster from the 1931 *Frankenstein* used as flashback scenes in *The Ghost of Frankenstein*, which starred Chaney and Lugosi. In that sense, these three titans of movie terror did, at least, appear on the same screen within a single motion picture.

11. In the Mary Shelley novel *Frankenstein* the Monster began his new life as a physically beautiful creature.

At least that is what the producers of the television movie *Frankenstein: The True Story* (Universal, 1973) would have us believe. The following is Victor Frankenstein's own description of the Monster in the novel as the creature first awakens (the reader may decide whether or not the creature resembled "beautiful" actor Michael Sarrazin):

"Beautiful! Great God! His yellow skin scarcely covered the work of muscles and arteries beneath; his hair was of a lustrous black, and flowing;

his teeth of a pearly whiteness; but these luxuries only formed a more horrid contrast with his watery eyes, that seemed almost of the same color as
the dun-white sockets in which they were set, his shriveled complexion
and straight black lips."

Beautiful?

Let the reader be the judge.

12. Character actor Dwight Frye acted only in two Universal Frankenstein movies, the original *Frankenstein* (as Fritz the hunchbacked dwarf,
a character adapted from one of the same name in an early stage play)
and its sequel *Bride of Frankenstein* (in which some of his filmed scenes
were deleted for the final cut of the film).

No, Frye also had small roles—"villagers" with lines to say—in both
*The Ghost of Frankenstein* and *Frankenstein Meets the Wolf Man*. He was
also filmed in scenes shot for *Son of Frankenstein*, which inevitably found
their way onto the proverbial cutting-room floor.

13. No Universal Frankenstein movie footage was ever shot in color.

That statement, of course, excludes any of the theatrical and television movies based on *The Munsters* situation-comedy series and also the
above-mentioned *Frankenstein: The True Story*.

As already stated, the third movie in the series, *Son of Frankenstein*,
was intended to be made in Technicolor. At least some test footage was
shot in this process. Even when watched in its filmed black and white version, *Son of Frankenstein* has a different overall look than all the other
entries in the Universal series. The picture does not always exhibit the
stark blacks and whites of the other Universal movies, but rather rich gray
tones (even the Monster's skin tones)—suggestive of color movies printed
on black and white film stock. Furthermore, the sets are relatively simple,
some of them even Spartan, as are sets in such early 1930s color horror
films as *Dr. X* and *Mystery of the Wax Museum*. The fact that the Monster's skin was green, and a reddish-brown fur vest was added to his otherwise all-black wardrobe, in this film also supports an intent to shoot in
color. As mentioned above, reportedly a reel of color footage turned up
during the 1980s or 1990s, only to mysteriously vanish.

14. The confusion of referring to the nameless Monster as "Frankenstein" began with the 1931 Karloff movie.

Surprisingly perhaps, this confusion goes back much further—more
than a century earlier, in fact, to the time of the very first Frankenstein stage

play in 1823, just half a decade following publication of the first edition of Mary Shelley's novel. Actor Thomas Potter Cooke, who played the "Demon" in the play *Presumption; or the Fate of Frankenstein*, continued to enact the role for many years. In the first play he was listed in the program as simply a blank (    ). It was not long before Cooke began to refer to his stage role not as a blank or even as a "Demon," but as the far more prestigious "Frankenstein."

Interestingly, Peggy Webling's 1927 *Frankenstein* play, upon which the 1931 film was somewhat based, also referred to the Monster as "Frankenstein."

15. Actor Glenn Strange played the Monster in four Universal Frankenstein movies.

It was *three* Universal Pictures—*House of Frankenstein, House of Dracula* and *Abbott and Costello Meet Frankenstein* (although the actor did later play the Frankenstein Monster in various personal and television appearances).

Confusion over a possible *fourth* Universal movie appearance, however, arose from a certain publicity photograph issued by Universal–International to hype their 1953 movie *Abbott and Costello Meet Dr. Jekyll and Mr. Hyde*, which featured a Frankenstein Monster wax statue (played by an actor) that comes to life when exposed to a wild electrical wire. At least one official still of this Monster—shaking hands with Boris Karloff, who played Dr. Henry Jekyll in the Abbott and Costello film—came with a typed caption on its back identifying the Monster's portrayer as Strange. The face that showed through the Monster's make-up, however, was clearly not that of Glenn Strange. A phone call to Glenn confirmed that he was definitely *not* the tall guy with the Monster make-up in Abbott and Costello's Jekyll and Hyde movie.

The Monster also did not resemble Eddie Parker or Gil Perkins, who, coincidentally, *did* have other roles in this picture, Parker performing Karloff's Mr. Hyde scenes and Perkins being knocked off a bicycle-built-for-two by Costello's character transformed into another Hyde monster. Nor did the Monster's face suggest Dale Van Sickel, who wore the famous make-up in the 1941 Universal comedy *Hellzapoppin'*. (Although Van Sickel appeared in *Abbott and Costello Goes to Mars*, also made in 1953, he seems not to have lent his stunting talents to *Abbott and Costello Meet Dr. Jekyll and Mr. Hyde*.)

Who was the actor masquerading as the Monster this time?

The man's name, unfortunately, was not included in the cast lists

Original Universal Pictures Frankenstein Monster Boris Karloff greets an "old friend" in this publicity still from *Abbott and Costello Meet Dr. Jekyll and Mr. Hyde* (1953). Although official Universal publicity identifies the actor in this exaggerated Monster make-up as Glenn Strange, it is actually bit player Charles Hamilton wearing the familiar guise.

compiled at Universal. Recalling how Van Sickel also played himself in one scene in *Hellzapoppin'*, I studied *Abbott and Costello Meet Dr. Jekyll and Mr. Hyde* to see if there were any other characters in the film having the size and facial contours of the wax-museum Monster. Sure enough, an actor fitting that description appears as one of the London bobbies in the film's climactic chase sequence. The late film historian George Turner tentatively identified that performer as "a Hollywood bit player named Chuck Hamilton." George's memory and knowledge of motion pictures and movie actors was virtually without error. Had this Frankenstein mystery at last been solved?

Further research proved that an actor named Charles Hamilton had appeared in various "B" film productions during the 1940s, including serials such as *The Shadow* (1940) and *Captain Midnight* (1942), both made by Columbia Pictures and, for easy reference, conveniently available on videotape. Review of the first few chapters of *The Shadow* found Charles Hamilton prominently featured as a henchman named Roberts. The tall actor's facial features perfectly matched those of the man behind the Frankenstein Monster make-up in the Abbott and Costello Jekyll and Hyde movie. Hamilton's role as the character had, at last, been verified, this long-standing mystery solved.

Curiously, then, *Abbott and Costello Meet Dr. Jekyll and Mr. Hyde* features a total of *four* actors who, at one time or another, wore the Frankenstein Monster's make-up in a Universal motion picture—Eddie Parker, Gil Perkins, Charles Hamilton and, of course, Boris Karloff. There is also the possibility that Dale Van Sickel, who worked that same year with the comedians in *Abbott and Costello Go to Mars*, was among the many uncredited stunt performers appearing in *Abbott and Costello Meet Dr. Jekyll and Mr. Hyde*, which would then bring the total up to *five*. (As a side note, the Jekyll and Hyde film also features a gag with Harry Wilson, a bit player and sometime stand-in for actor Wallace Beery; in 1958 Wilson would play the creation in Astor's *Frankenstein's Daughter*.)

16. Actor Boris Karloff made his screen debut in the 1931 Universal Pictures' version of *Frankenstein*.

By the time he played the Monster in *Frankenstein*, Karloff—then age 44—had played in more than 70 movies and serials, more than half of them silents, starting with a bit part in the Douglas Fairbanks comedy adventure *His Majesty, the American* (United Artists, 1919). Karloff's entire motion picture output during his long career would number in excess of 150 titles.

17. In Mary Shelly's *Frankenstein* novel, Victor Frankenstein was either a doctor or a baron or both.

Victor Frankenstein was neither doctor nor baron. He was simply a young student who never quite acquires the noble title of "doctor." The closest he ever came to being a baron was his membership in a rather prominent Swiss family. "I am by birth a Genevese," he begins his narrative in Chapter I, "and my family is one of the most distinguished of that republic. My ancestors had been for many years councillors and syndics, and my father had filled several public situations with honour and reputation."

18. The Frankenstein Monster, according to Mary Shelley's account, was created and given life in an old German castle.

Although Victor Frankenstein did impart life to his giant creation in Ingolstadt, a real town in Germany, that accomplishment did not occur in any castle. Frankenstein's laboratory was located in the simple quarters of an apartment, surely a rather unimpressive setting when compared with the myriad castles and watchtowers that have emblazoned themselves on the memories of the moviegoing public over the years.

19. From the very first Universal Frankenstein motion picture in 1931, the lumbering giant was referred to *on screen* as "the Frankenstein Monster."

Unlikely though it may be, the first on-screen reference to the character by that well-established name was in the later film *House of Frankenstein*. Until that time the creature was simply referred to as "the Monster,"

In the original edited version of *Frankenstein Meets the Wolf Man* (1943), the Monster (Bela Lugosi), as in this scene, had conversations with "Wolf Man" Lawrence Talbot (Lon Chaney, Jr.). When Universal personnel laughed during a studio preview of the movie, reportedly because the Monster spoke in Lugosi's thick Hungarian accent, the character's dialogue was promptly snipped out before the film's theatrical release. The Monster did speak, however, in several other Universal films.

"Frankenstein's Monster," "the Fiend" or some other such designation. *House of Frankenstein* was also the first movie in the series to refer to the Wolf Man character on screen as "the Wolf Man."

Incidentally, both names were spoken for the first time in a single sentence by actor George Lynn, playing the gendarme Gerlach, who is telling Dr. Niemann (Boris Karloff) why he cannot exhibit his Chamber of Horrors in the town of Frankenstein, a place that has had enough horror since, some years back, "the dam broke and swept the Wolf Man and Frankenstein Monster to their destruction."

20. The only instances of the Frankenstein Monster speaking in the Universal Pictures series were in *Bride of Frankenstein* and at the climax (with Bela Lugosi's voice dubbed-in over Lon Chaney, Jr.'s physical presence) in *The Ghost of Frankenstein*.

Although Universal's version of the Frankenstein Monster is generally thought of as a grunting, snarling or even entirely silent brute, he has emoted dialogue in other movies made by that studio. In *Hellzapoppin'* the Monster spoke with courtesy to Martha Raye. He *would* have spoken, again with Lugosi's voice, in *Frankenstein Meets the Wolf Man* had his dialogue not been deleted before the film went into release (although some scenes still show his mouth moving, allowing for big-screen lip reading by the audience). And, of course, the Monster did have a few lines acknowledging Count Dracula as his "Master" in *Abbott and Costello Meet Frankenstein*.

There are undoubtedly other myths and misnomers concerning the Frankenstein Monster and his story, but those will have to wait their turn to be—like the watchtower laboratory at the end of *Bride of Frankenstein* and the dam in *Frankenstein Meets the Wolf Man*—exploded.

# X

# FRANKENSTEIN ON
# THE HOME-MOVIE SCREEN

From 1953 through 1969 my main hobby was making amateur horror, science fiction and fantasy movies. Although these films would span various genres (*e.g.*, dinosaurs and Godzilla-type creatures, and super-heroes like Spy Smasher, Spider-Man and Captain Marvel), most of them fell into the categories of "classic movie monsters (Frankenstein's Monster, Dracula and the Wolf Man) and "teenage monsters" (the Teenage Frankenstein and Teenage Werewolf). I worked just about every job possible on these mini-epics—producing, directing, financing, acting, creating the stories (although none had what could be realistically termed a "script"), operating the camera (in scenes not featuring me, of course), doing the make-ups and special effects, making the props, building the sets (both full scale and miniature), "doubling" other actors, editing, doing the credits titles, and taking care of whatever other tasks might yet remain.

As I was one of the relatively few monster-movie fans doing this sort of thing, especially during the Fifties, and because I had friends (especially Larry Ivie, Larry M. Byrd and the late Ron Haydock) who were in the position to publicize these films in the monster-movie magazines (*e.g.*, *Famous Monsters of Filmland*, *Castle of Frankenstein* and *Fantastic Monsters of the Films*), I became rather well known during those years as an amateur filmmaker.

Because of the notoriety I was getting in the professional monster magazines, sometimes publishers of non-professional, privately published magazines called fanzines asked me to write first-hand accounts about these little movies. One of these articles, titled "Characters I Have Shown," appeared in the premiere issue of Phil Goodman's *Exciting Wonder Stories* (not dated, although the publication came out in 1963). About my films featuring such characters as Frankenstein's Monster, the article was amateurishly written and suffered even more from poor editing. A later article, "Terror of the Teenage Werewolf," appeared in the April 1963 edition of *The Transylvanian Newsletter*, published and edited by Harvey Ovshinsky. Although the editing was much better in this publication, my original writing was just barely an improvement over its predecessor. Neither of these original articles gave more than cursory information about the films or the making of them, but they did possess the germs for the expanded piece that follows.

The following article is, compared to all the others in this collection, the one that required the most rewriting and expanding. Using the two fanzine articles as barely more than a blueprint, I wrote most of what follows, as they say, from "whole cloth." It is, therefore, virtually an original piece of writing in itself that owes very little to its fan publication roots.

To anyone wishing to learn more about any of my amateur movies featuring the monster characters discussed herein, I direct you to the following websites:

www.donaldfglut.com
www.geocities.com/williewerewolf/sitemap.html
www.angelfire.com/tv2/supermanontv/sitemap.html

(To see what making these films, at least in part, inevitably led to, please visit: www.frontlinefilms.com.)

✳　✳　✳

Horror, science fiction and fantasy have traditionally been favorite genres for makers of amateur motion pictures. These genres appeal to young filmmakers because of the challenges and opportunities they afford in attempting to create Hollywood-style special effects and bizarre make-ups. As a teenaged amateur moviemaker living in Chicago, I too focused upon those kinds of films. In fact, almost all of the many amateur movies I had made over the years have featured strange characters with origins rooted in professional Hollywood movies of those genres.

Three infamous creatures from Hollywood films have appeared in countless amateur movies, including a number of my own. This trio of fearful favorites is, of course, Frankenstein's Monster, the vampire Count Dracula and the Wolf Man (or variations thereof). When I started making these 16mm films I was not really that interested in becoming a producer, director or actor. The truth is that I mostly wanted to *show*—as opposed to *make*—movies featuring those venerated characters on my own home-movie screen, anytime that I wanted. At that time the old Universal Frankenstein, Dracula and Wolf Man films were still playing in theaters (as Realart reissues) or just beginning to enjoy their first run on television (thanks to Screen Gems' release of their "Shock" packages of those old horror pictures to the small screen), and none of those films, either in full-length or condensed versions, were yet legally available to private collectors for home viewing.

I made my first amateur Frankenstein movie in 1957 at the age of about 13 years old. Entitled *Frankenstein Meets Dracula*, this was a very short color movie, shot in my family's basement, with my friend Victor Fabian playing Count Dracula and me lumbering about as the Frankenstein Monster. As I had not yet learned how to do an appropriate make-up for the character, I wore a Don Post full-head rubber mask (the one that sold for $3.50 in the middle to late 1950s), which proved to be stiflingly hot under the light-bar illumination required to shoot indoors. Dracula's costume consisted mainly of a stringy piece of black cloth masquerading as a cape. The film stock (and then processing) required was "expensive" (under four dollars) for a teenaged filmmaker of the Fifties; thus, several of the actors also had to chip in for the hundred-foot (about three and a half minutes) roll.

The plot of *Frankenstein Meets Dracula* was simplicity defined: Dracula revives Frankenstein's Monster (via some home-made laboratory equipment, like flashing lights and spinning wheels) in Frankenstein's castle and gains hypnotic control over the creature. After the Monster kills someone, another person enters the castle and drives a stake through Dracula's heart. The Monster attacks Dracula's killer, who then bludgeons the Monster (to death?) with a hammer.

That initial movie was quickly, the same year, followed by my first sequel in this "series," *Return of the Wolfman*, also made in color. Once again Fabian played Count Dracula and I donned the sweat-producing mask to play the Frankenstein Monster. Wayne Moretti, as the Wolf Man, became the subject of my first attempted horror-movie make-up and on-screen transformation, the latter extremely crude ones at that. Equally crude were my first attempts at showing Dracula's transformation into a vampire bat, accomplished through various simple cuts.

Lawrence Talbot (the Wolf Man) opens the film by robbing Castle Frankenstein, at the same time removing the stake from Dracula's skeleton and inadvertently reviving the vampire. Dracula is promptly up to his evil business, biting Talbot and then reviving the Frankenstein Monster. When Talbot seeks Dracula's help to cure his werewolf curse, he transforms into the hairy lycanthrope, only to fight the Monster. Toward the end of this very simple plot, Talbot becomes human again, shoots the Monster (to death?) and stakes Dracula.

When it came time to do the next sequel, *The Revenge of Dracula* (1958), a number of things had changed. In an attempt to make the movie look more like the Universal movies currently playing on television's *Shock Theater*, I decided to film it in black and white. Furthermore, *Horror of Dracula*, the benchmark vampire movie from England's Hammer Films, made in color and starring Christopher Lee as a more dynamic Count Dracula, had recently opened. Thus, although *The Revenge of Dracula* was to be shot without color, I was most anxious to play the Count this time—and more like Lee than like Bela Lugosi or John Carradine of the Universal movies. Friend Charles Martinka this time wore the hot Don Post Frankenstein Monster mask.

Again the plot was a very simple one. Dracula returns to life and, once more, revives the Frankenstein Monster. When Dracula's thirst for blood forces him to make an attack near dawn, two people trail him back to the castle. The Frankenstein Monster kills them both, then inadvertently ignites a fuse that sets fire to the castle (actually a cardboard miniature). Dracula, meanwhile, is reduced to bones by the morning sunlight.

As it turned out, *The Revenge of Dracula* required only half the amount of film (a one-hundred-foot roll) purchased to make it. With another hundred feet left to play with, I decided to forge immediately ahead—that same day, if my memory is accurate—with another movie. I decided to shoot a "prequel" to my Frankenstein saga showing how the Monster came to be. Shot as *the Horror of Frankenstein*, I would eventually call this film *The Frankenstein Story*, its opening title literally clipped from an article appearing in the first issue of *Famous Monsters of Filmland* magazine.

The story would open with Dr. Frankenstein, helped by his hump-backed assistant, Ygor, creating the Monster. After the Monster comes to life in the scientist's castle, Ygor befriends the creature, turns him against his maker and then sets out into the world. After Ygor forces the Monster to kill a teenager who made fun of his hunchbacked appearance (a scene "inspired" by one in the Universal film *The Ghost of Frankenstein*; I would frequently work scenes into my movies that I had recently seen on *Shock Theater*), the terrible duo return to the castle, followed by the boy's vengeful brother who sets fire to the building.

For this movie I again donned the rubber Don Post mask, with my friends Charles Martinka as Dr. Frankenstein and Wayne Moretti as the heavily bearded Ygor. A softball stuck under Moretti's T-shirt gave him an overly exaggerated hunchback look. Unfortunately, in making this film I encountered a problem quite the opposite of my experience with its predecessor. Somehow the film jammed in the camera for about the first half of the shoot, the result being that only the second half went through the camera, leaving *The Frankenstein Story* without the most important part of its story.

Weeks went by before I raised the budget for another roll of black and white film (cheaper by about half the cost of a color roll of equal length). By that time I was able to enhance the look of the Frankenstein laboratory, including Fourth of July sparklers among the life-giving gizmos. Unfortunately, Moretti had gone off on a vacation, forcing me to substitute another actor, a cousin visiting from Pennsylvania (Louis Csurics), in the role of Dr. Frankenstein's assistant. For some reason I stuffed newspapers under Ygor's shirt (possibly Moretti had owned the softball), which produced a noticeably less elevated "hump." When I spliced in the old footage with the new, Ygor's back seemed, at the end of the laboratory scene, to shoot up between shots. Ever resourceful (and economical; I did not want to shoot half the movie over *again*), I spliced a title card in between the two Ygors, never intending or realizing its humorous effect: "Radiation causes Ygor's back to grow." This was, after all, shot during the late 1950s when such radiation-caused growth spurts were not uncommon in fantastic films.

*Return of the Monster Maker* (1958), another black and white opus, was influenced by the movies *I Was a Teenage Frankenstein* (1957) and *Frankenstein 1970* (1958), both of which I had recently seen in movie theaters. In this entry, Dr. Frankenstein (Martinka) returns from the "dead" and promptly decides to create a "new monster." Aided by Ygor (Wayne Moretti) and the Frankenstein Monster (this time Bert Ott, again in that ubiquitous Post mask), the doctor sets out to bring back the component parts. The new creature (played by me, wearing a popular "horror mask"— a decayed corpse bearing some superficial resemblances to the Teenage Frankenstein Monster, which is why I originally intended to title this movie *The Teenage Frankenstein*) comes to life amid the usual laboratory display, then goes wild, finally battling the original Monster as Dr. Frankenstein switches on the gas that apparently kills them all.

*Return of the Monster Maker* actually seems to have been censored by someone at the laboratory (the processing lab, not Dr. Frankenstein's) before the film was returned to me. The movie opened with a scene suggested by a similar one in the movie *Son of Frankenstein* (seen, for the first time by me on April 12, 1958, on *Shock Theater*). In that movie Wolf von Frankenstein, played by Basil Rathbone, encounters his father Henry Frankenstein's coffin, upon which someone has crudely written the words "maker of monsters." Offended by this desecration, Wolf crosses out the word "monsters" and replaces it with "men." Apparently my use of the term "maker of men" equally offended someone at the lab, for when the film returned to my hands, the shot featuring those words was missing, a physical splice in its place.

Intrigued by the idea of a Teenage Frankenstein, I next reworked the basic idea of *Return of the Monster Maker* (at the same time economically recycling the "horror mask") for a movie that was both a sequel and a more elaborate "remake," which I simply titled *The Teenage Frankenstein* (1959, a year, as shall be shown, that would be my most prolific in terms of making movies featuring this growing cast of horror characters). This black and white movie proved to be my most ambitious yet, including more location photography, improved make-ups and special effects, and my first screen attempt to create an actual make-up for my returning role as the Frankenstein Monster. The recently released Hammer sequel *The Revenge of Frankenstein* also provided some inspiration in the more graphic display of floating eyeballs (ping pong balls) and an exposed brain (clay sculpture) that now enhanced the Frankenstein lab.

Shot during the winter, the film had a more involved and developed plot than any of its predecessors in my series. Larry Talbot (Victor Fabian) saves Dr. Frankenstein (Martinka again) from the gallows on the condition that the scientist cures him of his werewolf affliction. Talbot relates to Frankenstein his past experience with Dracula (Gene Gronemeyer). Meanwhile, the Frankenstein Monster has an encounter with a blind hermit (inspired by the recently *Shock Theater*–screened *Bride of Frankenstein*), whom, fearing fire, he kills when the sightless man strikes a match to light his pipe. Returning to Castle Frankenstein, the Monster, having known brief friendship, forces Dr. Frankenstein to build him a friend. Talbot, if he is to be cured, must help the doctor get the body parts. In the end Dr. Frankenstein brings his teenaged creation (played by Bert Ott) to life as Talbot changes into the Wolf Man. The original Monster and the werewolf fight again as the Teenage Frankenstein, upon seeing his hideous reflection, strangles Dr. Frankenstein and then blows up the castle.

Although the next sequel, *Slave of the Vampire* (1959), did not feature the Frankenstein Monster, it did mostly take place in the ruins of Frankenstein's castle. In terms of make-up and costuming especially, this entry was certainly an improvement over any of its predecessors in the series. The story was based on *Return of the Vampire*, which had its Chicago television debut on (naturally) *Shock Theater*, August 15, 1959. Victor Fabian played Count Dracula and I, for my first time, was the Wolf Man, wearing make-up—consisting of brown greasepaint, black wig, black and brown crepe hair, spirit gum and nose putty—that required as much time and effort to remove as it did to apply. In this movie the Wolf Man is Dracula's slave, attacking and bringing back victims for his master. When the vampire denies the werewolf his freedom, the man-beast attacks him, most of the film consisting of a fight between the two monsters, climaxing with the Wolf Man staking his former master.

A somewhat "profound" realization came to me in 1959, a year when "teenaged monster movies" were all the rage in theaters. To date my amateur movies had featured teenaged "actors" trying their hardest to portray adult—even very old—characters. Now, given the current popularity of films like *I Was a Teenage Werewolf* and *I Was a Teenage Frankenstein*, we had the opportunity to, at last, play characters of the same age as ourselves. Once I figured that out, a new "series" of films was born in my imagination.

The first of these was the winter-filmed *The Teenage Werewolf* (1959), inspired by actor Michael Landon's *I Was a Teenage Werewolf*, which started the youth-oriented monster craze in 1957. One week after completing a "prehistoric monster" movie, *Dinosaur Destroyer*, I went to work on *The Teenage Werewolf*, a black and white opus that would start a chain reaction of sequels.

In this "origin tale," deformed, sinister and quite mad Dr. Macabre (Ray Strezewski) transforms teenaged Tony Rivers, via hypnosis, into a werewolf, which attacks him and then goes out on a killing spree. The monstrous wolf boy apparently meets his death when, pelted by snowballs, he falls off a garage roof. I played the Teenage Werewolf in make-up inspired both by Henry Hull's in the *Shock Theater*–telecast *WereWolf of London* (re-run January 31, 1959) and that of Sandra Harrison as the vampire in the recent (1957) theatrically-screened *Blood of Dracula* (a kind of distaff *I Was a Teenage Werewolf*). Considering the aggravation I experienced removing the make-up, using my fingernails to scrape off the dried spirit gum to which the hair was affixed, I decided not to make any more such films. Little did I know, at that time, that the screen life of my Teenage Werewolf was just beginning—and that the make-ups would inevitably become more elaborate, time-consuming and uncomfortable.

*The Teenage Werewolf* was quickly followed in 1959 by a number of "teenage monster" films. *The Teenage Apeman*, made soon afterwards and in color, tenuously "crossed over" into my old Frankenstein series. In this movie Dr. Macabre (Wayne Moretti), using Dr. Frankenstein's laboratory equipment, transfers the brain of a teenager (played by Bert Ott) into the head of a gorilla. After making the ape's face more human in appearance, the mad doctor brings his creation to life utilizing the familiar Frankenstein machines. I played the Teenage Apeman, inspired by a similar (albeit adult) character portrayed by J. Carrol Naish in the movie *Dr. Renault's Secret*, shown on March 14, 1959, on *Shock Theater*. *The Day I Vanished*, also shot in color, was an adolescent version of *The Invisible Man,* with me playing a teenaged Griffin, who goes invisible and insane. Some of the invisibility effects were achieved utilizing a device I had purchased that allowed two simultaneously shot images to be combined in the camera.

My teenage monster series really kicked into high gear that year with the color *I Was a Teenage Vampire* shot in the summer. Dracula's teenaged son leaves his Transylvanian castle and sails to the United States in search of new blood. His victims are members of a teenage gang called the Vandals. When they discover what he is, he barely escapes them by turning into a *Son of Dracula*-inspired mist (the scene shot through a fish tank filled with water, into which milk was poured). While the Vandals have a "rumble" with a rival gang, the Teenage Vampire tries reaching his grave via a stolen motorcycle, only to be destroyed by the rising sun.

However, it was Tony the Teenage Werewolf that became the more recurring star of this series. He came back to my home-movie screen two more times in 1959, both in color, and finally sporting a more authentic home-made mask (to obviate some of the discomforts associated with doing the make-ups) with full facial hair, patterned after Michael Landon's. In *Return of the Teenage Werewolf* we learn that Tony (me again) had survived his fall and is now wandering in a dazed state through an alley. After killing again and then attacking a teenaged girl, the werewolf is run down by an onrushing car driven by two irate teenagers.

Next followed *The Teenage Frankenstein Meets the Teenage Were-wolf*—inspired by the recently released *How to Make a Monster*—with me again wearing the old "horror mask," and Paul Klug, in the mask I had designed for the previous entry in the series, as the young lycanthrope. Tony returns from the grave, kills again and then joins the Vandals gang, which has been amusing itself in the woods by beating up on a local disfigured hunchbacked character. The hunchback, Gregore Frankenstein (Wendel Tillman), grandson of Dr. Frankenstein, has brought to America the Teenage Frankenstein Monster. Energizing the creature, Gregore uses him to exact revenge on the gang. Tony, not surprisingly, transforms again and, as the Teenage Werewolf, savagely kills Gregore. Witnessing the brutal death of his master, the Teenage Frankenstein attacks his shaggy adversary. As the two adolescent monsters battle with one another, they are finally trapped when a dropped cigarette starts a forest fire.

But that was not to be the end of either teenage monster. The wolf-boy (again played by me) returned once again, this time back in black and white and with a full make-up rather than a mask, in *Revenge of the Teenage Werewolf* (1960). Tony turns up at the beginning of the movie, transforms into his hirsute alter ego, then tallies up his greatest-ever quota of human victims. Originally this picture included a lengthy drag race that had absolutely nothing to do with its plot. It was subsequently deleted, allowing the Teenage Werewolf to continue his mayhem until being shot to death by another teenager in a Chicago alley.

Virtually everyone from my "classic horror monsters" and "teenage monsters" series, plus a couple of other fiends, appeared in my color "epic" of 1961, *Monster Rumble*. I played a total of seven roles in this multi-monster bash—the Teenage Dracula, Teenage Frankenstein Monster, *original* Frankenstein Monster, the Wolf Man (all in full and vastly improved make-ups), a hooded executioner and a couple of decomposing corpses. Added to this monstrous mix were the Teenage Werewolf (Tom Werner), Reese Renfield (Wayne Moretti) and a real, almost eight-foot-tall robot named Fido (played by itself).

Much longer than any of the other entries, *Monster Rumble* centers on the son of Dracula's return from his previous death. The vampire makes a slave of Reese Renfield and an ally of surviving Teenage Werewolf Tony Rivers. Tony believes that the Teenage Vampire will cure him of his werewolf problem, but Dracula's son has another agenda. Reading first of the creation of the original Frankenstein Monster (in a long flashback sequence

The author in his own make-up as the Frankenstein Monster for the "flash-back" sequence of *Monster Rumble* (1961), a color amateur movie bringing together numerous "adult" and "teenage" horrors.

including Charles Martinka, by now typecast as my Dr. Frankenstein, and Rich Hagopian as Ygor), and then of the Teenage Frankenstein's "death" in the forest fire, the vampire decides to make the latter his obedient slave. Finding and re-energizing the teenage monster's body, the vampire takes it to his castle, hidden in a swamp, and subjects it to the power of Dr. Frankenstein's machines (this time also including a real Jacob's ladder and other new electrical devices). While the Teenage Frankenstein gets stronger, the now-insane Renfield turns on his master, contaminating his coffin as the sun rises and driving a stake through his heart. About the same time, the Teenage Frankenstein breaks loose, and a fleeing Renfield finds himself hopelessly trapped between that horror and the transformed

The author as the Teenage Frankenstein, doing battle with the (off-screen) Teenage Werewolf, in the 1961 amateur production *Monster Rumble.*

Teenage Werewolf. The two teenaged horrors battle to the death, blowing up the castle (a miniature made from plastic "American Bricks," then exploded utilizing firecrackers, with the camera shooting the blast—one take only—in slow motion) in the process. A cameo appearance by the hairy gray hand of the Teenage Apeman brings an end to this teen-monster rally.

A neglected teenage fiend resurfaced in my 1962 film *The Invisible Teenager,* a sequel to *The Day I Vanished.* I played Griffin again, this time escaping from a mental institution (I sneaked these scenes "on location" at a real place) to have his revenge on an old foe. One of the highlights of this movie was a game of pool in which the invisible Griffin wins (by cheating naturally). All of Universal's old Invisible Man movies had at least one scene wherein the unseen one, swathed in bandages, unravels the gauze to reveal—nothing. I accomplished this with some success in much the same way. Wearing black beneath my wrappings and standing in front of a black curtain, I shot the scene, then wound the camera back and shot the background for the scene. The effect worked fairly well for an amateur attempt.

The Teenage Vampire would return from his destruction only once more, this time without the company of any other monsters, adult or adolescent, in the much shorter black and white film *Dragstrip Dracula* (1962). The character (again with me in the role) is revived, the stake removed from his heart, just long enough to kill a few more victims and then be trapped again by the rising sun. The only really original aspect of this movie was an improved "bat to man" transformation, which I shot through a pane of glass. I animated the bat's flying, then hovering in the center of the frame, by affixing a series of black paper cut-outs to the glass sheet, photographing each increment of movement separately as one would a series of cartoon drawings or a stop-motion model. The actual transformation was achieved by painting a growing mass of black on the glass descending from the bat image, again shooting the scene a frame at a time. Finally, I removed the glass and, black cloak raised, I took my place in the scene, lining myself up to the position where the images had been on the glass. The transformation complete (all accomplished "in camera"), the son of Dracula then walked away.

I was already 19 years old and in my freshman year at college when *Dragstrip Dracula* was filmed. In less than a year I would technically no longer be a teenager, and more "mature" activities (such as fraternity parties) would soon replace my adolescent fascination with teenage gangs and rock 'n' roll–based monsters. It was time to move on to other subjects for my amateur movies, like heroes out of the comic books and the old movie serials.

My versions of the teenage horrors never again returned. Yet two of their adult counterparts did—just once—in a five-chapter serial, shot mostly in Southern California in color, entitled *The Adventures of the Spirit* (1963). Returning in this production were the Wolf Man (played in one of the then brand-new Don Post "custom masks" by both Bob Burns and myself), Dr. Frankenstein (played by CBS-television resident make-up artist Billy Knaggs) and the Frankenstein Monster (portrayed by none other than Glenn Strange, who had played the character in the Universal motion pictures *House of Frankenstein*, *House of Dracula* and *Abbott and*

The author as the blue-masked Spirit (left), Bob Burns as the mighty Superman and Glenn Strange (wearing a Don Post Frankenstein Monster mask, the original late 1940s issue) as Frankenstein's Monster, together in Strange's Glendale, California backyard one sunny day in June 1963 filming "Frankenstein's Fury," episode four of the five-chapter amateur movie serial *The Adventures of the Spirit*. (Photograph by Kathy Burns.)

*Costello Meet Frankenstein*). Other Hollywood notables appearing in the serial included science fiction and nostalgia author Jim Harmon and Lionel W. Comport, the latter a renter of animal performers to motion picture and television production companies.

　　*The Adventures of the Spirit* was mostly made during a summer vacation in Hollywood, California, with the remaining scenes shot later that season in Chicago. Its inspiration was my good friend (and honorary "big brother") Bob Burns, both a professional actor and a collector of authentic props and masks from horror, science-fiction and fantasy movies. Bob graciously agreed to let me use some of them in an amateur movie, at the same time performing before the cameras in one or more roles. *The Adventures of the Spirit* gave us both an excuse to put some of Bob's unique and treasured collectors items before the cameras once again. They included the "silver" wolf's head from the cane used to dispatch Larry Talbot at the climax of *The Wolf Man*, the actual costume worn in Republic's *Captain America* movie serial, and various props (*e.g.*, an alien head from *Invasion of the Saucer Men*, an extraterrestrial bat-like creature and communicator from *Not of This Earth*, a rubber mask worn in long shots by the bandaged horror of *The Mummy's Tomb*, and an "Id Monster" animation drawing from *Forbidden Planet*, etc.). And there were considerably more.

The *Spirit* plot was typical of the old cliffhanger adventures: A black-hooded and cloaked master villain known only as the Phantom Avenger plots to conquer the world using a gang of monsters (including the Frankenstein Monster, the "Mad Mummy," the Wolf Man and even a giant robot). The Spirit, a masked crime-fighter, opposes the Phantom Avenger at every turn, sometimes aided by such heroic friends as the Green Hornet, The Shadow, Captain America, Superman and Rocket Man. Finally defeating his arch foe mask to mask, the Spirit removes the ebony hood, revealing him to be the famous Phantom of the Opera.

Following *The Adventures of the Spirit*, there were some plans during the next few years to make a couple additional movies featuring the Frankenstein Monster. While still living in Chicago in 1963 or 1964, I had begun to think of shooting *Frankenstein vs. the Wolf Man*, taking advantage of the Don Post "custom" Frankenstein Monster and Wolf Man masks that were available at the time. I even did some drawings, suggesting a poster for this planned project. In 1966 or 1967, a few years after permanently moving to California in 1964 to attend the University of Southern California's cinema school, I wrote for an assignment a script for an intended short film, titled *To Be Frank*, in which the Frankenstein Monster (again intended to be someone wearing a Post "custom" mask) stalks out of the university's medical building and, entirely unnoticed by everyone on campus that he encounters, sits down and cries, realizing that the world and its real-life horrors have passed him by. A little girl (like the one he drowned in the 1931 *Frankenstein* movie), feeling sorry for him, comforts the Monster. Alas, neither of these projects was to be realized (although the title of the USC project was later recycled for a short story published in *Famous Monsters of Filmland*).

However, the other films were all completed during those more innocent days when amateur Frankenstein movies could be shot in a single afternoon in a basement or the backyard, with a group of enthusiastic friends playing the parts, utilizing home-made costumes and laboratory apparatus—and, most important of all, a real love for the old movies that inspired them.

# XI

# "THIS IS YOUR LIFE, FRANKENSTEIN'S MONSTER"

Having been one of those monster-movie fans who "grew up" reading Forrest J Ackerman's *Famous Monsters of Filmland* magazine, it was always a thrill having an article published in its pages. The following article, originally titled "This Was His Life," was the first one written by me to appear in "*FM*," in issue number 56 (July 1969), which was a special Boris Karloff tribute issue following the actor's recent death that same year. The article, about Karloff being the honored subject of the very popular *This Is Your Life* television program, was also slated to be included in Ackerman's paperback book *The Frankenscience Monster* (Ace Publishing Corporation, 1969), but was pulled at the last moment due to space constraints.

For various personal reasons, I wrote the article under a pseudonym, Victor Morrison, which was adapted from the names of two actors who had played the mysterious crime-fighting hero known as The Shadow—Victor Jory, in the 1940 Columbia movie serial of the same title, and Brett Morrison, who played the character on the popular radio series.

The article was written, in those days before home video recorders and cable TV, entirely from memory. I had seen the show telecast live back in 1957 and it made some lasting impressions, one of which was Karloff's upcoming birthday, November 23. From that moment on I made it a practice to send the actor a birthday card (I don't know if he ever actually received them, as the autographed photographs I would subsequently receive turned out to have been signed by someone else), continuing this tradition until he died.

In more recent years, edited-down reruns of *This Is Your Life* have been shown on the American Movie Classics cable–TV channel. These reruns included the Boris Karloff show, which has turned up a number of times, sometimes to coincide with Halloween. Watching the actual show again after the passage of decades was testimony to the impact seeing it for the first time so long ago had upon me. Most of what I had originally written back in 1969 did, in fact, prove to be quite accurate.

✳   ✳   ✳

During the 1950s, one of the great honors bestowed upon a famous personality on television was to hear his or her name spoken, then, looking up (usually with a curious expression) to hear the familiar voice of Ralph Edwards announce....

"This is your life!"

This honor—to have one's life revealed on the very popular NBC TV series *This Is Your Life* to an entire nation of viewers—was reserved for the giants of public life, the motion picture stars, the sports heroes, the great humanitarians.

That the greatest terror star of them all should receive such tribute on network television just days before his birthday that November night should not be surprising. It was, however, a tremendous surprise to the soft-voiced Englishman when Ralph Edwards, the show's host and also producer, prompted Karloff to look up from some paperwork he was doing, to hear....

"This is your life ... Boris Karloff."

To those watching *This Is Your Life* at home, it may have seemed strange to see such a broad, warm and even grateful smile appear on the face that three times in the past had been buried behind the greasepaint, high forehead and metal clamps of the Frankenstein Monster. Now, every trace of things terrible had vanished. This was Boris Karloff the man, Karloff the feeling human being, receiving his deserved thanks for his contributions to the establishment of a veritable genre of motion pictures.

After being ushered away to the NBC studios, Karloff's familiar image filled the television screen in the form of a number of stills from the movie *Frankenstein* and *Son of Frankenstein*, two of the films (especially the former) that owed him so much, and to which he owed much also.

Ralph Edwards proceeded with his biography of Karloff, discussing his pre-movie career with a theatrical troupe in Canada, and then relating biographical information that, in later years, would become preserved in the memories of the actor's fans, recounting the terror master's portrayals of such fantastic characters as Frankenstein's Monster and the Mummy.

Two specific incidents on the program were especially significant and interesting to fans of Karloff's Frankenstein motion pictures.

First, Karloff was given a set of doorknobs from one of his old dressing rooms. Again viewers saw that warm Karloff smile. But the actor did not let the matter end right there. Instead, his quick mind clicking away in search of a possible laugh, the actor placed the doorknobs to his neck, simulating the tiny electrodes that decades earlier had protruded from that of the Frankenstein Monster.

Doorknobs held to the neck, however, were still not the authentic article. The introduction of one of the show's guests from Karloff's past would prove to be even more memorable. This guest was the very man who, in a sense, helped to create the Frankenstein Monster as much as had Dr. Frankenstein himself ... and also the living corpse Im-Ho-Tep in *The Mummy*, the twisted-faced killer Bateman in *The Raven*, and other bizarre characters portrayed by Karloff.

He was the man with whom Karloff himself worked out the final make-up that would become a popular icon, that of the Monster in the 1931 Universal horror classic *Frankenstein*.

Jack Pierce!

The make-up genius of the 1930s and 1940s, who died the year before Karloff's death, was on the show because he was an integral part of the actor's life. And while Karloff had already been given that pair of ersatz neck "plugs," now he would receive from Pierce the authentic articles, the twin electrodes via which life was electrically infused into the movies' Frankenstein Monster.

Nearly two decades had passed since Boris Karloff had worn these tiny "bolt-like" gizmos, the last time being back in 1939 when they brought new power to the Monster in *Son of Frankenstein*. True to form, Karloff accepted this gift from Jack Pierce and placed one of the electrodes against his neck.

Boris Karloff's sense of humor was hinted at on his *This Is Your Life* presentation when one of the guests related a typical incident involving the actor during the 1930s. Karloff had been invited to a large Hollywood

Boris Karloff and monster creator Jack Pierce in the make-up room at Universal Pictures sometime after the filming of both *Frankenstein* (1931) and *The Old Dark House* (1932). Pierce was one of the guests to pay tribute to Karloff in 1957 when the English actor was surprised by host Ralph Edwards on the television show *This Is Your Life*. (On April 3, 1974, Christopher Lee was similarly surprised, with Peter Cushing among the guests, on the British version of this popular program.)

party at which the guests were attired in tuxedoes and evening gowns. When the actor arrived, he was dressed accordingly—except for the one additional item he had brought along with him. He had brought with him something that looked suspiciously like … a toolbox! What made the other formally dressed guests react in astonishment and then laugh was the fact that the object in Karloff's hand really *was* a toolbox. The actor then marched straight into the kitchen, removed his jacket, sat on the floor, opened his box and proceeded to tinker with the plumbing!

Boris Karloff had been paid, over coast-to-coast live television, the homage he deserved by members of his family and by old friends and colleagues. Indeed, it was a wonderful birthday present; yet, it was something else, for it showed the actor that to his peers and fans he was so much more than just a Frankenstein Monster, a Mummy or a mad scientist. He was Boris Karloff and loved primarily for that simple fact.

And it was Karloff the man that Ralph Edwards addressed with those famous words, "This is your life."

# XII

# FRANKENSTEIN SINGS—
# AND DANCES, TOO

The first stage play based upon Mary Wollstonecraft Shelley's novel *Frankenstein; or, the Modern Prometheus* opened on July 23, 1823, at the English Opera House in London. Entitled *Presumption; or, the Fate of Frankenstein* (it would subsequently be re-titled many times), the play combined music with the dramatized horrors. Mary Shelley actually attended a performance of this play. Whether or not she experienced any of the myriad other stage adaptations of her popular story has apparently not been recorded; had she attended any of those later performances, Ms. Shelley would surely have been surprised as to the number of variations on her story that would be offered.

As early as the 19th century, comedies and musicals based on *Frankenstein*'s theme would prove popular on the stage, and continue to find audiences into the 20th century and, presumably, beyond. During the late 20th century I was able to attend various performances of some of these stage presentations. Among my favorites was *I'm Sorry, the Bridge Is Out, You'll Have to Spend the Night*, which I saw in a dress rehearsal during its original 1970 run at the Hollywood's Coronet Theatre. Accompanying me at that performance was *Famous Monsters of Filmland* magazine editor Forrest J Ackerman. In some ways this spoof of horror movies, with its innocent young couple forced to spend the night in a castle filled with monsters and other eccentric characters, presaged the later *Rocky Horror Show* (and its movie adaptation *The Rocky Horror Picture Show*).

The show had special importance for me. Not only did it affectionately spoof some of my favorite movie horrors—Frankenstein's Monster, Dracula, the Wolf Man and the Mummy, to name some of its cast of weird characters—one of its authors happened to be Bob Pickett, better known to me as Bobby "Boris" Pickett. In 1963 Bobby "Boris" Pickett and the Crypt-Kickers had recorded the novelty song "Monster Mash," which went on to become a classic, reissued over the years (and returning to Top 40 charts) as a single, included on countless album collections, and "covered" by other artists. Pickett, talking rather than singing his lyrics in an imitation of Boris Karloff's familiar voice, became a kind of fringe rock star as a result of that song, going on to record other similar songs, such as "Monsters' Holiday," "Transylvania Twist" and "Irresistible Igor."

When "Monster Mash" first hit the popular-music charts, I was living in Chicago and playing in a rock 'n' roll band called either the Servels, a name inspired by a brand name I saw on a refrigerator, or the Bel-Aires, from the car (we couldn't make up our minds). At the time I was still shy about singing in public, and so I was content to play my electric guitar and keep my mouth shut. The arrival of "Monster Mash," however, lent me an opportunity to *talk* rather than sing into a microphone and, at the same time, do my own imitation of Pickett impersonating Karloff. Sometimes I performed the song with added anonymity, my face hidden behind my rubber "custom" Wolf Man mask made by the Don Post Studios.

I met Bob Pickett for the first time at a later performance of *I'm Sorry, the Bridge Is Out, You'll Have to Spend the Night*, staged in 1976 with an entirely new cast by the Department of Theatre Arts at Pasadena City College. We met again at the second Famous Monsters Convention held in Universal City in 1995. The hosts of the convention wanted Pickett to perform "Monster Mash" at the event's banquet. Originally he declined, and so I was recruited to reprise my own Pickett-as-Karloff impersonation. I rehearsed the song prior to the convention with a live full orchestra and with popular movie "scream queens" Brinke Stevens and Linnea Quigley as back-up singers.

Happily, at the penultimate moment, Bob agreed to perform his own song. It was the first time I had ever seen Pickett perform "Monster Mash," and that experience was more of a thrill to me than performing the song myself.

There have been other performances of *I'm Sorry, the Bridge Is Out, You'll Have to Spend the Night*, and, no doubt, there will be more. The show was even adapted to the motion picture medium under the title *Monster Mash: The Movie* (original title: *Frankenstein Sings*), starring Bob Pickett himself as Dr. Frankenstein, preserved on video by Turner Home Entertainment and released in 1996. But it is still the premiere version of this show, the one I attended at the Coronet in 1970, for which I have the most fondness.

The following article may have been originally intended for *Famous Monsters of Filmland*, although I no longer remember why it was not published in that magazine. Instead it was printed, titled simply "I'm Sorry, the Bridge Is Out, You'll Have to Spend the Night," in *Monsters of the Movies* number 4 (December 1974), illustrated with photographs taken by the author during that dress rehearsal.

* * *

Monsters galore stalked the stage of the Coronet Theatre in Hollywood in the spring of 1970. Horror film stalwarts such as Frankenstein's Monster, Count Dracula, the Wolf Man and the Mummy joined other ghoulish fiends to star in a play spoofing the much-revered Universal horror pictures of the 1930s and, especially, the 1940s. The play, a musical comedy that opened on April 28th of that year, was *I'm Sorry, the Bridge Is Out, You'll Have to Spend the Night*, a revealing title that instantly conjures up any number of old (and much beloved) monster-movie images and clichés.

*I'm Sorry, the Bridge Is Out ...* was written with love and admiration for those old Universal horror movies by Sheldon Allman and Bob Pickett. (Remember when the latter author billed himself as Bobby "Boris" Pickett and imitated Boris Karloff and Bela Lugosi on such "monster rock" recordings as "Monster Mash," "Monsters' Holiday," "Monster Swim" and the album *The Original Monster Mash*?) Allman and Pickett disinterred the hoary Universal creatures and, for about one and a half hours, placed

Dr. Victor Frankenstein (Stan Zalas) leads the non-towering Frankenstein Monster into his "secret" laboratory in the 1970 premiere presentation of the musical play *I'm Sorry, the Bridge Is Out, You'll Have to Spend the Night,* enacted at the Coronet Theatre in Hollywood. (Photograph by the author.)

them into enough familiar situations to entertain any hard-core monster-film aficionado.

Among the monstrous cast of characters of *I'm Sorry, the Bridge Is Out ...* were the following:

Count Ladislav Dracula, originally portrayed by Peter Virgo, Jr., and then by John Ian Jacobs (who, oddly enough, enacted the role of the Frankenstein Monster during the first few nights of performances) doing a nearly perfect impersonation of "original" movie Dracula Bela Lugosi.

Dr. Victor Frankenstein, played by Stan Zalas (a Boris Karloff fan who had seen the British actor playing Captain Hook in a stage production of *Peter Pan*), sustaining throughout the play a commendable impersonation of the famous horror icon.

The Frankenstein Monster, played by Steve Dalen, wearing greenish make-up in the Universal Pictures image (but *sans* neck electrodes), applied by Peter Colby, with the actor barely standing as tall as most other members of the cast.

The Wolf Man, alias Prince "Rex" Talbot, portrayed as an effeminate Gypsy by Bob Benveniste.

And the Mummy, actually actor Peter Soul, completely unrecognizable beneath yards of concealing bandages.

The play also showcased such undesirables as the Egyptian high priest Dr. Nassar (Greg Aveco), Countess Dracula (Gloria Dell), the doting Mom Talbot (Natalie Ritschel), Dracula's insectivorous slave Renfield (originally Tony Lane, then replaced by Chuck Cypers for the version attended by this writer), Dr. Frankenstein's early stitch-faced creations Sam and Charlie (Scott Holloran and Lou Claudio, respectively), a bevy of vampire girls (Susan Maura Burns, Jeannette Jensen, Jaynene Ewing, Claudia Kadley, Wanda Flaton and Kathy Landau), plus a couple of unsavory body snatchers (Alistair Hunter and Keith Lawrence) and their stolen cadaver (Lou Laudio).

But while the two above-mentioned grave ghouls were stealing their corpses, some of the best scenes in the play were stolen by the Quasimodo-like Igor (first played by Richard Miller, but by Tony Lane in the version seen by this writer), a slovenly hunchback who hobbled about the stage and chortled his lines in a gravelly voice.

The only "normal" characters in the play were the "perfect" young couple of brave, handsome John Wellgood (John Landon) and his bride-to-be, pretty and innocent Mary Helen Herriman (Janaire). It was this couple that provided the monsters and fiends with their respective motives of mayhem.

*I'm Sorry, the Bridge Is Out, You'll Have to Spend the Night* opened with Dr. Victor Frankenstein remorsefully confiding in his assistant Igor that his lovable Monster requires (no surprise here) a new brain.

Outside the gloomy castle, meanwhile, a terrible storm rages, destroying the bridge that crosses the river. Thus are John Wellgood and Mary Helen Herriman forced into that classic "old dark house" story predicament—they have to take refuge in this dreary house of mystery and monsters.

*So* innocent (and apparently also poor-sighted), in fact, are John and his fiancée, that neither of them even suspects that the white-faced Count Dracula or the sinister Dr. Frankenstein, not to mention the grotesque Igor, are up to any foul play—even when the doctor continually and reflectively glances at the young man's cranium, making mental notes and calculations.

Soon, Dr. Frankenstein works out his "perfect" plan:

John's brain will be transplanted into the head of the Frankenstein Monster. Igor's brain will then be plopped into the then vacant head of John's perfect body (as a token favor for the hunchback's years of loyal service). The Monster's bodyless brain will then find a new home in Igor's skull. Everything would come out neat and tidy in the end—that is, if not for the *other* inhabitants of the castle.

Count and Countess Dracula, for example, desire the young couple for their warm and innocent blood.

Mom Talbot covets Mary Helen as a catalyst by which her son, the Wolf Man, can be cured of his lycanthropic curse and, simultaneously, develop a liking for … girls.

Dr. Nassar and the Mummy prefer that Mary Helen be the sacrificial victim of the Egyptian deity Amen-Ra, god of the sun.

To complicate Dr. Frankenstein's plans even more, the lecherous Igor yearns for Mary Helen for more mundane and, in his own way, more personal reasons.

Therefore, John and Mary Helen become the human targets of every creature in the house, with the various fiends and monsters vying for their bodies, souls and other physical and non-physical attributes.

At one point in the storyline, Mary Helen is bitten by Count Dracula and, like Renfield, made the King of Vampires' obedient slave. At the same time John is menaced by the beguiling Countess Dracula, who stands before him with raised arms, revealing the bat-like cut of her ebony gown.

The Mummy and Frankenstein's Monster meet in one of the funnier scenes in the Cornet's presentation of the show. Neither character has the power of speech, yet they find themselves having the need to communicate with one another. This they accomplish through grunting, snarling and stiffly moving their once-dead arms. Eventually their awkward movements metamorphose into a rock 'n' roll dance, thereby bridging the communication and (in this case, millennia-old) generations gap, just before departing through a secret passageway leading to Dr. Frankenstein's laboratory.

The ending of *I'm Sorry, the Bridge Is Out* … seemingly frees the young human couple from their terrible predicament. Dr. Frankenstein's science manages to cure Prince Talbot of his werewolf affliction. Igor sets the clocks back, tricking Dracula and his wife into staying up past dawn, the vampire twosome being destroyed when the curtains are opened to let in the morning sunlight. Most of the other fiends are eliminated by the vengeful living Mummy when the bandaged one witnesses Dr. Frankenstein's experiment and realizes it is replacing his own sacrifice of Mary Helen to the Egyptian sun god.

Yet everyone who knows and loves the old monster movies also is cognizant that classic terror characters such as the Frankenstein Monster and Count Dracula never *truly* die. Somehow they always manage to survive even the most presumably equivocal modes of destruction—in order to appear, usually whole and entire, in the subsequent sequel. For that simple reason (so chorused the ubiquitous villagers), the entire grisly cast returns to life with enough energy to sing through the finale. They have come back, the belted out lyrics tell us, because their many fans *want* them to return. (In "real life," of course, that is also the reason for the characters' survival from one film entry to the next.)

This first version of the play was directed by Maurine Dawson, who had already worked with an all-star horror-movie cast (including Basil Rathbone, Lon Chaney, Jr., Bela Lugosi, John Carradine and Tor Johnson) in *The Black Sleep*, a 1956 black and white fright film that in many ways harkened back to the Frankenstein and Dracula films of old. In 1969 Ms. Dawson made her own dramatic documentary, *Tales of Blood and Terror*, a rare film released in England by Titan Films and featuring three separate versions of the vampire Dracula.

*I'm Sorry, the Bridge Is Out, You'll Have to Spend the Night* did not, in its initial run, enjoy the same immortality as its line-up of star creatures. The play was relatively short-lived, not for lack of appeal, quality or entertainment value, but for lack of adequate publicity. For a while there was talk of filming this first version of the show for a Halloween television "special," a project that did not, unfortunately, materialize. Equally unfortunately, most avid fans of the old Universal monster films at the time were not even aware of the play's existence. Had they attended the show, this writer suspects that they would not have been sorry that the bridge was out ... and would have been most glad to spend the night with their old and creaky friends.

# XIII

# FRANKENSTEIN
# IN FOUR COLORS

In 1973, science-fiction author, Edgar Rice Burroughs authority and friend Dick Lupoff informed me that he and comic-book historian Don Thompson, another friend of mine, were planning a follow-up to their successful hardcover book *All in Color for a Dime*, which was published in 1970 by Arlington House. That book consisted of a collection of articles about comic books, comic-book characters and their creators, each piece written by a different well-known author. All of the articles had previously appeared in *Xero*, a mimeographed yet highly regarded fanzine (or fan-published magazine) issued during the 1960s by Lupoff (although the pieces were heavily revised for book publication).

Like the Frankenstein movies of Universal Pictures and Hammer Films, *All in Color for a Dime* demanded a sequel. The follow up, another hardback to be published by Arlington in 1973, would be appropriately entitled *The Comic-Book Book*. Unlike the first book, however, which had already exhausted the supply of *Xero* articles, the second book would comprise all-new articles written especially for the collection.

Knowing of my passion for old Frankenstein-related comic books, particularly those created by Dick Briefer for the Prize Group, Lupoff asked me if I'd care to contribute a chapter about those four-color adventures. Naturally I accepted the offer, submitting to him what was originally titled "Frankenstein Meets the Comics."

*The Comic-Book Book* was eventually reprinted as a Krause Publications trade paperback in 1998. Between the publication of the first edition and the new softback, one of its editors, Don Thompson, regrettably passed away. The lion's share of the piece that follows was revived and revised with the well wishes of Dick Lupoff.

Around 1999, my friend Roy Thomas, an authority on the Justice Society of America (a team of comic-book super-heroes whose adventures were originally published in *All-Star Comics* from the early 1940s through early 1950s), asked me to write a short piece on the super-heroes featured in *Prize Comics*, who, for one issue only of that periodical, teamed up to battle Dick Briefer's Frankenstein Monster. The article was included, along with other guest-written pieces, in Roy's book *The All-Star Companion* (TwoMorrows Publishing, 2000). As that article contained information relevant to my coverage of the Briefer material but not otherwise used in *The Comic-Book Book* article, I have worked most of its content, albeit slightly revised, into the following text.

❊　❊　❊

Dr. Victor Frankenstein stared at the giant white-skinned form stretched before him on a platform in his laboratory. The creature was at least 15 feet tall, assembled from parts of many corpses and covered with a sheet.

In his enthusiasm, Dr. Frankenstein thought he had created a perfect man.

A lightning storm raged in the bleak heavens as Frankenstein eagerly manipulated the controls of his laboratory apparatus. After the giant humanoid received the life-giving jolts of electricity, it sat up on the platform. Victor stared into the face of his living creation, oblivious to the ghastly features he himself had stitched together. Perhaps it was his plan to give this being a new face, someday. But with the absentmindedness of most such unorthodox scientists, he had overlooked that single detail.

The face of this being was that of a hideous monster. The dead white flesh barely covered the contours of the misshapen skull. The blood-gashed forehead was high, with stringy black hair hanging in uneven lengths almost to the wide shoulders. The two bulging eyes rarely looked in the same direction. A skeletal stub, which Victor assumed to be a nose, was set up between those eyes. The lips were torn to reveal a set of ugly teeth. Despite the proximity of the wretched face, the scientist failed to recognize the potential horror he had created.

The actual blame for the creation of *this* Frankenstein Monster falls upon Richard Briefer. A previous appearance of the infamous Monster had been an adaptation of the Universal motion picture *Son of Frankenstein* in the premiere issue of *Movie Comics* (April 1939), published by Picture Comics (now DC Comics, the publisher of *Superman* and *Batman*). But this was presented as a one-shot combination of retouched movie stills and artwork. It was Briefer who took the Frankenstein concept and, for the first time ever, developed it into a comic-book series.

Seemingly Richard (later just Dick) Briefer was a fan of the novel *Frankenstein; or, the Modern Prometheus*, written by Mary Wollstonecraft Shelley and first published in 1818, and of the series of Frankenstein movies (including the afore-mentioned 1939 film *Son of Frankenstein*) then being made by Universal Pictures. Both seemed to have greatly influenced his comic-book work.

Before he actually utilized that concept of a scientist creating a monstrous living being, Briefer began to do his own experimenting. Briefer had already been writing and illustrating the *Rex Dexter, Interplanetary Adventurer* series in *Mystery Men Comics*, a four-color comic book published by Fox. Rex was kind of a poor man's Flash Gordon who rocketed about the universe battling extraterrestrial menaces. In the fifth issue of *Mystery Men Comics* (December 1939), the space hero defeated a fiendish robot having a squarish head, sunken cheeks, straight black hair that hung in bangs, and a pair of electrodes protruding from its head. Obviously this robot was patterned after the Frankenstein Monster stalking through the Universal Pictures series; also, it was virtually the face of Briefer's own future Frankenstein Monster.

Taking the basic facial structure of Universal's Frankenstein Monster (high forehead, straight black hair with bangs, scars and powerful physique) and altering it enough to avoid any problems with copyright infringement, Briefer put his own version of the character into a comic strip and tried selling it professionally. Briefer was not one of the upper echelon of comic-book writers and artists, nor would he ever be, occasionally "ghosting" for other talents on such features as the very popular *Captain Marvel*. His style was simply too loose and often unfinished-looking to compete with the work of some of the fine draftsmen then seeing their work printed. Therefore, Briefer took his intended series to Feature Publications' *Prize Comics* (the title which gave that comic-book line its name of the Prize Group), where he sold it under the title *New Adventures of Frankenstein*, supposedly written and drawn by "Frank N. Stein." (Naturally no one believed that the pseudonym was a real name. Fans of *Rex Dexter* could immediately recognize Briefer's style, which during the 1940s would be applied to a few more strips, including *Pirate Prince* in *Silver Streak* and *Daredevil Comics*, published by Lev Gleason.)

*Prize Comics*, which made its debut in March 1940, was one of the more successful magazines in the forties primarily featuring super-heroes. National, Timely and Fawcett led the field in the super-hero business. *Prize Comics*' star characters included the Black Owl, who did his best to imitate National's (now DC Comics) Batman; Doctor Frost, who controlled coldness as kind

The first page of the third installment in the *Frankenstein* series by "Frank N. Stein" (aka Dick Briefer), published in *Prize Comics* number 9 (Feature Publications, February 1941). In this story an evil midget, after removing a bullet from the Monster's head, befriends the giant and uses his talents in committing crimes. The tiny man would return in a number of subsequent stories while the Monster's size would, over time, considerably diminish.

of an opposite of Timely's (now Marvel Comics Group) Human Torch; the Great Voodini, who seemed to have been a fan of Mandrake the Magician of newspaper-strip fame; and Power Nelson, a futuristic imitation of National's Superman, who traveled to the twentieth century to perform his super-heroics. Of course, none of the *Prize* heroes could compete with the original characters that inspired them. It would take an ugly antihero like the Frankenstein Monster to give the magazine its special distinction.

Briefer's *Frankenstein* strip debuted in *Prize Comics* number 7 (December 1940). When the *Prize Comics* version of the Monster came to life in Frankenstein's laboratory, its movements were sporadic. Inadvertently the creature knocked his creator unconscious, then he fled the castle to find his place in the world. As would be expected, the hideous being was persecuted wherever he went. He experienced happiness for the first time in his short life when he came upon the cabin of a blind man who fed and befriended him. When the blind man's son returned to the cabin and found his father in the company of a 15-foot-tall horror, he blasted the creature with a shotgun. The Monster was driven away by an angry mob that attacked him with clubs and stones. Briefer adapted these first four pages from the plotline of Mary Shelley's novel. The Frankenstein castle and fantastic laboratory reflected Briefer's own interest in the Universal movies and were an attempt to present on paper what was already familiar to filmgoers.

It should be mentioned, however, that at the time that Briefer produced his first Frankenstein comic-book tale, he did not—unlike the many writers and artists of illustrated stories that would follow him—have the tradition of a long list of Frankenstein movies upon which to pattern his stories. In 1940, for example, Universal Pictures had filmed only *three* movies in its Frankenstein series—*Frankenstein, Bride of Frankenstein* and *Son of Frankenstein*. Thus far the Universal version of the Frankenstein Monster had not yet met such other horror stalwarts as the Wolf Man and the vampire Dracula. This forced Briefer to be more original in his story ideas, and his character's encounters with such familiar horror figures as werewolves, vampires and zombies would not occur until much later.

Readers of the Shelley novel had been led to believe that the Frankenstein story was set in an earlier century in the wilds of various places in Europe. But those who read the *Prize Comics* version might have been surprised to learn that the Frankenstein Monster had been created not far from Manhattan ... in 1940!

After the Monster committed the cardinal sin of throwing two children into a lion's cage, the fiend caused some more destruction, then climbed to the top of the Statue of Liberty. Obviously, Briefer was also drawing on the popular images created by past monster movies. Anyone who had seen King Kong ascend New York's Empire State Building could not help making the association. Atop the Statue of Liberty, the Monster snatched people from the giant crown and dashed them to their deaths. Luckily, with the coincidence typical of the comic books, Victor Frankenstein was in the vicinity with his fiancée, Elizabeth. Victor reached the crown and then leaped upon his murderous creation. He missed the Monster, however, and landed in Miss Liberty's left hand. Surprisingly, instead of crushing his maker, the Monster gently placed him within the Statue's crown. After the police aimed their guns and opened fire, the bullet-ridden giant plummeted—again, like Kong—to an apparent death beneath the waters off Bedloe's Island.

Later, Victor wondered why the Monster had saved his life. Suddenly there was a crash of glass and the giant fiend threatened through the broken window. "I *spared* you to *live*—to live in *misery* also—to *watch* and *see* the *suffering* and *grief* that *I, your creation,* will cause the *human race.* You will *chase* me, but *never get* me! I go now, always *haunting* and *tormenting* you!"

Victor was still brooding over the horror he had unleashed upon the world in *Prize Comics* number 8 (January 1941). Realizing that such misery was the result of creating a soulless being, Frankenstein resolved to destroy his Monster in the most practical way he could devise. He would build another! And this second creation would be even less human than the original. This monster would have the head and paws of a giant crocodile and the brain of a madman! (By now, Frankenstein should have known better.)

The reptilian horror and the Frankenstein Monster fought atop New York's Radio City. Although the crocodile-man should have been the winner of their battle, the Monster killed his foe and escaped via an elevator shaft into a subway excavation. Apparently Victor had not considered the consequences had the reptile-man and not the Monster won.

The Frankenstein Monster had become the greatest super-villain in *Prize Comics.* As the *Prize* super-heroes were occupied with their own, usually lesser, adversaries in their own features, someone was needed to battle the Monster on more equal terms. Victor Frankenstein was, by then, becoming so neurotic over the Monster's every new crime that disposing of the brute would obviously have to become someone else's responsibility. While not equaling the Monster in size and raw strength, this new adversary would have enough courage and sheer "goodness" to combat even so terrible a fiend.

A young boy named Denny happened to be the sole survivor of an automobile crash caused by the Monster. Denny's parents were killed in the wreck and Victor Frankenstein felt responsible. The boy's legs were injured, and only the surgical skill of Frankenstein saved him. But Denny was forced to remain in a wheelchair. Frankenstein resolved to cure the boy completely, while seemingly aging 20 years under the strain. While the

Monster commanded the criminal underworld and continued to wage his war against humanity, Denny received periodic treatments. During the 10 years following his cure, Denny lived as the ward of the spirit-broken Dr. Frankenstein, training himself (à la Bruce Wayne, who would become the Batman) to physical perfection. Wearing a black riding outfit and a pin with a picture of his pet bulldog Spike, the young man became a super-hero of sorts with the single purpose of destroying Frankenstein's Monster.

Briefer may also have been a fan of the old Bulldog Drummond stories and movies. Drummond was an amateur sleuth aided in his adventures by a valet named Tenny. Just as Briefer had once applied the Frankenstein concept to *Rex Dexter*, so did he seemingly apply Bulldog Drummond and the similarly sounding name "Tenny" to *Frankenstein* (the "New Adventures" and "Frank N. Stein" had been dropped). The Monster had threatened to demolish New York's subway system. But Denny heroically intervened, defeating the Monster's hired thugs and finally capturing the giant. When a reporter photographed Denny running from the scene and found the bulldog pin which had fallen from his black outfit, the following headline ran in the morning newspaper: "Bulldog Captures Monster!" With the bulldog emblem on his chest, "Bulldog Denny" vowed to be the eternal enemy of the Frankenstein Monster.

The decade in which Denny grew into Bulldog Denny also affected the Monster. In his original Briefer conception, the Monster was too large and powerful to be defeated by one of even Denny's prowess. During those years the Monster had somehow grown considerably smaller. And although he was still a hideous creature to behold, his face lost many of the gruesome features it possessed when the being first came to life.

When Victor Frankenstein was finally written out of the strip to be replaced as the Monster's main antagonist by the more appealing Bulldog Denny, the Monster assumed his maker's name. Briefer had tried to remain accurate by not calling the Monster "Frankenstein." But the public had already been, for many years, confusing the Monster with its maker in terms of names, and Briefer finally went along with this trend. Frankenstein, as the Monster was now called, continued his battles against humanity, at one time even (literally) going to Hell to team up with the Black Owl's demonic adversary Doctor Devil (*Prize Comics* number 22, July 1942), until Bulldog Denny demonstrated his goodness by defeating both villains.

The United States had entered World War II. Bulldog Denny knew that in Germany there existed a "monster" far worse than the one created by Dr. Victor Frankenstein. Thus, the hero was called to Washington for defense work in *Prize Comics* number 24 (October 1942). But Frankenstein was still at large and a terrible threat. Before he left for Washington, Bulldog Denny called together a strange group whose combined efforts, he hoped, would demolish the creature now called Frankenstein.

Cross-overs (that is, a character from one strip appearing in another character's feature) were rare among the varied strips in *Prize Comics* during the 1940s, as they were in most comic books of that era. As stated above, *Frankenstein* had already overlapped with *The Black Owl*; moreover, with *Prize Comics* number 34 (September 1943), the Black Owl's feature would for the rest of its run be merged with the book's "Yank and Doodle" to become a single strip starring all three super-heroes.

Only once, however, did the *Prize* heroes join forces as a team to tackle that greatest menace outside of the Axis powers—Frankenstein. The story, titled "Utter Failure!!," appeared in Briefer's *Frankenstein* strip in *Prize Comics* number 24 (October 1942). Oddly enough, the *Prize* editors seemed not to realize the historic significance of this tale nor its potential as an ongoing series. Furthermore, not so much as a mention of the team-up appeared on the cover.

In a scene not unlike many featuring the popular Justice Society of America in All-American's/DC Comics' *All-Star Comics*, a group of famous heroes were called together by Bulldog Denny. With Denny about to leave for Washington on that defense project, it was now up to *Prize*'s finest to tackle the Monster. Seated around the table and addressed by Bulldog Denny were a number of heroes who had been respectively battling evil in their own *Prize Comics* features. There was the Black Owl, in reality wealthy idler and playboy Doug Danville, who put on a blue-and-red costume with cape and owl mask to battle injustice, utilizing only his developed strength and skills. Also seated at the table were Yank and Doodle, in reality Dick and Rick Walters, who donned star-spangled costumes to become "America's Fighting Twins" (junior versions of Timely's Captain America) to fight for Uncle Sam. There was Doctor Frost, who had no secret identity, wore a blue-and-green outfit, and used his freezing abilities to put evildoers on ice. The Green Lama, a character adapted from the pulp magazines, and a radio series, wore a monk's green garb and used supernatural powers to combat evil. Finally numbering among this group were the General and the Corporal, the bumbling stars of a humor strip then being run in *Prize Comics*.

All of these stalwarts had their own "favorite" villains in *Prize Comics*. But none of them had ever encountered so enduring a bad guy as Frankenstein. As in *All-Star*, the heroes agreed to battle their mutual enemy and then rushed off as a group, shouting in unison, "Let's go!" (a cry which might have become a trademark slogan had this group concept continued). They then split up to fight Frankenstein, either one against one or two against one, each encounter with the Monster spanning its own required number of panels.

The Black Owl, once the most popular *Prize Comics* hero and usually featured on its covers (until the introduction of the equally popular Yank and Doodle some issues earlier), was the first of this heroic group to tackle Frankenstein. The costumed hero used his greatest weapons—his fists—on the Monster. But, unlike Bulldog Denny, the Black Owl was not experienced in battling the giant creature. The Black Owl would have been dashed off the side of a cliff if the General had not shot the Corporal from a cannon smack into the back of the Monster's head.

Using the powers that he had acquired in Tibet, the Green Lama spoke the mystic words, "*Om! Mani padme hum!*" Immediately the most loathsome of monstrosities appeared before Frankenstein. Unable to overcome these horrors, Frankenstein fled from them, running into the slamming fists of Yank and Doodle.

Being battered by two young boys in "Halloween costumes" was certainly the most degrading encounter of all for Frankenstein. But even though America's Fighting Twins gave the brute a workout, they could not accomplish what even Bulldog Denny had failed to do. Leaping at the Monster head first, Yank and Doodle fell to the ground with Frankenstein-sized headaches.

Exhausted from the repeated assaults, Frankenstein fled from *Prize Comics'* one-shot imitation of the Justice Society of America champions. It took the chilly Doctor Frost but a single panel to do what all the other heroes combined had failed to do. As Frankenstein dove off a cliff to the water below, Doctor Frost simply gestured. Frankenstein's head crashed hard into a sea of solid ice, the impact knocking him cold.

Pummeled and battered by the various mystery men, Frankenstein seemed to be defeated. "Yes," commented the Black Owl, as he and the other victorious heroes looked down at the outstretched figure of the giant Monster, "I guess we're just an invincible bunch of guys!"

Indeed they were, or would have been, had they gone on to share subsequent adventures together. However, although these heroes were mentioned in the splash panel of next issue's "Frankenstein" installment of *Prize Comics*, they never teamed up again.

Even after such a crushing (and humiliating) defeat, Frankenstein revived and resumed his war against mankind. The *real* war was still going on, and patriotic readers knew that there were heroes whose courage and fighting ability rivaled even that of the Black Owl, the Green Lama and the rest of the *Prize Comics* roster of super-heroes. In the thirty-third issue of the magazine (August 1943), Frankenstein was captured by the combined might of Uncle Sam's armed forces.

Frankenstein was about to enter a new phase of his artificial life. He had already lost his stark white complexion in favor of a more normal flesh tone. A scientist named Professor Carrol, believing that Frankenstein had never been given a chance in life because people hated him for his appearance, defended him in court. Despite the horrendous crimes perpetrated by the Monster for so many years, the giant was given over to the scientist for treatment and rehabilitation.

Professor Carrol's transformation of Frankenstein into a decent citizen involved special injections, hypnosis and psychiatric treatments, plus the services of a plastic surgeon, barber and tailor. Carrol changed the beast into a mild-tempered "Mister Frankenstein." The world would soon somehow forget that this was once a terrible and murderous demon. Perhaps there was good reason to overlook his crimes. After all, could Frankenstein's evil acts really compete with the atrocities currently being performed by the Nazis?

Dick Briefer began to change his artistic style. His drawing had always been slightly "cartoony." There was nothing wrong in being cartoony, especially since such a style gave the artist's work a particular individuality, a quality otherwise lacking in so much comic-book art. Briefer must have realized that a horrible Frankenstein Monster out to destroy humanity was hardly frightening considering the real overseas horrors of those wartime years. He began to exaggerate further his drawings until the overall tone shifted to almost that of a humor strip.

"Mister Frankenstein" was more than a mere giant-sized human being. He was an American who now felt the urge to do what virtually all American comic-book heroes were doing in 1943—fight the Nazis. With Frankenstein added to the list of *Prize Comics'* champions, other comic-book companies' heroes, and even movie heroes battling the Germans, it seemed like Hitler and his maniacs had little chance for survival.

In *Prize Comics* number 34 (September 1943), Briefer did one of his rare non–*Frankenstein* stints for that magazine, drawing the final installment of *The Green Lama* (replaced the next issue by *The Flying Fist and Bingo*, another superhero feature). The issue was also significant in that *The Black Owl* and *Yank and Doodle* were combined into a single feature.

At the same time, Frankenstein began his new life by attending school, starting in the first grade. The entire flavor of the magazine was changing. Emphasis was now being placed on youth (the Black Owl playing second banana to the much younger Yank and Doodle), most significantly with the introduction of *Buck Saunders and His Pals*, another of the popular "kid gang" type features by the prolific team of Joe Simon and Jack Kirby. There was hardly room anymore for the gore and horror so prevalent in the early *Frankenstein* stories. Still, there was a considerable helping of murder and violence interspersed with the humor of a bumbling giant in grammar school.

Frankenstein fought Nazi spies on the home front until *Prize Comics* number 39 (February 1944). The Gestapo captured the giant, drugged him, and entrusted him to a Nazi scientist who promptly undid all the positive miracles that Professor Carrol had accomplished. For a while Europe was haunted by a hideous creature wearing a Gestapo uniform who brutally killed anyone failing or refusing to raise an arm and exclaim, "Heil Hitler!" However, eventually Frankenstein escaped his special Nazi treatments and regained his red-white-and-blue memory and sense of patriotism. For a while he worked as an undercover agent against the Nazis, sabotaging trains and wiping out German troops from the sidelines, until he was discovered and forced to flee for his unnatural life.

For a while, Frankenstein came under the influence of a female vampire named Zora, who turned him into a kind of Jekyll and Hyde character. By day he was the nice "Mister Frankenstein"; by night, however, he was the destructive beast set upon the world by Victor Frankenstein. Eventually Frankenstein drove Zora away with garlic and was able to settle down to a more peaceful existence.

More changes were taking place in the pages of *Prize Comics*. Many of the once-popular super-heroes were forced to surrender their feature spots to a new assemblage of humor strips. Within a few issues, features like *Ham and Eggs*, about a pig and a rooster, respectively, *Sir Prize*, knight of the Castle Booboo, *Peter Pelican and Grouper*; and *Caveman Frolics* dominated its pages. With the end of World War II the editors of *Prize Comics* apparently felt that their audience would prefer to breathe more easily and see gags instead of violence. People wanted to laugh.

With the new format of *Prize Comics* established, Frankenstein was given a stitched cut running vertically down the middle of his high forehead. His face had already changed to a caricature of its former appearance. The peg of a nose simply could not have been placed any higher above the eyes and still be a nose. These changes were gradual and there was no real break in story continuity. And yet the creature now claiming to be Frankenstein was, in fact, the *same* monstrosity that had once terrorized New York City and threw innocent children to the lions.

Frankenstein was no longer a mildly humorous strip but outright comedy using funny versions of the old horror characters. This creature with a transplanted heart of gold now lived in a ridiculous world of inane vampires, werewolves, mummies, ghouls and related fiends. And this horror-humor strip predated a similarly themed television series, *The Munsters*, by about 20 years.

When *Frankenstein* became a humor strip, Dick Briefer went wild in his stories and art. His already loose style "exploded" to the point that he often did not pencil his work but inked right from scratch. He worked so fast that when he used up his supply of drawing board he scribbled his pictures on the back of wallpaper. To further economize, Briefer, when using the standard drawing board, cut it in half in order to get two pages of finished artwork for every one page of board.

Frankenstein became so popular in this humorous incarnation that the publisher of *Prize Comics* awarded the big guy his own 48-page comic book. *Frankenstein* number 1 appeared in 1945 ("By Popular Demand!" the cover boasted). With this new

Cover drawn by Dick Briefer for the second issue (Crestwood Publishing, 1945) of Prize Publications' *Frankenstein* comic book, played strictly for laughs. This scene reprises the brand new "origin" Briefer concocted for the Frankenstein character appearing in the first issue, published earlier that same year.

book, Briefer was able to do something perhaps he should have done much earlier—give Frankenstein a new origin in a possible attempt to sever his connection with the former gruesome Monster. That was fine for new readers of the feature. But for those trying to reconcile the original *Frankenstein* strip (wherein the Monster was created in New York by Victor Frankenstein) with the new version running in both *Frankenstein* and *Prize Comics* it provided only confusion.

In the new origin, "Frankenstein's Creation" in the premiere issue of *Frankenstein*, an anonymous mad scientist tried to eliminate his boredom. The scientist's black cat enacted the role of Fate by accidentally knocking a book from the shelf. The mad scientist stared at the book through his thick spectacles. It was a copy of *Frankenstein* by Mary Wollstonecraft Shelley.

Inspired by the novel, the mad scientist resolved to create "the most terrible beast man or animal has ever known!!" Taking his shopping list to a shady undertaker, he purchased such necessary ingredients as "two eyes, two ears, a forehead, half a nose, some lungs, a stomach, a half pound of hair, black preferably—quarter pound of cream cheese—" Even mad doctors can mix up their shopping lists.

After Frankenstein (as the creation was called again) came to life in the scientist's laboratory, the latter injected him with a drug capable of giving a rabbit the ferocity of a lion. To the mad scientist's disappointment, Frankenstein loved flowers and animals, and would no more think of attacking the human race than of harming an ant. After escaping an explosion, which destroyed the mad doctor in his castle, Frankenstein set out to resume the absurd existence he was already enjoying in the pages of *Prize Comics*.

Frankenstein soon took up residence in a haunted-looking old mansion in Mippyville (the house given to him by the mayor), where he was at home with the bats and spiders. He eventually married his dream woman, a ghastly creature who proved to be a domineering social climber and nag. After a quick divorce, Frankenstein went back to a solitary life. Later he joined a type of commune of freaky characters, such as the hag Awful Annie and other weird creatures.

Yet more changes began to occur within the *Prize Comics* pages. Westerns were enjoying new popularity due to the influence of motion pictures, radio and that new medium of television, the latter successfully running a seemingly endless stream of old theatrical cowboy films. The publishers of *Prize Comics* agreed that sales might be increased if cowboys replaced "funny animals," *Yank and Doodle* ("starring" *The Black Owl*) and

*Frankenstein.* Thus, *Prize Comics* number 68 (February-March 1948) opened with *Harry Tracy, Last of the Western Badmen.* It was also the last issue to feature *Frankenstein, Yank and Doodle* and other familiar strips, including Dick Briefer's one-shot *Max the Magician,* which was even more loosely drawn than his *Frankenstein.* In April of 1948, the 69th issue of *Prize Comics* became *Prize Western.* The following year, *Frankenstein* number 17 (January-February), the cover of which depicted "Franky" high above the city, standing before a huge clock and about to be impaled by a madman using a clock hand for a spear, was the final issue of this humorous series. Frankenstein and its association with Dick Briefer seemed defunct— at least for the next three years.

But, as in other forms of popular media, comic-book trends run in cycles. During the early 1950s a new phenomenon emerged to replace the super-heroes that had dominated the color pages since the late 1930s. The super-heroes, with the exception of a few seemingly immortal characters like Superman and Batman, were hanging up their tights, capes and masks to go into retirement. Readers no longer wanted stories of mystery men zooming through the air and thwarting crime. Instead, they craved tales of vampires, werewolves and zombies told and drawn in realistic fashion. The more grisly the scenes depicted, the more blood and dismembered limbs, the better. The new heroes were crypt and vault keepers who chortled gleefully as a vampire sank its fangs into the throat of a busty young woman, or as a hen-pecked husband chopped his nagging wife up into little pieces and used them in some twisted method of revenge.

The time was right for the return of the Frankenstein Monster, but not the blundering boob who preferred sniffing daisies to snuffing out human lives. The Prize Group decided then to continue *Frankenstein* with the 18th issue (March 1952), again with Dick Briefer writing and drawing. But Briefer's drawing style had to be considerably revamped in order to meet the standards established by the other companies already publishing horror comics. Despite the gore, the current readers of comic books would not have accepted the more cartoony Frankenstein of the early *Prize Comics* issues. Briefer had to discipline himself.

*Frankenstein* number 18 began an entirely new storyline, with Briefer's individualistic art style debuting in its more "sophisticated" form. Though still not up to the caliber of some of the artists working at the competition, especially those employed at the prestigious EC publishing house, Briefer's drawings were always his own, always original, and presumably never copied or "swiped" from other existing sources. And this new style was entirely appropriate for the new *Frankenstein* series.

Briefer's latest and final version of the Frankenstein Monster was still based on his earlier concepts. The "beast," as Briefer sometimes referred to him in the captions, still had a high forehead, flat head, and a ridiculously small nose between his eyes. Among the innovations were an open wound with torn stitches that revealed the skull underneath, and a torn, lipless mouth that exposed the misshapen teeth even when the brute's mouth was closed. There were more ghastly features about Briefer's 1940 Frankenstein Monster, but the 1952 version was even less pleasant to behold owing to the more realistic style in which he was rendered.

As before, Briefer took care not to bring down the wrath of Universal Pictures for using their copyrighted Frankenstein Monster's face. The basic features vaguely suggested the Boris Karloff Monster, although some of the more obvious trappings were changed. Karloff's stitchless scar was moved from the side of the forehead to the center, for example, and all of the Universal Monster's metal clips and electrodes were avoided.

In "The Rebirth of the Monster" in *Frankenstein* number 18, two villagers broke into the castle of Frankenstein, which had not been opened in a century (this clearly setting the new series apart from the 1940s strip), to learn if the old legends about Henry Frankenstein creating a Monster were true. (After 11 years of "Victor," Briefer now chose to use the name "Henry" for the Monster's creator, in conformance with the character's name in Peggy Webling's stage play of 1927 and the 1931 movie starring Karloff.) They find, lying on a slab next to the skeleton of its creator, the giant Frankenstein Monster. The sudden rush of cold air that accompanied the villagers' entrance would also bring them death, for it revived the beast. Both men were promptly crushed by the creature's enormous hands.

Reborn, the Frankenstein Monster ravaged the nearby village. Bullets did not stop the Monster, for Henry Frankenstein had given him a leathery flesh that sealed as soon as a bullet penetrated it. In these small European towns (especially ubiquitous in Universal's Frankenstein movies, on which Briefer obviously patterned his 1950s series) no one ever thought to call out the army to blast apart the marauding giant. Apparently it was more "fun" to take up blazing torches and garden rakes and clubs and form a mob to pursue and destroy the Monster.

The great-grandson of Henry Frankenstein flew to Europe from the United States intending to destroy his ancestor's creation. Believing the similar-looking descendant to be his creator, the Monster relaxed his guard, only to receive a burning torch in the face. In agony, the Monster jumped into the water. Frankenstein realized that he had been spared in order to experience the horror and know the guilt that would result again from the acts committed by his ancestor's creation.

Briefer's earlier versions of the Frankenstein Monster were anything but reticent. This new version, however, was apparently designed more for the benefit of readers familiar with the Universal movies, wherein the Monster was usually speechless. They could more readily accept this new conception, who never so much as uttered a word or was given even a single thought balloon to reveal what he might be thinking. The Monster's thoughts remained a mystery to the readers, and this technique worked.

Young Dr. Frankenstein pursued the Monster, who had stowed away aboard the doctor's America-bound ship. In the United States the doctor last saw the Monster destroying some foreign spies before the laboratory in which they were hiding blew up in *Frankenstein* number 19 (summer, 1952). Inevitably he was written out of the series, leaving the Frankenstein Monster to roam across the countryside, encountering such creatures and fiends as American

Cover drawn by Dick Briefer for the twenty-first issue (Feature Publications, October-November 1952) of *Frankenstein,* which had been revived as a straight horror comic book earlier that year while continuing the numbering from the last issue of the humorous series. The cover has nothing to do with the story inside the magazine, which combined elements of two classic science-fiction novels, *The Island of Dr. Moreau* by H.G. Wells (mad doctor turns animals into humans), and *The Lost World* by Arthur Conan Doyle (surviving prehistoric reptiles).

Indian zombies, a scientist who "devolved" lizards into dinosaurs and evolved a wildcat into a beautiful young woman, and a Mexican werewolf.

Seemingly, Briefer assumed that his new audience had not read or at least would not remember his earlier stories in *Prize Comics* and the comedy version of the *Frankenstein* comic book. He never stole the poses for his artwork, but he did reuse or at least adapt material from his own past plots. The sources did not really seem to matter. Briefer had already adapted stories from his first *Prize Comics* series into the funny series. By the 1950s, basically he had *two* past series offering material that he could retool into "new" stories.

"The Monster's Mate" in *Frankenstein* number 23 (February-March 1953) was based on a similar story from *Prize Comics* number 26 (December 1942), in which a scientist created a female horror for the Monster, only to see her destroyed by the usual mob of angry townspeople. In the new story, the Monster, now mysteriously back in Europe (Briefer never told us which country), befriended an ugly giantess who had wandered away from a circus. When the woman is killed by another band of townspeople, the Monster, as did his 1940s predecessor, lashed out at them with a terrible vengeance. This story was only partially based on the *Prize Comics* tale, as the original involved the actual creation of a female being. *That* part of the story was eventually adapted to *Frankenstein* number 28 (December-January 1954), "The She-Monster," in which yet another mad doctor brought a murderess back to life as a companion for the Monster.

In the 30th issue of the comic book (April-May 1954), now with the cover title *The Monster of Frankenstein*, Briefer had a sculptor pour molten bronze over the Monster in order to create a perfect life-sized statue of the giant. When the bronze hardened, the still-living Monster ripped his way out, grabbed the whimpering sculptor and poured liquid bronze down his throat. This time Briefer hit the proverbial jackpot. The basic theme had already been used in both the original *Prize Comics* series and in the humorous *Frankenstein* book.

Briefer's plots were now showing less imagination than those of earlier years. It was becoming standard (and expected) to see the Monster naively trusting some questionable character who only planned to use the giant for his own evil or selfish ends, probably eventually also to eliminate the beast in some grisly fashion. The Monster would invariably learn of the treachery and then inflict upon his "friend" the same kind of horrible death. Indeed, the stories were gradually becoming almost parodies of the stories that began with *Frankenstein* number 18. The relative lack of care and originality hardly mattered anymore, however. A "monster" more powerful and destructive than any created by Henry or Victor Frankenstein had appeared to threaten the comic-book industry and its characters and themes.

Comic books in general, but especially horror and crime titles, were being attacked by one of the most heinous of "monsters"—censorship. Primarily through the crusading efforts of Dr. Frederick Wertham, a psychiatrist, in a series of magazine articles and in his 1954, best-selling book *Seduction of the Innocent*, people were "informed" that comic books constituted one of the greatest threats to modern civilization. Wertham cited case upon case wherein emotionally disturbed children, many of them from questionable home environments, had read comic books just previous to their embarking on careers as juvenile delinquents. Naturally it followed, Wertham pointed out, that virtually every delinquent child in the country was made that way because he or she read comic books. It certainly seemed logical to parents searching for an excuse for their own failure to raise their children correctly. (This was years before it was likewise "proven" that television, motion-picture and videogame violence were the real culprits in so corrupting children.) A scapegoat was needed and comic books conveniently provided one. Some horror and crime comics published at the time *were* in bad taste. But the whole industry was under attack, and with the mass panic spreading (so that dealers were afraid to place horror and crime comic books on their display racks), the publishers finally tossed in their towels, coffins and torture devices.

The Comics Code Authority was established, forbidding the necessary ingredients of the horror books. By the beginning of 1955 there would be no more horror comics in the grand 1950s tradition.

The publishers of the Prize Group of comic books saw the hysteria coming and knew that their *Frankenstein* title had no future. Since its 20th issue, only one *Frankenstein* story was run per book, the others being non-series horror and science-fiction "fillers." With the 30th issue, two *Frankenstein* stories began appearing per book. These tales were originally scheduled for issues that would, unfortunately, never be printed. The gruesome *Frankenstein* could never pass the taboos of the Comics Code Authority, and the publishers were trying to use up their inventory stories while they still could.

The cover of *Frankenstein* number 33 (October-November 1954) was historical and mildly nostalgic. The art was a serious version of the cover of the last issue of the funny series, with the Monster about to be hand-harpooned in front of a giant clock. The last story in the book, "Frankenstein and the Plant," was about another mad scientist who developed a carnivorous plant whose buds assumed the shape of its last meal. Not surprisingly, the story ended with the plant's buds looking exactly like the face of the mad scientist who provided its most recent dinner. The story had been done before, back when Frankenstein was a friendly oaf. There was no longer any reason for Briefer to show much originality. *Frankenstein* number 33 was the swansong issue.

Dick Briefer proved that a monster could survive in a world of super-heroes (at least those in the Prize Group lineup). He took an established character, Frankenstein's Monster, adapted it to the tastes of contemporary comic-book readers, and eventually evolved that character from a hideous monstrosity to a patriotic American citizen to a bumbling clod and finally to a misunderstood misanthrope in a world of prejudiced human beings. This final incarnation of Briefer's Frankenstein Monster was the present writer's first encounter with the character in *any* form, back in the early 1950s. I had always been enthralled by the very concept of the Frankenstein story and was delighted to find that the Monster had his own comic book series. Unfortunately, the one book that I bought from a newsstand for a dime was its second-to-last issue. Yet that single issue of *Frankenstein* had appeal, as did the Universal movies featuring the character that I would experience just a few years later. Years would pass before I would be able to acquire a complete run of Dick Briefer's *Frankenstein* series (*not* for the original cover prices!) and discover that the artist had been developing his feature since the 1940s.

Comic books numbering in the thousands have used the Frankenstein Monster or theme, including series and individual stories published throughout the world. But Dick Briefer's version, enduring from 1940 through 1954, was the only one possessing the required appeal to make it a success for such a long period of time. Perhaps the drawing and even the scripting were not up to par with some of the competition. Nevertheless, to those of us who had read Mary Shelley's *Frankenstein* or seen the Universal Frankenstein movies, Briefer's series (including the funny version) had all the correct elements.

With the arrival of the Comics Code Authority, the Prize Group ceased all publication of horror comic books. Editorship of their line eventually changed over to Joe Simon and Jack Kirby, who continued doing romance stories, mystery tales and a few other genres of books before the Prize Group went completely out of business. Briefer freelanced, working for companies like Marvel Comics, until he, too, unfortunately vanished from the comic-book scene.

Dick Briefer's *Frankenstein* was not the only illustrated book utilizing the character—or variations thereof—to come out during the early 1950s.

While Briefer's Frankenstein Monster waited in comic-book limbo for his return in 1952, the American Comics Group (ACG) introduced its own series, *Spirit of Frankenstein*, in *Adventures Into the Unknown* number 5 (June-July 1949). The ACG horror stories were always rather tame by comparison with most of those published by other companies. In this series, Dr. Lambert Pardway resented his young colleague Dr. Warren for the fame he had acquired in the scientific world. The latest achievement of Dr. Warren was inventing a giant humanoid robot with a bald head and plastic "skin." The crafty Pardway talked Warren into placing his brain into the robot following his death. Inadvertently, Warren created another Frankenstein Monster, with the robot controlled by the evil mind of Pardway. For two years this series appeared randomly in *Adventures Into the Unknown*. But to readers familiar with Briefer's work and the movies, this series simply did not represent Frankenstein. In the 16th issue (February 1951), just slightly more than a year before Briefer's return to the theme, *Spirit of Frankenstein* was discontinued.

Among the best and most successful Frankenstein comic-book stories other than Briefer's were those that did not attempt to create a new or competing series.

One of the best and most faithful comic-book adaptations of Mary Shelley's *Frankenstein* is the one originally published in *Classic Comics* number 26 (Gilberton Company, December 1945). Illustrated by Robert Hayward Webb and Ann Brewster, this version was reprinted many times, even as the title became *Classics Illustrated*, and eventually with newly painted cover artwork.

In December 1945, *Classic Comics* (later to become *Classics Illustrated*) devoted its 26th issue to a straightforward adaptation of Mary Shelley's *Frankenstein*. The script was faithfully written by Ruth A. Roche and interpreted visually by artists Robert Hayward Webb and Ann Brewster. Like Briefer, Webb and Brewster used some of the physical characteristics suggested by the Universal movie Frankenstein Monster, this time including placing "bolts" at the neck and joints. But the creature was given an almost black skin and was barefooted, perhaps in an effort to make it different enough to avoid a lawsuit. Ms. Roche was obviously familiar with the original novel. Her breakdown as interpreted by the artists remains a veritable storyboard for some future definitive movie version of *Frankenstein*, if it is ever filmed.

The now-legendary Entertaining Comics (EC), which produced the best written and illustrated four-color horror comics during the early 1950s, published a number of significant Frankenstein-type stories, but only one of these, "The Monster in the Ice!" in *Vault of Horror* number 22 (December–January 1951–1952), featured the original Monster. The story, written by EC editor Al Feldstein and illustrated by "Ghastly" Graham Ingels, told of the discovery of the Frankenstein Monster in a block of Arctic ice. Anyone who saw the Monster's face went mad. That was understandable. In attempting to only suggest the Universal Pictures concept, Ingels created one of the most hideous versions of the character ever to appear on a comic-book page. The Monster's eyes bulged from the sockets, enormous tusk-like teeth protruded from the mouth and scraggy hair hung from the deformed head. Most other EC Frankenstein tales had relatively pleasant-appearing "monsters." Jack Davis, with his ability to infuse humor into an otherwise gruesome story, had a mad scientist create his own Frankenstein Monster for a museum exhibit in "Mirror, Mirror, on the Wall!" in *Tales from the Crypt* number 34 (February–March 1953), with Davis presenting his own adaptation of the Universal Monster. Interestingly, most of this story was related from the creation's point of view, from his first awakening in the scientist's laboratory to his final death in a hall of mirrors, where he is frightened to death by his own multiple images. In the 40th and last issue of *The Vault of Horror* (December 1954–January 1955), in Feldtsein and Ingels' "Ashes to Ashes!" the Frankenstein line created a perfect baby girl following generations of developing what was originally merely a blob of earth. There was no longer any need to adapt the Universal Monster, for the Frankensteins had at last created a being of perfection, only to be returned in the end to its original elements by a bullet fired by a jealous suitor.

The EC Frankenstein stories were always extremely well written and drawn by some of the best comic-book artists in the business. They usually climaxed, after a storyline emphasizing plot and characterization, with a shock or surprise ending. The comic books produced by Timely and Atlas (both now the Marvel Comics Group) in the 1940s and early 1950s did their best to compete with the ECs, but generally stressed action and monsters over literary content. Atlas has the distinction of publishing more unrelated or non-series Frankenstein stories during that period than any other comic-book company.

Patriotic super-heroes Captain America and Bucky battled the revived Monster in "The Curse of Frankenstein," published in *USA Comics* number 13 (summer, 1944). In this opus, the Monster was eventually lured into a bog of quicksand (a fate similar to that suffered by Universal's Monster in *House of Frankenstein*, a movie released that same year). Although creatures purporting to be the original Frankenstein Monster continued to appear in that company's comic books, it was obvious that they had not read the *USA Comics* story, or at least had faulty memories. For example, in *Blonde Phantom* number 14 (summer 1947), in the story "Horror at Haunted Castle!" the beautiful golden-haired heroine fought a Baron Frankenstein who looked exactly like the Monster. In the early 1950s the original Frankenstein Monster appeared in *Marvel Tales* number 96 (June 1950) in "The Return of the Monster," illustrated by Syd Shores, who drew the character with pointed ears, fangs and claws. In "The Monster," drawn by Paul Reinman for *Marvel Tales* number 106 (April 1952), a very Universal-looking Monster attacked a motion-picture crew shooting a film in the Frankenstein castle. Jim Mooney drew another Universal-type character for "The Monster's Son" in *Strange Tales* (September 1952), which showed that the brute was really a scientific genius capable of creating an offspring. Arguably the best of these stories was "Your Name Is Frankenstein!" written by Stan Lee and drawn by Joe Maneely for *Menace* number 7 (September 1953). In this story the Monster, after years of digging his way to the surface from a swamp bog (inadvertently connecting, albeit tenuously, this story with the creature with whom Captain America and Bucky tangled), found the humans he tried to save as uncaring as always, and preferred to return to the earth. Perhaps the most unusual of these stories was "The Lonely Dungeon" in *Mystery Tales* number 18 (March 1954), which proved that it was really the Monster who created Dr. Frankenstein, and who was, in turn, built by the caretaker of his castle (who had also created many other such monsters).

In March of 1963, Dell Comics published a version of *Frankenstein* rather freely adapted from the 1931 Universal movie of the same title. Three years later, the second issue of Dell's *Frankenstein* (September 1966) appeared on the newsstands. But, now drawn by artist Tony Talarico, this was not exactly the same Frankenstein image that had appeared in the movie or in the first issue. "Frankenstein," as he was called, was now a super-hero (taking part in the 1960s resurgence of such characters) who wore a tight-fitting red costume, sported a white crew cut and fought criminals. (Other traditional horror characters that also became costumed do-gooders at this time, courtesy of Dell Comics, were Dracula and the Werewolf.) Frankenstein adopted the secret identity of Frank Stone. But when a menace appeared on the scene, Frank yanked off his rubber human mask and became the heroic Frankenstein, pitting his superhuman strength and stamina against the forces of evil. The stories were simply executed, illustrated by an artist known for his speed with a pencil. The series was an ill-conceived idea to begin with. It died with *Frankenstein* number 4 (March 1967), with Frankenstein revealing that his familiar green countenance was also a false face. Someday his real face would be shown, he promised, but that day never came. No one seemed to be sorry about missing its revelation.

Frankenstein's Monster has also been a series character in foreign countries. *Frankenstein*, published by Edicao la Selva from 1959 to 1960, was one of two series issued in Rio de Janeiro. Some of the stories, done mostly in the Dick Briefer school, borrowed heavily from both Briefer's old plots and artwork. The Monster, now called simply Frankenstein again, was portrayed as a brutal killer who met up with a number of mad doctors, vampires and other fiends. A second series from Rio de Janeiro, published in 1969 by Editora Penteado and running only two issues, featured some mild horror tales labeled "adults only." Perhaps this was due to many South American horror comics featuring the sexy adventures of Dracula, the Mummy, the Wolf Man and even the Phantom of the Opera also being published at that time.

During the 1960s, the old-style horror comic books provided the basic format for a large number of horror magazines, their stories usually printed in black and white (rather than the traditional four colors), pioneered by Warren Publishing Company's *Creepy*, and later *Eerie* and *Vampirella*. As these publications were not officially classified as comic *books*, but comic *magazines* (standard magazine size), they did not have to subscribe to the Comics Code Authority and adhere to its censorship requirements; thus, they could go all out when it came to horror. A suitable place for the Frankenstein Monster had been created. Like the stories published before by EC and Atlas, the Warren Frankenstein tales had no real plot or character continuity with each other. Each of them was a complete story in itself that, like the EC opuses, led to a final shocking ending.

The first actual series to appear in one of these magazine's was Skywald Publishing Corporation's *Frankenstein Book II* in the third issue (May 1971) of *Psycho*, a magazine similar to *Creepy* and *Eerie* in format. Written and illustrated by Tom Sutton (under the pseudonym of Sean Todd), this new series began after the climax of the Mary Shelley novel. The Monster, a more ugly version of the Universal creature, and one given to long dissertations (like the original conception in the novel), salvaged his creator's corpse from the icy waters of the Arctic and used his superior transplanted brain to turn Frankenstein himself into a resuscitated horror. The Monster was exhibited along with a company of human oddities in the next issue's "Freaks of Fear!" (September 1971). In Paris the Monster met Quasimodo, the famed Hunchback of Notre Dame. The third installment, "The Sewer Tomb of Le Suub!" in *Psycho* number 5 (November 1971), pitted the Frankenstein Monster against an octopus-like behemoth in the sewers beneath Paris. The creative effort devoted to this series was appreciated, although the long-winded dialogue of the Monster quickly became stultifying.

In 1972 Marvel Comics began publishing the excellent *Monster of Frankenstein*, a new comic-book series adapted (in its early issues) from the Shelley novel, originally done by writer Gary Friedrich and artist Mike Ploog. The series joined Marvel's *Werewolf by Night* (also drawn by Ploog) and *Tomb of Dracula*, comic books now permitted again thanks to a slight relaxation in the Comics Code rules as revised the previous year. Very shortly after, DC introduced *The Spawn of Frankenstein*, a shorter page-count Frankenstein series in the pages of *Phantom Stranger* number 23 (January-February 1973), written by Marv Wolfman and drawn by Mike Kaluta. Both the Marvel and DC versions of the Frankenstein Monster represented the original character, and both series began with their respective Monster being chipped out of the polar ice where Mary Shelley's story had left him. However, the Marvel series, at least when it began, was set in 1898, while DC's series was set in contemporary 1973.

During the succeeding years, numerous Frankenstein-related stories have been published in comic books and comic magazines, some of them comprising their own series. However, of all such stories published since the first in that 1939 premiere edition of *Movie Comics*, Dick Briefer's efforts remain, for many aficionados, the most memorable, even though they were far from the most literary or artistic. There was something compelling in that flat head, those sunken cheeks and that impossible nose set between the eyes in Briefer's versions of the Frankenstein Monster. Briefer's character, whether battling Bulldog Denny in the subway tunnels under New York City, napping in the garden outside his haunted house, or enacting some horrible vengeance upon some human being who had feigned friendship only to exploit his misplaced trust, had power—a strange charm by which the series endured in its original form until the coming of the Comics Code Authority. (Thankfully, Briefer's stories, like the immortal Monster they featured, are, to this day, still sometimes reprinted in one format or another.)

Victor (or Henry) Frankenstein had created a being charged, as the movies showed us, with eternal life. Dick Briefer's version of the Monster, at least during his comic books' original run, was somewhat less immortal. Still, the character had survived and thrived in those old publications for almost 15 years. When compared with other characters bearing the name of Frankenstein who lumbered through their illustrated adventures, that was quite an impressive accomplishment.

# THE MONSTER
## OF FRANKENSTEIN
## (ALMOST) RETURNS

In 1959 an enterprising young writer, film scholar and fantastic films buff named Calvin Thomas Beck published and edited a magazine with the title *The Journal of Frankenstein* (although the editing was credited to one "Victor Frankenstein IV"). The magazine, published out of Beck's home in North Bergen, New Jersey, was his attempt at creating a magazine that could compete in the then very lucrative "monster magazine" market. Unlike the competition, however, *The Journal of Frankenstein* was targeted at an older, more intellectual and sophisticated (and, in an East Coast sort of way, "hipper") audience than the general readers of *Famous Monsters of Filmland*, *World Famous Creatures* and *Monster Parade* (to mention some of the other magazines).

*The Journal of Frankenstein*'s simple black and white cover boasted a familiar logo. Comic-book readers had seen that word "Frankenstein" for years. It had been clipped off the *Frankenstein* comic-book series created during the late 1940s by artist and writer Richard (Dick) Briefer.

Although the goals set by Beck for *Journal* were lofty enough, the "sophisticated" market he hoped would buy his magazine did not respond accordingly. Nor did poor distribution help to launch this title. As a result, *The Journal of*

*Frankenstein* number one proved to be the publication's only issue. Beck would, however, make a successful comeback in 1962 with the more commercial *Castle of Frankenstein.*

Dennis Druktenis revived *The Journal of Frankenstein* in 1999, starting off the new series of magazines with issue number two, and continuing with the black and white covers and retaining "Victor Frankenstein IV" as its editor. As the magazine sometimes featured Frankenstein-related articles not directly associated with motion pictures, I thought its pages might be ideal for an article I wanted to write regarding Dick Briefer's Frankenstein comic book and my own involvement in its attempted revival. The following article first appeared in *The Journal of Frankenstein* number four (2000) under the title "The Return of the Monster of Frankenstein."

✳    ✳    ✳

My first real introduction to the Frankenstein Monster was not through the famous Universal movies of the 1930s and 1940s, nor from the original novel, Mary Wollstonecraft Shelley's *Frankenstein; or, the Modern Prometheus.* It was in a comic book—to be precise, issue number 19, dated summer 1952—of the unpretentiously titled *Frankenstein* from Feature Publications (also known as the Prize Group of comics).

There was no way I could then have imagined that someday I—in collaboration with artist Brian Thomas, who would not be born for a couple decades yet, and whom I would not meet until much later—would be professionally involved with returning the title character of *The Monster of Frankenstein* (as *Frankenstein* was cover-designated for its last four issues) to his artificial life.

But first, some background...

Horror comic books, many of them gruesome and gory in the extreme, were in vogue in those early Fifties days, and already "grownups" were grumbling about the alleged "harmful" effects these were having on us innocent young people. Books like *Tales from the Crypt, Chamber of Chills* and, of course, *Frankenstein* were blamed for everything from child psychoses to juvenile delinquency. The present writer was just eight years old when I saw that 19th issue displayed on a rack at our local confectionery store. A year or more would pass before I worked up the courage to actually flip through it and eventually be allowed by my mother to purchase one of those four-color "forbidden books." But the vivid image on that cover—a giant, husky, grotesque-looking manlike figure stalking past an old, probably haunted house—would forever remain in my memory.

The character seemed to be about eight-feet tall, clad in blue pants and jacket, a red T-shirt and brown slip-on shoes. His skin was flesh-colored. His head was absolutely flat, topped with straight black hair that hung in unkempt bangs over a rather high forehead. An ugly gash literally split the forehead, the stitches broken to expose the whiteness of the skull underneath. The cheeks were sunken, cadaverous, and the mouth was torn and twisted into a horrible perpetual scowl that revealed the uneven teeth. Most intriguing was his pug nose, which was located high between the bulging eyes.

Though horrible to behold, there was something oddly intriguing, even compelling, about this strange creature, and it was hard to look away (even for a young boy whose comic-book diet consisted mainly of the more sanitized exploits of Superman, Tarzan, Little Lulu and Donald Duck). I would soon learn that this giant "man," whose adventures were detailed on the pages of this comic book, was Frankenstein's Monster— or, as we kids called him in those less enlightened times, just "Frankenstein."

Over the next couple of years I continued to see the *Frankenstein* comic books on the newspaper stand and confectionary-store racks, sometimes paging through them. Their cover illustrations would make lasting impressions on me, although I'd still not read any of the stories these covers were selling. The distinctive *Frankenstein* logo also had an impact and was instantly recognized when I saw it again in 1958, "borrowed" for the premiere issue of *The Journal of Frankenstein*, a one-shot magazine published and edited by Calvin Thomas Beck, and also its 1999 revival, as well as for a number of other later publications.

The first *Frankenstein* issue I actually bought, took home, then read until the pages were in tatters, was number 32 (dated August 1954). Two of the book's three stories were actual "Frankenstein" tales, set in modern times, and both signed by someone named Dick Briefer. The second "Frankenstein" story, a nine-pager titled "The Beautiful Dead"—involving the Monster, a wax dummy of a beautiful woman and an equally lovely corpse—ranks, in this writer's opinion, as one of the best-plotted short horror tales ever published in a comic book. Its final panel, showing the effects of decay on the once-gorgeous dead woman, her eyes bulging from a bony green face, her mouth gaping wide, was an image I would never forget. Of equal impact was the story's penultimate panel, capturing the

Monster's own horrified reaction to the rotting corpse. That was the only issue of *Frankenstein* I purchased off the newsstand. The succeeding issue I never saw on the racks; and, unfortunately, *Frankenstein* number 33 would prove to be the last issue, being among the many victims of Dr. Frederic Wertham's anti–comic book campaign of the 1950s. And just as the Monster in this series could not survive fire, his illustrated adventures would not live through the advent of the Comics Code Authority, an industry censorship board that banned, among other "offensive" subjects, horror in American comic books. Thus, *Frankenstein* went the way of the legendary *Tales from the Crypt* and others titles that sold so well during the early 1950s. (Needless to add, juvenile delinquency did not become extinct in the wake of the horror comics' demise; rather, television, as would movies and video games in future decades, became the next scape-goat.)

For several years, that single issue constituted my main exposure to the Frankenstein Monster character, with Briefer's depiction of him, as far as I knew, the definitive one. As a very young boy I purposely avoided seeing Universal's Frankenstein movies, which still played frequently in theaters, for fear that the Monster would look like it did in the comic book, and that was one hideous face I did not relish seeing blown up on a big theater screen. For the same reason I turned down or at least avoided opportunities to visit the annual Halloween haunted house set up by a local florist, as I knew that "Frankenstein" was its star attraction. In fact I would not see my first two Frankenstein films, *House of Frankenstein* and *House of Dracula* on a triple bill with *The Mummy*, until late August 1956. I had, however, become a fan of the *Frankenstein* comic book, but, unfortunately, by then it was too late.

In 1957, in a way attempting to "fill the gap" left by the departure of the horror comic books and also to realize my own creative urges, I started writing, drawing and sometimes also coloring my own rather gruesome amateur comic books, many of them featuring the Frankenstein Monster. These stories were more or less a melding of both Briefer's and Universal Pictures' versions of the Monster. Most of the Monster's poses in these crudely executed tales were copied directly from the paucity of Briefer printed artwork available to me at the time. To keep more in tune with the character I had seen on the movie screen, I "doctored" the Monster's face—giving him the correct forehead scar, neck electrodes, and so forth— so that he looked more like the Universal version.

But producing my own comic-book stories about Frankenstein's Monster was not enough. I really wanted to read and own Dick Briefer's original books. That meant that I had to graduate from the status of typical comic-book *reader* to the arguably loftier position of comic-book *collector*.

Tracking down back issues of *Frankenstein*, even during those early post–Comics Code days of the late 1950s, was difficult. "Used books" stores were not yet specializing in old comic books, and mail order dealers were still, for the most part, a phenomenon of the future. A few years after *Frankenstein* ceased publication, I managed to obtain a coverless copy of issue number 31 (June-July 1954) in one of those three-for-a-dime packs then sold in grocery and "mom and pop" stores. Not until the early 1960s did I find another issue (this time with a cover, yellowing in the window of a Chicago used book store), *Frankenstein* number 23 (February-March 1953); it cost me a whopping four dollars and, disappointingly, had only one "Frankenstein" tale ("The Monster's Mate"), but it started for me a collecting adventure that would, but not until the early or middle 1960s, fetch me the entire 16-issue run.

The *Frankenstein* comic book, I would learn, was both written and drawn by Dick Briefer. The concept, at least an early and less refined version of it, really began in the seventh issue (December 1940) of *Prize Comics*, featuring an even bigger and more hideous Monster (mostly just called "Frankenstein") created by Victor Frankenstein about a decade before the start of World War Two. After numerous adventures, this version of the Monster—a crafty, articulate being (the 1950s character did not speak) who enjoyed killing humans—gradually evolved into a gentle, oafish comedic character (kind of a precursor to Herman Munster). The Prize group finally gave this humorous "Frankenstein" his own book, titled *Frankenstein* (including a brand new and rather different origin for the title character), which successfully lasted for 17 issues (1945–49).

Later, the *Frankenstein* comic book was revived, picking up the original numbering with issue 18 (March 1952). The series had been transformed into a straight, outright horror series in which Dick Briefer introduced a brand new version of his Monster. These stories, in keeping up with current comic-book trends, were often quite graphically gruesome. Frequently they climaxed with the Monster enacting some ghastly revenge on someone whom "the beast" had naively trusted, only to be inevitably used or betrayed (a standard Briefer plot that may have been influenced by the 1945 Universal Pictures B-film *House of Horrors*, wherein the Creeper, a grotesque killer played by Rondo Hatton, carried out the murderous desires of an insane sculptor). Although this mute incarnation bore certain physical resemblances to his predecessor (*e.g.*, flat head, sunken cheeks, and between-the-eyes pug nose), he was clearly a separate character altogether, established in his debut story ("The Rebirth of the Monster") as at least 100 years old (long before the Second World War). And while I loved all of Briefer's Frankenstein efforts, it was this early 1950s version that I most preferred. (For more details on Dick Briefer's "Frankenstein" series and stories, see this author's books *The Frankenstein Legend: A Tribute to Mary Shelley and Boris Karloff* [Scarecrow Press, 1973] and *The Frankenstein Catalog* [McFarland and Company, 1984].)

Over the years, myriad comic-book series, as well as individual stories, would be based on the Frankenstein theme. Some of these would be fairly successful, others not. None, however, would ever achieve the success, longevity and popularity of the body of work produced by Dick Briefer over a period of fourteen years. Remaining a fan of Dick Briefer and his work, I learned during the early 1970s that this very prolific creator was living in Hollywood, Florida, no longer doing comics but making his living by painting portraits (of human beings, not monsters). In 1973, through comics historian and friend Shel Dorf, I acquired Briefer's address and began corresponding with him. This was shortly after the "Collectors Showcase" prompted Briefer to reproduce as acrylic paintings some of his old comic-book covers, including *Frankenstein* numbers 7 (May-June 1947, still part of the "funny" series) and 18. (I would eventually purchase these excellent pieces from Briefer for my own "Frankenstein" collection.)

In Briefer's first letter to me (dated November 19, 1973), his handwriting the same as that familiar byline on so many of his old stories, he stated, "With all this nostalgia you and others are absorbed with, I feel more alive and appreciated today than I did back in the '40s and '50s." How true. Regarding his personal fondness for and interest in his "Frankenstein" work, Briefer wrote to me: "I started *Frankenstein* in *Prize Comics* back in about 1940 as a serious series, *á la* movie, version for quite a spell. I found myself bored with it until I started sneaking little cute bits of humor in it here and there, and in 1945 it became the humorous, *á la* Charles Adams [sic], character and plots that I enjoyed doing (writing and art) until that folded ... (and after it flopped in comic magazines, the publisher gave me the rights to try to get it syndicated in daily [newspaper] strip form, which never was accepted). Then, after a lull, it went back to a serious affair for about two years which I again hated to work on."

From subsequent letters I also learned that Briefer was *not* the big fan of his material that I was. "You've got to understand," Briefer stated in one letter, "that I am not turned on about my past comic work—there is no nostalgia at all."

And he was really not interested in getting back into comics. "I could never get myself to the first step of buying illustration board, India ink and brushes." Nor was he interested in having "to think out anything new—just reproduce something I did in the past which has its own value," namely, those paintings based on his old covers.

To my surprise (and disenchantment), my long-time hero expressed no fondness at all for his 1950s *Frankenstein*, the version that was my favorite. Briefer admitted, however, that he might be coaxed out of comics retirement back to the world of panels, line art and dialogue balloons, at least on a part-time basis, but only under certain conditions. "I think of all the blank pages facing me off the drawing board that had to be filled with boxes of drawings and lettering, etc., not to mention script. But I would like to do another COMIC Frankenstein in the old vein if I could make the time and it paid well."

Over the next couple years Briefer and I discussed again trying to sell his old *Frankenstein* newspaper strip, featuring the funny version of the character, with me picking up the writing end of it once his already-completed continuity (based on stories from his old comic books) ran out. The idea of my working with someone who had been an idol of mine since childhood was more than just appealing; therefore, I promptly began to concoct plot lines. Alas, the newspaper project would again reach a dead end. However, this was not yet the end of our possible professional working relationship.

In the early 1970s I began, on a freelance basis, writing scripts for the Marvel Comics Group, and in 1975 a story of mine was published in that company's humor title *Arrgh!* The comic book's editor, Roy Thomas, asked me if Dick Briefer and I might like to revive Briefer's humorous *Frankenstein* as a possible continuing feature in *Arrgh!*

By 1974 I had already introduced the Frankenstein Monster as a continuing character to *The Occult Files of Dr. Spektor*, a comic-book series which I created and wrote for Gold Key Comics (a division of Western Publishing Company). As in the old Universal movies, this version of the Monster also crossed paths, now and then, with other fantastic characters. Occult investigator Dr. Adam Spektor, when he did encounter the Monster, tried his best to destroy him. Spektor's files were illustrated throughout this title's run by artist Jesse Santos. It was rewarding to this author writing my own version of the Frankenstein Monster into a series that was also of my own invention.

But actually working with the creator of the Prize version of the character was likened to the proverbial "dream come true." Naturally I was

An earlier introduction of the Frankenstein Monster, by the author, to a comic book series, this one in the sixth issue (Western Publishing, February 1974) of *The Occult Files of Dr. Spektor* (Gold Key Comics). The Monster would return again and again to menace this occult investigator. Interior artwork for this title was by Jesse Santos, who provided both the pencils and the inks.

interested. Briefer proved to be interested, too; and so, I quickly thought up a plot involving the preservation of the funny "Frankenstein's" nose in an ice cube, the cloning of his huge body from that nose, and the character—because of an electrical power failure similar to that which had just recently darkened New York—again emerging from this bungled experiment as a good-natured oaf. Unfortunately, Briefer, learning that page rates for comic-book art had not escalated to the heights he had anticipated since his leaving the business, bowed out of the project, and it then appeared that no version—neither serious nor funny—of his Frankenstein was about to stalk the comic-book pages again.

In later years, however, Dick Briefer and his Frankenstein monsters refused to stay dormant. The artist himself began to enjoy new recognition, largely thanks to the dedicated efforts of comics fan and historian Al Dellinges, who, in 1979 and 1980, began devoting considerable space to the artist/writer in such "fanzines" as *The Comic Book Art of Dick Briefer* and *Near Mint.* Also in 1980, Dellinges self-published *Frankenstein: A Humorous Daily Strip by Dick Briefer*, printing for the first time daily continuity from the unsold newspaper feature.

The Briefer Frankenstein Monster himself began to make new appearances, as in issues of the humor magazine *Cracked*. Comic books published by "independent companies" (*e.g.*, Eclipse, Caliber and Real Images) started to reprint some of the Briefer Frankenstein stories—including some from the serious 1940s series, the humor series (including some revamped by 3D-maven Ray Zone to be read, with red- and green-lensed glasses, in three dimensions) and the pre–Comics Code horror series. Bill Black revived the horrific early 1940s version of the Monster (although the character was sometimes drawn in the image of the 1950s character) for his independent AC line of comics, eventually renaming the character "Frightenstein" and making him part of the "Action Comics universe" of long out-of-print master villains and super-heroes.

One early 1990s afternoon in a Chicago suburb (years after Dick Briefer had passed away), at a wedding anniversary party for a couple working in the comic book business, I met a young Chicago-based artist named Brian Thomas. Brian and I shared numerous interests, including dinosaurs (Brian had recently illustrated the 1991 comic book *Dinosaur Island*) and the Frankenstein Monster. At the time, the majority of Brian's work involved drawing stories for the popular *Teenage Mutant Ninja Turtles* and various "Archie" comic books. When Brian subsequently mailed me a complimentary T-shirt illustrated by him, the artwork including a recreation of Briefer's funny Frankenstein character, our friendship was cemented for eternity.

Around this time, "revivals" of 1940s and 1950s titles (*e.g.*, *Airboy* and *Mr. Monster*) were popular in comic books, although the new adventures were presented with modern sensibilities, including the use of contemporary art styles and narrative techniques. There would also be new interest in the "Frankenstein" theme due, in part, to the publicity generated by actor/director Kenneth Branagh's 1994 big-budget motion picture *Mary Shelley's Frankenstein*. To me the climate in the mid-1990s was perfect to launch a revival of Dick Briefer's *Frankenstein*, the 1950s horror version, as an ongoing series, and my friend Brian Thomas seemed just the artist to collaborate on it.

Brian—himself a talented writer, with his own good ideas to share regarding the tone and direction of our proposed Frankenstein book—responded immediately and enthusiastically. It wasn't long before the two of us were actively at work developing the project. Brian began making drawings of the Monster, while I went to the canon of Briefer stories in order to understand just what made them—and their presentation of the Frankenstein Monster—so memorable.

In studying carefully and then analyzing the 1950s stories, I finally realized that, although this Frankenstein Monster bore some superficial similarities to the Universal Pictures character (*e.g.*, flat head and black bangs), the two versions of the character were, in many ways, very different. Perhaps this was a conscious effort of Briefer's to avoid any copyright or trademark-infringement problems with the film studio. The Dick Briefer Frankenstein Monster wore blue and red clothes and brown shoes, while the Universal character wore a black suit and raised black boots. Briefer's version sported neither the neck electrodes nor metal head clamps, which were familiar trappings of Universal's Frankenstein Monster. There were no scars, stitches or sewn metal strip on the wrists or arms and hands. Instead of a neat scar on one side of the forehead and another on the cheek, Briefer's creature had an unsightly, ripped-open seam running down the middle. In all, with his watery eyes, torn mouth and uneven teeth, Briefer's image of the Monster made Universal's gray-faced character appear almost handsome by comparison.

Beyond the Monster's physical appearance, the character also differed from his movie counterpart in personality, behavior, attitude and body language. Briefer's 1950s Monster never spoke, almost never made any kind of vocal sound (nor, unlike other comic-book Frankenstein Monsters over the years, was he given "thought balloons"; readers therefore never even knew what the giant was thinking). And unlike the Monster as portrayed in most of Universal's films, Briefer's creature got hungry and required food to survive. While the motion-picture character could seemingly stay awake and tireless forever, the comic-book version needed his sleep. Universal's Monster moved stiffly, awkwardly, often slowly; Briefer's was nimble and active, frequently running, jumping, leaping or climbing, and, when seated, slouching or lounging. And while Universal's character could be strengthened by a jolt of electricity, such a zap could literally knock Briefer's Monster unconscious.

Thus, as Brian and I proceeded with the project, we both knew that it was imperative that we consistently remain keenly aware that we were not doing that most familiar version of Frankenstein's Monster from the Universal motion pictures; nor were we doing Mary Shelley's original conception of the character. We were doing Dick Briefer's Monster of Frankenstein, which, in its own right, was a unique and valid interpretation.

We decided that our *Frankenstein* comic book would pick up directly from where Dick Briefer's series left off in 1954, then switch to an updated storyline in the present. Fortunately, both Al Dellinges, in his fan magazines, and Joe and Jim Simon, in their book *The Comic Book Makers* (1990), had already published material that Briefer had prepared for the intended but never-completed *Frankenstein* number 34. This included a cover (showing an old man with a Voodoo doll of the Monster, the real Monster looming in the background), an unlettered splash page (the Monster pursued across a bridge by a torch-carrying mob) with the story title "Witchcraft!" and also a lettered second page (the Monster escaping from his pursuers into the town's sewer system).

For added authenticity (and also as a respectful nod to Briefer) we incorporated redrawn and rewritten versions of those original unpublished pages into the beginning of our debut issue. Our opening story began in 1954 with the Monster being pursued by those same angry townspeople—symbolic

This page from the planned revival of Dick Briefer's *Monster of Frankenstein* comic book series was adapted by the author and artist Brian Thomas directly from an unfinished Briefer story intended for the title's never-published 34th issue. Set in 1954, this sequence features a character named Frederick who was physically patterned on Dr. Frederick Wertham, the psychiatrist whose writings of the period led to the end of such horror comics. (Copyright © D.F. Glut and B. Thomas.)

of the real-life pressure groups that were out to suppress and destroy horror comics—then escaping into the sewers (this sequence scripted and drawn by us in a writing and art style suggesting Briefer's own during the 1950s). Inadvertently put into suspended animation through actions engineered by a townsman symbolically resembling Dr. Wertham, the Monster sleeps for decades, inevitably reviving in today's world (the series then being presented utilizing modern comics' storytelling techniques).

Although our Monster of Frankenstein would then also exist in modern times, his world—like the one Briefer had envisioned for him—would mainly consist of unspecified places in Europe that still remained relatively "old-fashioned." Keeping faithful to Briefer's vision, we decided to keep the stories rather basic, eschewing the footnotes, cute editorial asides and other such distractions so common in today's comic books. Furthermore, the Monster himself would remain the *main* fantasy-based character. In other words, save for the occasional vampire (never one with the notoriety of a Count Dracula), zombie or mad scientist's new creation, there would be no super-heroes, costumed mutants or "cross-overs" with other famous characters.

I enthusiastically went to work, scripting in full the first six issues (three making up one complete storyline) and plotting several more. As in Briefer's earliest 1950s stories, our series would include a descendant of the Monster's creator who, in trying to restore the Frankenstein family name by "working on" the Monster, inadvertently unleashes more horror upon the world—with destroying his ancestor's creation then becoming his life's sole mission. The first story included something Briefer never revealed to us—the Monster's origin. Because Briefer's 1950s Frankenstein Monster was established in his first story as having been created circa 1850, his "universe" must then be one in which Mary Shelley's earlier *Frankenstein* novel (first published in 1818) did not exist. In relating via flashback our own version of this Monster's creation, I tried to write it the way Briefer himself might have, following up on various clues found in the early 1950s issues, and basing it in part on the origin Briefer *did* show for his horror Monster of the 1940s.

As I began to write the scripts (one of which had the Monster involved with a small-time European dictator), Brian Thomas also continued to work—penciling, inking and lettering several sample pages of the first story, creating model sheets for the character and also producing a possible cover. The latter was inspired by several of Briefer's own published covers, featuring a big close-up of the Monster's face; of course, it included the familiar original logo that had become a part of Frankenstein mythology. After considering and discussing numerous title possibilities for our revived series (we didn't want to simply call it *Frankenstein*, as that had become, in our estimation, too "generic"), Brian and I settled upon perhaps the most obvious one of all—*Monster of Frankenstein*.

In the late 1990s our revival of *Monster of Frankenstein* was scheduled to debut as a series from Mark Williams' and Ricky Rocket's company No Mercy Comics. Brian's cover, intended for the first issue, was even colored by Ricky. Within a month following acceptance of the series, however, Mike and Ricky decided, for economic reasons having nothing to do with our *Monster of Frankenstein* project, to withdraw from the comic-book business in pursuit of other endeavors. (Sadly, Mark, who returned to his former career in motion-picture special effects, died of cancer shortly after No Mercy folded.)

However, despite this temporary setback, *Monster of Frankenstein*, like its immortal title character, will not perish; and hopefully sometime during this new Millennium, Dick Briefer's enduring creature, who has appeared in comic books in one form or another for more than half of the last century, will be stalking and running and doing monstrous things once again.

The last page of the first intended story of *The Monster of Frankenstein*, as revived by the author and artist Brian Thomas. Set in the present rather than the Fifties, this sequence was drawn by Thomas in his own style and not based directly on Dick Briefer's. (Copyright © D.F. Glut and B. Thomas.)

# The New Adventures
# of Frankenstein

One of my pet projects as a fiction writer, almost since first attempting that profession in the middle to late 1960s, was a continuing series of novels featuring the Frankenstein Monster. The series, which I named "The New Adventures of Frankenstein," took a while to find its first publisher, after which–like the Monster himself–it found itself terminated and revived again and again. For a while it seemed as if the series had finally come to an end during the early 1980s until, more than two decades later, it found "life" anew via publisher/editor Dennis Druktenis and his "revived" *Castle of Frankenstein* magazine.

Dennis had a plan to attempt, in his own way, reviving via his own *Castle of Frankenstein* the so-called "pulp magazine format" that was especially popular in the United States during the early 1930s through the late 1940s–cheaply produced (and sold) magazines published on the cheapest "pulp paper," rushed out so quickly and frugally that the edges of the pages were usually left untrimmed. Those original pulp magazines–existing in that long-lost world of old-time radio shows, movie serials, Big Little Books and the earliest comic books–spanned numerous genres, including science fiction, romance, Western, mystery and detective, air adventure, heroic adventure and, among the most popular, *horror.* Many featured some of the most lurid cover art ever published, and some featured original stories on the

Frankenstein theme. In Dennis Druktenis' opinion, my Frankenstein novels constituted the ideal property to start off his "Pulps of Frankenstein" series of tomes.

The following article–originally titled "The New Adventures of Frankenstein Lives Again!"–describes the long and convoluted history of these stories, as first related in *Castle of Frankenstein* number 29 (2001).

\* \* \*

After more than three decades, "The New Adventures of Franken-stein"–a series of novels conceived by this writer during the late 1960s (the first of which was published in the very early 1970s)–lives again, thanks to Dennis J. Druktenis, the publisher of the equally revived *Journal of Frankenstein* and *Castle of Frankenstein* magazines. Like the star character of this series, the infamous Frankenstein Monster, the books themselves, over the years, have been retooled and revived, sometimes from what, more than once, appeared to be certain and permanent death.

The origin of the series dates precisely back to 1967, the year the present writer graduated from the University of Southern California. My professional author's career was just beginning. Among my strongest interests then were horror movies (mainly the Frankenstein films made during the 1930s and 1940s by Universal Pictures, with the then current Hammer Films' Dracula and Frankenstein series running a close second), the old movie serials (mostly the ones from Republic Pictures), "B" Western movies (starring the Three Mesquiteers, Roy Rogers, "Wild Bill" Elliott, etc.) and comic books (including super-heroes and the early 1950s pre–Comics Code *Frankenstein* series by Dick Briefer. Mary Wollstonecraft's novel *Frankenstein; or, the Modern Prometheus* had a special fascination for me. Also, I was reading a lot of "pulp style" novels featuring such heroic series characters as Tarzan, Doc Savage, The Shadow and the Spider.

One day during that year the idea struck me like a life-giving lightning bolt from one of those old Universal Frankenstein films: I would launch my career as a novelist with my own series of books starring one of my personal favorite fictional characters, Frankenstein's Monster. The series–which would chronicle the rediscovery and activities of the character in modern times–would be called, simply, "The New Adventures of Frankenstein."

My intent was clear from the outset. While remaining basically as true as was possible to Mary Shelley's original novel, my stories would mainly invoke the atmosphere, character types, plot situations and other trappings of the Universal movies (mist-shrouded castles, wild electrical laboratories, angry torch-bearing villagers, etc.). Like that series, "my" Frankenstein Monster would, as the series progressed, meet up with other familiar horror icons, such as Count Dracula, living mummies and an angst-ridden werewolf. And, despite the apparently thorough destruction of the Monster at the end of one novel, the character would always manage, somehow, to come back–meaner and sometimes stronger than ever–in the following sequel.

The stories would chronicle the Frankenstein Monster's modern-day adventures, although, like the Universal movies, they would often be set in various parts of Europe that were more or less "lost in time," where some people still sometimes traveled by horse and wagon and frequently behaved as if they were still living during the 1930s or 1940s. The first book would focus mainly on the Monster's discovery in the Arctic, after being entombed in ice for over 200 years following the events of the Mary Shelley novel. Subsequent "New Adventures" would have the creature cross paths (and sometimes tangle) with various other bizarre characters, from vampires, mummies, werewolves and a descendant of Dr. Jekyll, to robots, monster gorillas and even dinosaurs. Some characters, like the werewolf John Stewart and the vampire Dracula, would appear in more than one novel. The Monster's main nemesis, however, would be Dr. Burt Winslow, the heroic young scientist who would revive the Monster in tome number one, and then, haunted by guilt, spend much of the rest of the series trying to track down and destroy the murderous horror he unleashed upon the world. Winslow's assistant and girlfriend, the lovely Lynn Powell, would be sympathetic toward the patchwork brute.

Certain aspects of the Hammer series would be incorporated into the stories, too, such as the graphic gore, overt violence and sensuous women that the more staid Universal never allowed. There would be touches borrowed from some of my other loves as well, including the Republic cliffhangers (fistfights, gun battles, car chases, etc.), cowboy movies (train hold-ups, bar fights, Western-style jailbreaks, etc.) and the Briefer comic books (the Monster trusting the wrong people, a guilt-ridden scientist trying to track down and destroy the creature, etc.). Finally, as the *Batman* television program was still quite popular at the time the earliest books were written, I thought that my novels, to capitalize on then current "camp craze" promoted by that show, should be written somewhat "over the top."

Also, the books would not be lacking in personal "in jokes." The very name of the series was inspired by Dick Briefer, who, during the early 1940s, used "The New Adventures of Frankenstein" to describe his earlier *Frankenstein* stories in *Prize Comics*. Many of the character names would be "adapted" from the names of real-life friends (*e.g.*, "Lars Burrod," "James Judson," "Dirk Andersen" and "Kurt Allen" in *Terror of Frankenstein*). Gregore Frankenstein, the first-person protagonist of "My Creation, My Beloved," originally appeared as a grotesque hunchbacked character harassed by a local teenage gang in my amateur movie *The Teenage Frankenstein Meets the Teenage Werewolf* (1959). Tor, a Kong-sized gorilla from my amateur movie *Tor, King of Beasts* (1962), guest-starred in *Frankenstein in the Lost World*. The six new creations in *Bones of Frankenstein* all bear suspicious resemblances to various Frankenstein Monsters from old comic books, including the Briefer series of the 1950s. One of the most enjoyable to write books in the series was *The Return of Frankenstein*, which was, if one reads between the lines, a kind of "Western," complete with a masked-avenger/Zorro-type hero. As I like to think of most of my fiction–whether presented as novels, short stories, comic books or movie scripts–occurring in the same "universe," my Frankenstein series would feature names and places and items that readers might have already encountered somewhere else, such as Democracy Pictures, the Marshall Natural History Museum, the Dark Gods, the sorcery book *Demonomicon* and the vampire "bible," the *Ruthvenian*. And both *Frankenstein Lives Again!* and *Frankenstein Meets Dracula* include references to someone who "might" be Dr. Adam Spektor, a character I created and wrote for Gold Key Comics back in the 1970s.

The bottom line was that the novels would be *horror* stories, with all the blood and gore that normally goes along with such tales. At the same time, however, the stories were not meant to be taken *too* seriously. And laced through the ghastly events would be a sense of *fun*.

All of the above, then, constituted my basic plan regarding the novels' themes.

As to the actual appearance of the Frankenstein Monster himself, I opted to go back to Mary Shelley's own description of the character in her novel, supplementing it with *suggestions* of the Monster's look–though different enough to avoid any copyright or trademark problems–in the Universal and Hammer movies. As in the Shelley description, the Monster's cadaverous countenance would be hideous to behold, his yellow skin pressed close to the arteries and muscles underneath. His eyes, set in whitish sockets, would also be yellow. The Monster's lips would be straight and black, his teeth a pearly white. His hair would be long and flowing. Like the Universal character, my Monster would be a rather flat-headed being clothed in black, his raised boots making him appear even taller than his true eight-foot height. A crudely stitched (as in the Hammer movies) and metal-clamped scar would run across his somewhat raised forehead. Stitched scars would also mark the length of the right cheek and circumvent the neck and wrists. Electrodes, for conveying life-imparting electrical energy, would be set at the Monster's temples.

With both my goal and the Monster's "look" defined and locked in, I put my own non-transplanted brain to work and came up with themes and titles for an entire run of books, 10 of them novels and one a collection of Frankenstein-related short stories, some of the latter having direct continuity with the novels. They were: *Frankenstein Lives Again, Terror of Frankenstein, Bones of Frankenstein, Frankenstein Meets Dracula, Frankenstein vs. the Werewolf, Frankenstein in the Lost World, Frankenstein in the Mummy's Tomb, The Return of Frankenstein, Frankenstein and the Curse of Dr. Jekyll, Tales of Frankenstein* (the short-story anthology) and *Frankenstein and the Evil of Dracula.*

Some of the above titles were inspired by other sources. *Bones of Frankenstein* was a title I had read during the late 1950s or early 1960s in *Kodak Movie News*; it was a submission in that newsletter's amateur film contest. *Frankenstein Meets Dracula* was also the title of an amateur movie I made in 1957 wherein I portrayed the Monster wearing a Don Post full-head rubber mask, a ubiquitous item sold in novelty and magic shops of that era. *The Return of Frankenstein* was an earlier title for the 1935 Universal movie *Bride of Frankenstein*. (I didn't know then that *Frankenstein Lives Again* was also an early title for that film.) *Tales of Frankenstein* was the title of a television pilot film co-produced in 1958 by Universal and Hammer and released by Columbia TV subsidiary Screen Gems. As it turned out, the title *Terror of Frankenstein* would later become the American release title of the 1977 Swedish/Irish movie *Victor Frankenstein*.

I wrote–on a manual, non-electric typewriter–the original version of *Frankenstein Lives Again* in 1967, quickly following it with *Terror of Frankenstein*. By the time I was well into *Terror*, the first book's manuscript was already making the publishing rounds ... and promptly getting rejected by virtually everyone! Cover letters from editors generally stated that there was no market for a series of Frankenstein novels, or that the books were too "campy," that there was no current space in their publishing schedule to fit them in, and various other reasons. Nevertheless, as undaunted as Victor Frankenstein himself was in pursuing the secrets of life and death, I forged ahead and within about three years cranked out the entire 11-volume series. Sooner or later, I kept telling myself, some publisher would be smart enough to pick them up.

"The New Adventures of Frankenstein" got its first true spark of life when Luis Gasca, editorial director at the Buru Lan publishing company in San Sebastian, Spain (and a friend of my literary agent Forrest J Ackerman), in a letter dated December 24, 1969, wrote me that his company wanted to put out the entire series. The stories would be translated into Spanish by Eduardo Mallorqui. Gasca himself would write the introduction to the first volume, "El Monstruo de Don Glut." All of the books would be graced with cover and interior artwork by Esteban Maroto, an artist then basically unknown in the United States but who would soon, after his work on these books was seen by publisher James Warren, become a celebrity in Warren Publishing Company's line of black and white comic magazines. The only problem was that the books would be published in Spanish, a language I neither spoke nor read except for knowing a small number of obvious words. (I did, however, have a background in Latin and promptly invested in a Spanish-English dictionary.) At least (and at last), however, the series had been given *life*!

On April 15, 1970, Luis Gasca sent me a list of all eleven of the planned titles, some of them slightly revised in content and all translated into Spanish: *Frankenstein resucitado, Frankenstein y el robot, Los huesos de Frankenstein, Frankenstein y Dracula, Frankenstein y el hombre lobo, Frankenstein en el mundo perdido, Frankenstein y la momia, Frankenstein y el gorilla, Frankenstein y el Dr. Jekyll, El horror de Frankenstein* and *Frankenstein y el Vampiro.*

By late January I received copies of the first four covers, with the Maroto line art reproduced in full color. Everything seemed to be proceeding with the full power of Frankenstein's laboratory apparatus until, on the 15th, Gasca reported to me that the series might be in danger, not at the hands of torch-wielding townspeople or an exploding castle, but from a far more powerful threat–Spanish censorship! Spain, at the time, was still in the tenacious grip of the Franco regime, which strictly monitored the materials printed in that country, targeting in particular fiction having fantastic content. At that time the first book in the series was already with the censor, who was looking for specific passages that would be considered "offensive."

The first Spanish-language book was finally issued in February 1971, although I was never told what might have been amputated from it. That same year, on the high boot heels of the initial book, the first sequel

DON GLUT
FRANKENSTEIN
RESUCITADO

Cover of the first Spanish-language edition (1971) of the novel *Frankenstein Lives Again!*, with cover artwork (originally black and white and colored later) by a then virtually unknown artist named Esteban Maroto. (Soon Maroto would become an internationally known and highly regarded artist, known mostly for his contributions to the Warren Publishing Company's various illustrated horror magazines.)

appeared. On March 3, Gasca informed me of the bad news. The censor had come down very hard on the Frankenstein series, harder than any crumbling building or angry mob, and determined the second volume "has been tipped by 'cruelty and horror.'" (It was, after all, a *horror* novel!) The third and fourth books, apparently translated and ready for printing, and with the cover artwork completed, would *not* go to press. Enclosed with Luis Gasca's letter were the reports from the censor, the "Dirección Géneral de Cultura Popular y Espectáculos" of the "Ministerio de Información y Turismo," dated February 2, 1971. Material on five pages of *Los huesos de Frankenstein* and 18 pages of *Frankenstein y Dracula* had been deemed objectionable. According to Gasca, the deletions and changes required would have made the Frankenstein Monster in these stories "something like a good priest." As far as Spain was concerned, the Monster had been banished to the grave forever.

One trait I share with Victor Frankenstein, however, is that I rarely let anything I've worked on remain dead forever. For example, all along I had also been writing those individual stories that would, I hoped, eventually be collected under my title of *Tales of Frankenstein*. Before long at least some of these "tales" began to see print. "To Be Frank," a short story featuring the same Frankenstein Monster appearing in the regular "New Adventures" series, was published in *Famous Monsters of Filmland* magazine issue number 83 (April 1971), accompanied with a number of somewhat related photographs from Hammer's 1957 classic *The Curse of Frankenstein*. Following that in 1973, "F.R.A.N.K.E.N.S.T.E.I.N.," about a super-computer that becomes a kind of Frankenstein creation, was published in *Man and Monster*, one of the "Perry Rhodan" paperback series (Ace Publishing Corporation) edited by Forrest J Ackerman. *The Rivals of Frankenstein*, a paperback edited by Englishman Michel Parry and first published by London's Corgi Books in 1977, featured "Dr. Karnstein's Creation," a *Tales* entry about a Frankenstein-type vampire creation. (During the late Seventies, producer Milton Subotsky intended to include this story, as well as others from Parry's collection, in an anthology movie titled *The Rivals of Frankenstein*, a project that unfortunately never got made.) "Origin of a Superhero," about a future-world descendant of the original Victor Frankenstein creating a super-powered being, was included in Parry's *Superheroes* paperback, first published in London by Sphere Books in 1978. Finally, in 2001, "My Creation, My Beloved," about an ugly descendant of Victor Frankenstein creating a perfect female lover, but with unexpected results, was accepted to appear in the Forrest J Ackerman–edited anthology *Brave Nude World* (Sense of Wonder books).

Through Forry Ackerman, "The New Adventures of Frankenstein" rather quickly found a new home, this time in, of all places, the Netherlands. Forry had sent the Spanish editions of the first two books to the Dutch publisher of the periodical *Horror*. Unfortunately, I knew even less Dutch than I did Spanish, so again I would not be able to read my own work. The translations into this latest foreign language would be directly from the Spanish–and probably censored–versions from Buru Lan, so I cannot even imagine what the end result was like.

The first book, now titled "Frankenstein keert terug" and featuring a cover painting of Boris Karloff from Universal's original *Frankenstein* (1931) movie, appeared in issue number 24 of *Horror* (1974, although no date was posted). The second installment, re-titled "Frankenstein en da robot," with a tinted photograph of Glenn Strange from Universal's *House of Dracula* (1945) on the cover, appeared that same year in *Horror* number 28.

Within a year, "The New Adventures of Frankenstein"–like the Monster himself so many times before–was revived again (and yes, in *another* foreign language, but at least one for which I knew a small number of words), this time in the actual country where Victor Frankenstein created him. The German publisher Pabel Verlag agreed to publish 10 of the books (they passed on the anthology) in their magazine *Vampir Horror Roman*. The text would be translated from my original English manuscripts this time and not from the printed and watered-down Spanish editions. That lent me some time to revise and polish a bit of the original texts of the first two novels.

As published, the German editions were: "Frankenstein kommt wieder" (issue number 148 of *Vampir Horror Roman*, December 1975, with text translated by Sebastian Wieser), "Frankenstein Kampf mit dem Roboter" (number 153, January 1976, translator not credited), "Frankenstein und das blinde Mädchen" (number 157, February 1976, translation by Wieser), "Frankenstein trifft Dracula" (number 161, March 1976, translator not credited), "Frankenstein und der Werwolf" (number 165, April 1976, translated by Lore Strassl), "Frankenstein bei den Dinosauriern" (number 168, May 1976, translated by Strassl), "Frankenstein in Mumiengrab" (number 173, June 1976, translated by Eva Wagner), "Frankenstein und der Fluch des Dr. Jekyll" (number 357, December 1979, translated by M. Stocklj) and "Frankenstein Kampf mit Dracula" (number 370, March 1980, translated by Joachim Honnef). Most of these editions had original artwork, the last one credited to Prieto Murana, the "Jekyll" entry recycling the cover art from the British edition of *Terror of Frankenstein* (see below).

With all of these foreign-language editions of the stories, you can imagine my delight when receiving a phone call from Forry informing me that the novels were finally about to appear in *English*. Mews Books, a division of New English Library (NEL), had agreed to publish the series in the United Kingdom in paperback editions featuring cover art painted by Tony Masero. As my writing abilities were improving through time, I now had another opportunity to revise the original manuscripts, a task I performed (at last on an electric typewriter) on the first two books. Mews released *Frankenstein Lives Again* in January 1977, following it with *Terror of Frankenstein* in February, *Bones of Frankenstein* in July and *Frankenstein Meets Dracula* in December, the scheduling for these British editions overlapping with the series also coming out in Germany. For undisclosed reasons, although they were most likely sales related, NEL did not continue the series beyond number four.

Actually having the opportunity to *read* these books myself, once the paperbacks were issued, proved to be an eye opener. There I was in 1977 reading (in the case of the first two entries, at least) books that had essentially been, except for relatively minor changes, my first novels written a decade before. I was stunned at how "primitive"–even nonexistent– the writing style actually was (very few simple declarative sentences!) and amazed that NEL had agreed to publish the books without more major revisions. Worse, now the books were "out there" in the world where my English-speaking friends could *read* them. It was now clear to me why so many North American publishers had rejected these books so many years ago, and it had little or nothing to do with any shortsightedness on their part. Already in the back of my mind was a desire

Cover of the British edition of *Terror of Frankenstein*, published by Mews Books (New English Library) in 1977, with a cover painting (recycled for the German series) by Tony Masero. A total of four entries was published by Mews.

to rewrite the books–at least the first two–once again, but next time more extensively.

The opportunity to do just that came circa 1980 when, via Forry Ackerman once again, I was contacted by Hank (no relation to Frank) Stein of the Donning Company. Hank was starting a new series of books in trade paperback format. My name was fairly "hot" at the time, as my

The first American version of *Frankenstein Lives Again!* was published in 1981 by the Donning Company. Intended as a series, only this initial entry was issued. The cover painting is by Ken Kelly, a popular artist in the horror and science fiction genres.

novelization of the film *The Empire Strikes Back* had been a number one bestseller for about six weeks. Partly for that reason, Hank wanted to bring "The New Adventures of Frankenstein" into Donning's new line of books. It was Stein's wise request that I put *Frankenstein Lives Again!* (now including an exclamation point) "through the typewriter one more time."

That I did, hopefully improving the text, and at the same time working through various plot problems that had always been there and fleshing out the characters a bit more. The published book, featuring a dynamic cover painted by popular Warren Publishing Company artist Ken Kelly, and interior black and white drawings by an artist named Danforth, appeared in the bookstores in 1981. Unfortunately, the book line did not take off as successfully as Donning and Stein had hoped. The series was dropped, the Frankenstein project included.

Now, more than 30 years after it was first conceived, "The New Adventures of Frankenstein" has been revived yet again, thanks in no small part to the renewed interest in the character through magazines like *The Journal of Frankenstein* and *Castle of Frankenstein*. Dennis Druktenis, in launching his own series of "pulp fiction"–style "tomes," contacted me in July 2000 and asked if I would be interested in his reprinting the stories. As I had always envisioned these novels as "pulp fiction" anyway (I liked to describe them as "lurid potboilers"), because most of the stories had been out of print for many years and also because so few of them had ever been available in English, I agreed without too much hesitation. Besides, who could be a more logical publisher for "The New Adventures of Frankenstein" than the person who revived from the "dead" such classic titles as *The Journal of Frankenstein* and *Castle of Frankenstein*?

However, I only agreed to the project *if* I was allowed to rewrite the stories, to make them more *readable* and also bring them "up to date." Remember that the original manuscripts were written during the late 1960s through early 1970s. Oftentimes plot elements which presented major problems in the Sixties could be easily solved today via such taken-for-granted pieces of technology as cellular phones or home computers. While bringing in these modern wonders, I still wanted to maintain the ambiance that they were taking place when they were being read, yet in places in the world where time sometimes had the anachronistic habit of seemingly "standing still."

*Frankenstein Lives Again!*, having already been rewritten quite extensively for the Starblaze series, required almost no tinkering–just correcting the spelling of the town's name from "Ingoldstadt" to "Ingolstadt," and (as so many years had passed since the book was first written) stating that the Monster was created "more than two centuries ago" instead of "almost two centuries ago."

Of all the novels, *Terror of Frankenstein* required the most work. The story, with its "spy spoof"–inspired plot and gadgetry, reeked of the "mod" world of the late Sixties. The book presented other problems, too. Its arch villain, a Chinese Fu Manchu–type character, had to be "toned down" somewhat from his original "Yellow Peril" portrayal. *Frankenstein in the Lost World* also required major changes. Originally the person who hijacked Burt Winslow's rented Lear Jet was a "Black militant" (a character associated with the 1960s) fleeing from the law; he was replaced in the new version of the story with a more relevant Middle Eastern terrorist. Furthermore, that novel was written before the so-called "Dinosaur Renaissance" of the early 1970s, when the appearances and lifestyles of dinosaurs and other reptiles of the Mesozoic Era were reinterpreted based upon newly discovered fossil specimens and sometimes rather bold ideas regarding the physiology and behavior of those extinct animals. Thus, the giant sauropods in the story would no longer spend most of their time buoyantly lounging about in weight-supporting water, and pterosaurs actually flapped their wings rather that merely glided through the air.

The revised version of *Bones of Frankenstein,* produced by Dennis Druktenis (editor and publisher of the revived *Castle of Frankenstein* magazine) in the style of the old "pulp magazines," with cover artwork by Rick "Spine" Mountfort.

And, in all the books in which she appears, the character of Lynn Powell had to be better developed and given more to do than merely stand around looking beautiful and letting out the occasional scream.

How did I feel about rewriting these books again—*all* of them?

Frankly, it took a *lot* of time and effort, too much, really—despite that this go-round was accomplished using a computer—during which I could have been spending my time in more profitable, or at least more fun, ways. However, this rewriting was *entirely necessary.* Remember that Mary Shelley herself, my original inspiration, extensively rewrote and changed various story elements from her 1818 edition of *Frankenstein* for the new version printed in 1831, the latter being the text that is mostly read today. In that way, at least, I was in good company in rewriting my texts. (Besides that, hardly anyone seems to complain when producers of the stature of Steven Spielberg and George Lucas "re-do" their films, sometimes decades following their original theatrical releases.)

For those readers who care about such things, the editions published by Dennis Druktenis are the *true, authentic and authorized* versions. As the creator and writer of this series of "tomes," I reserve the right to declare these the "official" versions. If these new editions contradict the older versions in any way, the previous editions should be disregarded as to content, but not, I hope, thrown away. In fact, if a reader happens to acquire one of those earlier texts, no matter what the printed language, I advise that they should be regarded only as literary and historic oddities or "artifacts"; the stories themselves, as presented in those volumes, simply never happened *quite* that way.

Amen!

"The New Adventures of Frankenstein," improved upon and revived as the Monster had been so many times before, made its return "debut" in February 2001 when Druktenis Publishing & Mail Order, Inc. unleashed "Tome #1," *Frankenstein Lives Again!* Two months later came *Terror of Frankenstein*, with nine more books to follow, sold in bookstores, on newsstands, in comic-book shops and through the mail. As with the old "pulp magazines" published during the first half of the twentieth century, each "tome" boasted both cover and interior artwork, executed in a rather "sensational" style by artist Rick "Spine" Mountfort (replacing Scott Pensak, who had to leave the project due for personal reasons, but not before providing a painting of the Monster used in Druktenis' original advertisements for *Frankenstein Lives Again!*).

As to whether or not "The New Adventures of Frankenstein" would continue *beyond* the 11th book, *Frankenstein and the Evil of Dracula* ... well, we know that the Monster is immortal and that money (as that creature sometimes also does) "talks." Also, it only requires a sufficient number of requesting readers, plus, of course, the proper laboratory apparatus, to bring the big guy back.

# INDEX

Numbers in **bold** indicate photographs.